OPTIMISM AT ARMAGEDDON

Optimism at Armageddon

Voices of American Participants in the First World War

Mark Meigs

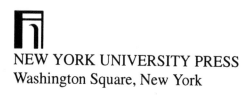

NEW YORK UNIVERSITY PRESS
Washington Square, New York

First published in the U.S.A. in 1997 by
NEW YORK UNIVERSITY PRESS
Washington Square
New York, N.Y. 10003

Library of Congress Cataloging-in-Publication Data
Meigs, Mark.
Optimism at Armageddon : voices of American participants in the
First World War / Mark Meigs.
p. cm.
Includes bibliographical references and index.
ISBN 0-8147-5548-8
1. World War, 1914-1918—United States. 2. World War, 1914-1918-
-Campaigns—France. 3. Soldiers—United States—History—20th
century. 4. United States—Civilization—French influences.
I. Title.
D570.1.M45 1996
940.4'0973—dc20   96-23869
                                                      CIP

Printed in Great Britain

In memory of
Robert Rodgers Meigs
Henry Howard Houston
and
Henry Howard Houston Woodward

For my father and mother

Contents

Acknowledgements   viii

Introduction   1

Chapter 1   "It's a great life if you don't weaken:"
             American Participants' Understanding
             of their Involvement in World War I   8

Chapter 2   "It's a great life if you don't weaken,
             but believe me there are few who don't:"
             The Meaning Americans Gave to
             Action at the Front in World War I   36

Chapter 3   "From a hayloft to a hotel where kings
             have spent their summers:" Americans'
             Encounter with French Culture   69

Chapter 4   "Mad'moiselle from Armentières,
             Parlez-vous?" Sexual Attitudes of
             Americans in World War I   107

Chapter 5   "A Grave Diggin' Feelin' in my Heart:"
             American War Dead of World War I   143

Chapter 6   "The best place to live on Earth:"
             Lessons for the Doughboys' Return   188

Conclusion   221

Notes   227

Bibliography   249

Index   259

Acknowledgements

Many organizations and individuals have contributed to this work over a long period of time. But the project truly started in Berkeley at the University of California, where the intellectual energy and generosity of the faculty and students have been a source of wonder and delight. There, Paula Fass, Suzanna Barrows, Carolyn Porter, James Kettner, Randolph Starn and Sam Haber read drafts of the manuscript and always gave advice and encouragement about the project. Jeffrey Lena, Reid Mitchell and Michael O'Malley, fellow students, but by now scattered on their own careers, gave invaluable help and critical readings as well as the support of friendship. At later stages, historians Charles Royster and Russell Weigley helped as well, reading early drafts with understanding.

A book needs all kinds of professional care and this one has been singularly blessed. Archivists and librarians across the United States and France have helped continuously, with patience and imagination. In France, town records in remote warehouses have been made available, and desks in busy town halls have been set aside for my visits. I must thank especially Dr. Richard Sommers and his assistant, David Keogh of the United States Army Military History Institute at Carlisle Barracks. They introduced me to the remarkable historical resources under their care. James Dallett, retired archivist at the University of Pennsylvania, has several times sent me references and photocopies of documents I needed. The anonymous readers for publishers sent excellent detailed critiques. Editors Niko Pfund and Annabelle Buckley have been encouraging right to the the end of the process of creating this book.

The author needs looking after as well. The family of Madame Geneviève De Bergh has welcomed me in its several branches across France. In Washington, Craig and Edith Eder opened their house to me.

The French Republic and the United States Marine Corps also supported this work. Through the French Embassy, I received a Chateaubriand Scholarship that allowed me to spend a year in France. The Marine Corps Historical Foundation awarded me a fellowship to complete my research in Washington, D.C.

My new colleagues in France, at the University of Paris Nord, and on the Research Committee of the Historial de la Grande Guerre, Péronne, have given me an intellectual home in France, without which I could not have finished this book. Hubert Perrier's doctoral seminars on intercultural relations have reanimated American issues for me with a new perspective. Annette Becker and Stéphane Audoin-Rouzeau of the Historial have raised my interest in and understanding of World War I to new levels. Finally, I must thank Divina Frau-Meigs for the completion of this book. At the earliest stages of research she lent me her car for trips. And since she has read, re-read, proofread, and advised on every version. I can only hope over a long life to repay this labor of love.

M. M.

Introduction

World War I has been a matter of unresolved interpretation for American participants from the first moments of their involvement to the return of the last soldiers and bodies of soldiers in the 1920s and even to the present day. The signs of the historical significance of the American effort were plentiful in Europe by the end of the war. American supplies had supported the allies. Americans had enlarged several ports in France and laid railroads to move goods and men to the Western front. There were camps, hospitals, and even a university of pre-fabricated buildings that had gone up with a speed and disregard for expense that astonished the French. They were abandoned or sold in 1919: solid, if ambiguous, testimony to the extent and importance of the American effort.

Nothing is more real than the death of individual people by the violent destruction of their bodies. But the disposition of those bodies, some returned to the United States, some arranged in cemeteries in France, commemorated in individual graves or by the collective symbol of the 'unknown soldier,' leaves the interpretation of that human loss ambiguous as well. The event has no obvious meaning in American history. On one level, the nation seemed to quit the isolation from European affairs that had characterised American foreign policy in the nineteenth century. But afterwards that policy revived. On another level, the war had been fought to a successful conclusion by the Allies with American help, but given the size of the United States, the contribution of Americans to the war, though essential at the end, cannot compare to the involvement of Europeans. At the same time because of the magnitude and stakes of the war effort – for a combatant soldier literally a matter of life and death – American participants were obliged to create meaning out of the materials around them. World War I is an opportunity for studying the creation of meaning in strange surroundings, adopting and accommodating beliefs to realities, testing a national identity against foreign identities.

That the experience of World War I differed for both America and Americans from the experience of the European combatant nations and combatants cannot be stated too strongly. European

1

soldiers may not have been generally enthusiastic for war, but few Germans or Englishmen or Frenchmen initially had doubts about why they fought, or later, that the actual experience of fighting the war changed Europe and their countries. Four years of trench warfare has become inextricably linked with the meaning of World War I to Europeans and the hegemony of the trench image has spread its disillusioning power back from the lines to symbolize the end of eras, cultures, world views and political systems. For Americans involved in the war, both the certainty of purpose and the position of the experience of combat as symbolic of the war's meaning must be questioned.

To pinpoint changes brought about in American society and culture by the war is difficult too. Americans arrived late, fought briefly, and quickly found themselves among the victors. The fighting that they did required as much courage as fighting done by others. The conditions in which they fought and the tactics used were comparable to the conditions and tactics used by European armies since early in the war. But while their numbers were necessary to the victory, the contribution of the American forces must be seen as only part of the long process of exhausting Germany. After some delays, Americans returned home to a country whose political climate rejected the continued international engagements that were the Wilsonian fruits of victory, embracing an agenda of "Normalcy" and isolationism. These "effects" of World War I on America seem to deny that the war had significant effects.

The "Great War" for the people of the United States must either be the Civil War where the nation's survival was at stake, or World War II whose victory set the stage of American foreign policy for the second half of the twentieth century and whose social upheavals so altered American society. To be usefully understood, the connection between the military facts of World War I and American society and culture must be seen in some more carefully constructed context than a catalogue of the war's cultural effects. No cataclysm like Pearl Harbor, but rather an accumulation of events, lead the country from neutrality to war. No clear military victory or cataclysm like the atomic bombs dropped on Hiroshima and Nagasaki put an end to the war either; the battles in which Americans fought were important as part of that general wearing away of all Germany. But the war nevertheless gives an opportunity to make a portrait of Americans

in war showing them straining the givens of their culture, and
using the materials around them – propaganda, history, literature,
religion, popular culture – to make sense of their experience.
A study of Americans in World War I must examine a great
many different kinds of sources and address many different kinds
of experiences beyond combat. For an American soldier, sharing
an initial young man's war enthusiasm with schoolmates, reading
the army's ubiquitous propaganda, going on leave at a French
resort town, visiting the cultural sites that he had learned in
school represented the distant background of his civilization, or
flirting with a French girl might have made as strong an
impression as his time fighting, and might have informed his
thoughts on the fighting. Studies of Europeans in the war tend to
demonstrate how the brutality of endless trench warfare altered,
drowned out, and eventually nullified these other possibilities of
experience. Americans who had experienced combat certainly
privileged that memory, but it colored, rather than obliterated,
the other aspects of their war.

The chapters that follow trace thematically the narrative of
Americans' experience of the war. They start with the reasons
Americans gave for volunteering, or the rationalizations and
understandings they came to upon being drafted into the army.
What combat meant to veterans appears in the second chapter.
Their cultural contact with France, through the tours that the
army arranged for the six months after the war, and their sexual
and sentimental contact with the French, follow in the third and
fourth chapters. The death of American soldiers and the
meanings attached to death in war are the subject of chapter five.
Soldiers' thoughts of home and the United States Army's preparation for their return conclude the study.

Each chapter juxtaposes "official" views, those expressed, for
example in *The Stars and Stripes*, and in army handbooks, General
Pershing's General Orders, and official unit histories, with less
official but widely disseminated sources: popular songs, jokes in
army newspapers, and also the postwar fiction that has come to
dominate our image of the war. These published sources find
their place with letters sent home, diaries kept clandestinely,
memoirs written after the war, and the answers of veterans of
World War I to the United States Military History Institute
World War I Survey, distributed in the 1970s. Not all these
sources appear in every chapter, nor does this by any means

make an exhaustive list of the kinds of documents used here. The sources of each chapter, however, span a range from the official and widely spread to the private.

Such an arrangement tends to expose "official" views and explanations as incomplete, misleading, even as cover-ups. The intention here is to go beyond this exposure, or even the ironic effect of the comparison, and do more than privilege private testimony over public. Adaptations of those official views to fit the needs of individuals reveal a far richer picture of American culture, when it stood at the threshold of becoming mass culture, than any single voice or any single type of source might.

The intention is to adapt Henry May's notion of "loss of innocence" to soldiers and nurses. Henry May addressed the question of American innocence and found its demise among intellectuals in the years before World War I. He defined innocence as "an absence of guilt and doubt and the complexity that goes with them." What had made innocence possible, for the intellectuals who concerned him, were beliefs in "the certainty and universality of moral values; the inevitability, particularly in America, of progress; and the importance of traditional literary culture."[1] When quite ordinary Americans in uniform learned the useful and positive vocabulary of progress from propagandists and the YMCA during a war that was infinitely destructive, they lost their innocence while gaining its appearance. Americans became sophisticated by adopting an official language of optimism and American superiority. Little suggested that they had enjoyed any prewar moment of innocence, and yet the language of innocence, of optimism, of uplift, was absorbed by these entirely practical Americans in the way they would have absorbed any formula that could help them through an alienating experience.

The war seems to have taught Americans these particularly American characteristics, and American success in the war seems, if anything, to have embedded this language of American progress in the vocabularies of large numbers of soldiers and nurses. Americans in World War I participated in a mass event: they were the object of the first highly organized mass propaganda effort in American history. Just how far they acted as a mass, and how they maintained some sense of individuality, is an indicator of the state of American culture in the early part of this century.

Though participants must have been quite aware that the propagandistic interpretation of events did not cover all the cases, they could use that language as they needed to. Thus, they accepted a difference between rhetoric and reality which colored the way they reported battle, their relations with foreign women, living and fighting in France, tourism, and even death. Their experience was both real to them and not. Guides, translators, instructors, educators and propagandists mediated their experience at every step. They sometimes resisted official interpretations as well. They placed limits on the messages they would repeat, and they said different things to different audiences.

Gerald F. Linderman, making a similar study of the motivations and especially the notion of courage held by soldiers in the Civil War, found that "they yearned for the end of the war, never realizing that it would truly end for them only years later, when they surrendered the war they had fought to the war civilian society insisted they had fought."[2] For World War I soldiers, the fighting war and the war for interpretation took place simultaneously. Linderman's sources, the letters, diaries and journals of Civil War soldiers of both North and South, are remarkable for their sincerity. The Civil War soldiers, a more literate group than their counterparts in World War I, made sense of their experience in modern war as best they could. No doubt they chose their words carefully when writing to parents and loved ones. But there was no Committee on Public Information to supply those words, and no censorship to eliminate unacceptable words. Linderman found that the thoughts of Civil War soldiers departed from ideas accepted by civilians, but he never suggested that they adopted one version of the war for expression that conflicted with their own observations. The World War I soldier-writer contended with both the propagandist and the censor. Thus, necessarily, he produced writing that did not always correspond entirely with everything he thought. He was forced into "doubt and complexity."

Historian David Kennedy, in his book on World War I and its lessons, addressed a far broader social and cultural context than Henry May did. At the level of popular culture, the level of most of the young people attached to the American Expeditionary Forces, he found a baffling persistence of nineteenth-century culture in the "romantic, upbeat view of war expressed in innumerable doughboy diaries and letters and memoirs." At the same time, he noted a loss of confidence in progress in general and a disillusionment with progressive aims, in particular among intellectuals. "This hole," Kennedy wrote, "in the fabric of American culture, further separating the intellectuals from the 'masses,' was one of the lasting legacies of the war."[3] David Kennedy's observation marks a point of departure for this examination of those often strangely upbeat texts.

Another, more concentrated look at this literature in the context of a successful war, an extensive propaganda effort and a progressive social reform effort, all aimed at enthusiastic young American letter and diary writers, revealed the war as the occasion to learn a certain kind of American culture. In this light, the stresses of combat became another mnemonic device, acting with the novelty of foreign travel and the very impressionable age of American participants, to make the lessons of the war stick. David Kennedy called the optimistic rhetoric of so many American soldiers a "residue" of Victorian style, but for immigrants and the children of immigrants in the army, that optimistic, jaunty style might be an adaptation to the mainstream of America as learned from the YMCA. In an army that undertook to teach reading and writing to its immigrant members, a certain style might have nothing to do with the retention of older values.

The chapters that follow explore just how and why those baffling optimistic qualities became expressed in the writing of American participants in World War I. That quality is evidence of the penetration of a mass culture with standard responses to difficult situations. This culture penetrated at least far enough for soldiers to reproduce it in their writing, but they could also resist it, remaining individuals at the same time. They became complicated and modern.

In this sense, World War I could provide a model for the study of wars in which Americans have fought in this century. The displacements and stakes of war make it necessary for ordinary people to record thoughts in letters and diaries that under other circumstances would be lost. The gap between the official version of war, the version of the propagandists, and the accommodation of participants to that version can be a measure for studying changes in American culture using this opportunity. Before the twentieth century, as Gerald Linderman has shown, soldiers were alone with their comrades while adapting the culture with which they arrived in the military to a new situation. For World War II, the subject has not been approached. The evident urgency and drama of that war as a fight between good and evil has seemed to mark a moment in American history of remarkable unity, though studies of working people and of racial minorities have placed limits on that conclusion. During American involvement in the Korean and Vietnam conflicts, the official version of the war, the war fought by soldiers and the war as seen in print and on television, seem to have parted company. Perhaps these conflicts of interpretation were inevitable during these major and very real military engagements produced by the Cold War, a war eventually "won" by the more virtual strategies of deterrence and propaganda. Again no systematic study has been attempted. In the Gulf War the official and projected – near virtual – image of the war, obliterated the individual's version of the war and dominated the version in print and on television. The standard opinion provided by the military triumphed, at least until the present moment. Study of how that version of an American military operation was received by participants will provide a great insight on the elements that make up Americans' opinions at the end of this century, just as the present study attempts to shed light on that process at the time of World War I.

1 "It's a great life if you don't weaken:" American Participants' Understanding of their Involvement in World War I

Could we have spent a year in a fairer land, under a fairer sky?
Yes, of course, in America . . .

The Stars and Stripes
vol. I, no. 22, July 5, 1918, 4.

The different stages of neutrality, diplomatic mediation and of military preparedness that led the United States eventually into World War I are complicated but possible to reconstruct. Following the steps that lead individual people to rationalize their own participation in the war is more difficult. Historiography has neglected ideologies that motivated individual Americans during World War I for several reasons. First, the tortuous path the United States took towards war has seemed to provide no clear reason for individual Americans to have fought. Second, during World War I, Americans were saturated with ideological messages, provided by President Woodrow Wilson himself, the Committee on Public Information (CPI), and many other agencies. The means used by the CPI, through which all official war information was passed to the public, have since been regarded with suspicion and many of the messages themselves have proved hollow. Thus, to reconstruct the illusions of the war years looks like needless praise for propaganda. And third, the conscious ideological motivation for American soldiers has seemed a "nonsubject," since the publication of studies made of World War II soldiers, notably the four volumes of *The American Soldier* and the related work of Brigadier General S. L. A. Marshall, *Men Against Fire*, first published in 1947.[1] These exhaustive studies found that

8

in battle, American soldiers fought for the protection and the regard of the people nearest to them. They fought for "primary group cohesion." Ideology, larger causes, and such abstract notions as patriotism played hardly any role at all as GIs fought in World War II.

Nobody ever made systematic studies of fighting men before World War II comparable to the interviews and questionnaires gathered by sociologists, psychologists, and military experts for *The American Soldier*. Historians have tried, however, to assess the place of ideology and the larger purposes and causes among the motivations of Civil War Soldiers. Of these James McPherson, in his book *What They Fought For*, has found "ideological motifs that almost leaped from . . . many pages of the letters and diaries of Civil War soldiers." In *What They Fought For*, McPherson made the connection between ideology and fighting by examining the thoughts of men from volunteer units that did most of the fighting in the war. But in the citations he made, soldiers wrote of their thoughts on the war, or on political and economic issues of the day, as distinct from their thoughts about battle. Perhaps for this reason, his results have differed from those of Civil War historians who have addressed themselves to battle with results following more closely what McPherson has called the dominant paradigm set by *The American Soldier* and S. L. A. Marshall. The effects of peer pressure, group cohesion, male bonding, ideals of manhood and masculinity, concepts of duty, and many other aspects of a man's world view distinct from ideology were all important in the works of Bell Irvin Wiley, Reid Mitchell, and Gerald Linderman. These historians wished to find out what motivated men in battle and found that ideology or constitutional issues or the "Cause," though sometimes present, were not by any means dominant among Civil War soldiers when they were fighting.[2] The difficult examination of the relationship of ideology to questions of group cohesion in battle in the Civil War remains to be written and will be an important contribution to Civil War scholarship.

In World War I, American soldiers' reasons for fighting colored their thoughts about battle, making an unavoidable synthesis. The meaning of the war to soldiers and nurses built upon the layers provided by the manner in which America entered the war, the discourse of Wilson and the modified, more belligerent discourse of the Committee on Public Information, speeches they heard, movies they saw, and, of course, their own observations and experiences. The most important quality that soldiers' and nurses' memoirs all shared with the pamphlets and newspapers from which they received information was that they never stopped explaining why they fought and what they fought for, and they never completed their explanations.

The immediate causes of war for the European powers have become familiar signposts on the way to that Armageddon that had nothing to do with the eventual involvement of the United States. Various Bosnian crises culminated in the assassination by a Serbian anarchist of the Austrian Archduke Franz-Ferdinand at Sarajevo, the Bosnian capital, in June, 1914. Russia's commitment to other Slavic and Orthodox states led her to support Serbia in the ensuing debacle with Austria. Treaties, some secret, others known, connected Germany to Austria, France to Russia, Britain to Belgium, and Britain, France and Italy together. The necessities of German military strategy required her to attack France before attacking Russia.

This cultural, diplomatic and military Gordian knot, against a background of economic and colonial rivalries, provided the reasons for the failure of Europe's diplomats to prevent the war among all those countries. Americans, however, had years of the carnage and destruction that followed the declarations of war in which to consider their own participation and goals. The European diplomatic failure looked like grim tragedy from the western side of the Atlantic.

The events that actually lead to American involvement could hardly stimulate the necessary war commitment, and most were subject to differing interpretations that might divide Americans as much as unify them. An issue like America's financial dependence on an eventual allied victory could hardly motivate all Americans in the same way. The bankers and businessmen, who had extended credit to the Allies for the quadrupling of trade between them and the United States, had obvious reasons for desiring the victory of Britain and France. But other businessmen had been hurt by the Allied blockade of Germany that had reduced American trade there to almost nothing, by 1916. Farming and agricultural business had profited during these early years of the war. Nevertheless, Senator George W. Norris of Nebraska and other western politicians could appeal to the good sense of their constituents, deriding the idea of going to war "at the command of gold."

An issue like the commercial rights of neutral powers could move Americans to support either the central powers or the Allies. As both Germany and England tried to prevent American shipping to their enemy, Americans were initially made angry by both sides. The British, however, had a public opinion advantage. Their control of the sea lanes permitted them to halt American ships and inspect them for goods on their way to Germany, or even, on their way to neutral ports from which the goods could be shipped to Germany. Sometimes, American shipping was taken to British ports for inspection. These practices caused delays, and cost money, but did not cost lives. The Germans relied on submarines to blockade England. Their approach took American lives, most significantly when torpedoes sank the Lusitania on May 7, 1915. The public had been warned of the torpedo danger, and the ship carrying arms to England fell under the definition of a contraband carrier in international law, but the 1,198 passengers who drowned, of whom 128 were Americans, made Germany look like a brutal aggressor.

Yet, the sinking of the Lusitania was no Pearl Harbor. President Wilson continued to negotiate with Germany. He made proposals for a peace conference to the Allies and Germany and, by the Spring of 1916, he had won a pledge to abandon the submarine campaign from a German civil government anxious to keep the United States out of the war. Wilson's success in this negotiation helped him in his presidential campaign of 1916. After his re-election, he continued in his role of peacemaker, soliciting acceptable peace conditions from the belligerent countries and, when these proved unencouraging, he proposed his own plan for peace in a speech on January 22, 1917. He established the basis of his fourteen points for peace: that a League of Nations acting as a force for peace should be founded, that no one nation should dominate another, that arms should be limited, and that the end of the war should not result in the violation of the rights of the loser. He called for "peace without victory."

Initially, the German civil government had cooperated in these efforts for peace with more enthusiasm than the Allies. But even before Wilson's proposal of January 22, the German government decided to resume unrestricted submarine attacks in the war zone

around Britain. German military authorities had made the calculation that Germany could win the war of attrition by starving
Britain of supplies, and they doubted President Wilson's ability to
bring both sides to the bargaining table.

Germany's resumption of submarine attacks against American
shipping finally brought the United States into the war. There
was no diplomatic surprise in this. The German ambassador had
warned his government what the probable outcome of the
resumption of submarine warfare would mean. But, according to
German military calculations, Britain would most likely collapse
before intervention from the unprepared United States could
become effective. Wilson, willing to negotiate everything but the
sinking of passenger and merchant ships, continued to keep lines
of communication open, but soon sinkings had started again.
These new losses of American life and property, coupled with the
discovery of German diplomatic efforts to distract the United
States by exciting Mexico into reclaiming the southwestern
United States – the discovery of the famous Zimmerman note –,
brought Wilson to ask congress for a declaration of war on April
2, 1917.

No one was surprised by Wilson's move to war, yet this was a
great shift from the administrative stance of seeking peace at
almost any cost to one committed to total war. For several years
a preparedness program had been underway in the United States,
but the United States was not prepared in any military sense for
a war of this scale. Cultural, ethnic, linguistic and historic
traditions attached the United States to Britain and France. And
among the college-educated, especially among the college-educated in the East, there was even enthusiasm for the war – it was
largely from this population that the early volunteers for ambulance services had already departed for Europe. Large populations of Irish or German descent, however, had no historic
reason to fight for the Allies. And for many other Americans,
the power structure of northern Europe was a matter of
indifference. Samuel Eliot Morrison recalled these regional differences:

> At the western university where I was teaching when the war
> broke out in Europe, it seemed to the average student as unreal
> as the Wars of the Roses; returning to Harvard early in 1915,
> one was on the outskirts of battle . . . sympathy for the Allied

cause was unconcealed; not for a moment was Harvard neutral in thought or deed.[3]

There never was any serious possibility of the United States going to war on the side of Germany. While seeking peace through 1916, Wilson had made it clear that acceptance of his proposals by the Allies and rejection by Germany would lead America into war with Germany. The real alternative had been neutrality, but that had proved impossible to maintain for a country that traded with all the belligerents. The United States had been inexorably led into war, but with no unifying cause to stir men to risk their lives. President Wilson's war message of April 2, 1917, spelled out American war aims in superb optimistic humanitarian terms; he painted a picture of a reformed world, but he did not provide language to move men to fight.

> Without rancor and without selfish object, seeking nothing for ourselves but what we shall wish to share with all free peoples, we shall, I feel confident, conduct our operations as belligerents without passion and ourselves observe with proud punctilio the principles of right and of fair play we profess to be fighting for ... We shall fight for the things we have always carried nearest to our hearts – for democracy ... for the rights and liberties of small nations, for a universal dominion of rights by such a concert of free peoples as shall bring peace and safety to all nations and make the world itself at last free![4]

When as old men in the 1970s, veterans answered the US Army Military History Institute's World War I Survey on the subject of their enlistment, the complications of America's involvement and the fine vision of Wilson's rhetoric had almost disappeared. They were likely to answer: "patriotic reasons," "I wanted to serve my country," "natural desire for adventure," or some variation of these answers. Whether they enlisted or were drafted made little difference fifty years after the event.

Regional, ethnic, and racial differences were not readily apparent either in responses on the questionnaire. Veterans of the Thirty-sixth Division of volunteer Oklahoma and Texas National Guard units, whose surnames suggest native born origins, answered the Survey question, "Why did you enlist?" with patriotic and personal reasons. "I thought it my duty. I thought I was needed." "I felt that it was my duty to serve my country.

My country needed every able-bodied man to help save the world for democracy." "Desire to serve my country, and too, everybody who was anybody was doing it." One said, "Death of Mother. Impetuosity of youth."[5] Presumably, this last man felt freed from family ties to pursue adventure in war. Duty, adventure, peer pressure, patriotism, all terms difficult to place in a specific historical context, played at least as important a role as the Wilsonian notion of saving the world for democracy.

German-Americans responded to questions about enlistment in much the same way, but perhaps with a stronger memory of enthusiasm. In a sample taken from units recruited in areas of the United States having a high proportion of German immigrants, twice as many veterans with German surnames remembered joining the army enthusiastically as remembered that event with neutral or negative language. Otto Gerstner of the Thirty-second Division, recruited largely from Michigan and Wisconsin and having a large number of German surnamed members, explained that, as his parents were German immigrants, he felt a patriotic responsibility to join. His patriotism grew because his family's new country fought its old country. Laverne Hoffman called his impulse to join a "natural desire for travel and adventure." Men with German surnames often wrote of duty to their country and patriotism. Many succumbed to the pressure of friends joining up, perhaps indicating that the fever to join could overtake a largely German community as easily as any other. The most negative responses among men with German surnames simply said "drafted," or "conscripted," and left it at that. No one voiced any doubts about fighting their ethnic relatives, "To help defeat the enemy," wrote James Gitchell as his reason for joining.[6]

Educational levels seem to have affected the degree of enthusiasm remembered by soldiers. A crude division between education levels – calling all those who listed their occupation before the war as student, clerk, or salesman more educated, and those who called themselves farmer or laborer less educated – revealed that more than half (56 per cent) of the better educated group remembered enlisting enthusiastically, while less than half (41 per cent) of farmers and laborers remembered that spirit.[7] Really negative memories of induction almost invariably came from farmers and laborers. Among German-surnamed men who responded to the US Army Military History Institute's Survey, however, a remarkable 66 per cent remembered enlisting with enthusiasm, and the most negative memories were the laconic and neutral single word "drafted."

African-American veterans responded to the question on the Survey about reasons for enlistment expressing personal hopes that could expand to include hopes for their race and nation. Private Henry I. Craven wrote, "Would be good for me and I would be helping my country." Private Edward Jackson suggested that being in an all African-American organization had helped them fight for America, "To help protect my country. I enjoyed it. All negro national guard units. We are proud of our part we played for our country. We were under white officers." The most enthusiastic response came from corporal Lloyd Blair, of a unit with black junior officers. "I thought it was the best. After learning my duty I loved it. I tried to get others to join." He stated that he "loved" the leadership of the unit. "We had colored officers. We couldn't get along with the white too much. Pregesty [Prejudice?]. I got a whipping it took about 25 to do it. I knocked down every one I hit with either right of left."[8] His testimony seems to indicate that high morale among African-American units could bring them into conflict with white authorities. But conflict with Whites was no reason for not serving.

The format of the enlistment portion of the Military History Institute's questionnaire encouraged quick responses like "duty" or "patriotism" that seem clear but that are open to interpretation. In the context for these words created from the popular discourse around soldiers at the beginning of American involvement in the war, however, patriotism means participating in the formation of a unified United States from the diverse material of the American population and their history. With the exception of African-American veterans who sometimes wrote in racial terms, and a few German Americans who referred to their ethnicity, the hopes expressed for their war experience by individuals in the US Army Military History Institute Survey, fifty or more years after the event, usually do not show any desire that service in the war will identify them, or their group, more closely with the nation. Through the simple patriotism of their responses, moreover, they expressed a memory of this identity as fully accomplished. By the 1970s, when they wrote, that assimilation perhaps seemed complete, and their words look like the expression of an individual sentiment of loyalty to the United States.

In 1917 and 1918, however, the opportunity afforded by war to heal racial, ethnic, and sectional splits certainly interested the organs of propaganda along with magazine writers and movie makers, though sometimes in a conflicting manner. Many speeches and articles described how one or another group of Americans moved closer to the center of American society by means of the war. A war like World War I, in which few Americans had an obvious stake, could join various elements of American society in a common project.

Just how the immigrants and others who had been on the fringes of American society participated was an important test for America's ability to assimilate new immigrants. George L. Bell, Executive Officer of the State Commission of Immigration and Housing for California, stated it thus:

> In a critical time like the present in making a program for the defense of our State and Nation we must make new inventories of our resources. We are in a sincere doubt as to whether to put our 15,000,000 immigrants and their 10,000,000 children in the asset column or in the liability column. We are thus puzzled about one-third of the total population of the United States!

According to Bell, the war made an excellent opportunity and test for assimilation.

> It might be said that this [war] is a great adventure in democracy, and in making a program of defense we should keep clearly in mind that we are aiming at the ultimate defense of the world. When we work for the defense of our nation then, and particularly in the work of Americanizing the many races, let us realize that we are but making a working model for a greater thing ... Let us, by the Americanization processes ... mold our many races into one great, common, democratic ideal. Then, only when we have succeeded, let us apply to the many nations what we have done with the many races.[9]

Bell's words attached some domestic foundations to the larger international abstractions of Woodrow Wilson. Defense of the land and Americanization come to mean the same thing. By assimilating, immigrants would help defend the country, and through participation in the defense of America, immigrants could assimilate American democratic values. Later, the world would learn from that model. Wilson had spoken of the fantastic example American morals and conduct could set for the world. The rhetoric of men like Bell showed how that example would come to pass. Willing participation in the defense of America would be sufficient.

Enthusiasm for the war in Europe could wipe away differences between generations as well as between ethnicities. All American history could be recast marching towards the same goal, making the world safe for American ideals. Photographs of a Southern Civil War veterans' march in *The Red Cross Magazine* were captioned as follows:

> The American Spirit: The Gray Clad Warriors of 50 Years Ago have given way to the Khaki clad warriors of today, but their spirit goes marching on. It seemed to me as I watched old men and young men together that the younger generation had absorbed the splendid spirit of the older men and that the former, too, were not afraid to lay down their lives for their country and for the cause of liberty and true democracy. Every now and then a stalwart figure dressed in Khaki strode by, the upright, erect carriage and elastic step a strange contrast to the bent carriage and feeble step of the veterans, who fifty years ago heard the call and answered, giving their all for the cause they believed in.

In this paragraph, "the cause of liberty and true democracy" may have motivated either the "Gray Clad Warriors" or the "stalwart figures in Khaki." That shared commitment made the young men worthy of their history, and helped the defeat of the separatist South recede a little further as both groups of southerners moved towards the center of American history once more.

The American Red Cross Magazine presented photographs of Americans of different ethnic backgrounds: Germans, Irishmen, Italians, and a photograph of a Native American. The caption for all these men read: "100% American," and "Indian transformed in a few generations into a defender of his America."[10] War training had removed the hyphen from these minority-Americans. Participation of Native Americans in World War I, like participation of southerners, held out the promise of placing a former enemy of the American State into the American mainstream.

After the war, the Boston Hampton Committee, an organization for the promotion of the Hampton Institute, an educational institution for African and Native Americans, published "A Brief Sketch of the Record of the American Negro and Indian in the Great War." This pamphlet underlined these same points. Native American participation in the war legitimized it as a suitable enterprise for Americans, and participation in the war brought African and Native Americans into the fold of the American state.

The pamphlet insisted that Native Americans were enthusiastic about the war: "Before we entered the war, 12,000 Indians enlisted in the Canadian Army and went overseas, thrilled at the prospect of defending the British Empire," and this number included men from the United States who crossed the border to join. The pamphlet estimated that "there were 5,000 Indians serving in our forces, it means that one out of fifty has pledged his life to defend the principles of liberty and humanity for which our country entered the war . . ." The *Indian Leader* of Lawrence, Kansas, implying a social hierarchy in Native American society, showed that the "best" Indians were in favor of the war: "Every one of these boys belongs to an Indian family of prominence. Once antagonistic to the government, the Bullhead Indians present seried ranks in their devotion to Uncle Sam." The newspaper described a demonstration of loyalty to the United States Government on the Standing Rock Reservation when seven of their young men joined up. Just as *The American Red Cross Magazine* had mingled descriptions of Civil War veterans with young World War I soldiers, the *Indian Leader* attempted to connect the later war with older campaigns: "Notable participants in this affair were: Mary Crawler, the only woman survivor of the fight against Custer . . ." Native Americans had become absorbed into the American state. Given their numbers, whether Native Americans went to war willingly or not made little difference to the outcome, but, as a symbol of the unifying effects of participation, they could legitimize the whole enterprise and give a historical context to a conception of patriotism.

The pamphlet contained the words of black Americans too, and they carried a clear message. African-Americans, and certainly their leaders, wanted something very specific from the State if they participated in the State's war.

Nearly 400,000 gallant black soldiers, "fruit and flower of the Negro race," have helped to make the world safe for Freedom and Democracy; many of them have fought, bled, and died that their country's ideals might triumph. If, in the hour of her travail and danger, the Negro has neither faltered nor failed in pledging his life, his labor, his money, his all in defense of his country's safety and honor, surely in the hour of victory and prosperity he will not be denied fair treatment and recompense accorded other soldiers because of his valuable services and unswerving patriotism. The Negro asks full protection of the law to be left unhindered and unhampered in his industrial and commercial pursuits, to be given a fair deal and full opportunity to educate his children, and to work out his own destiny – being loyal to his family, to his community, to his country, and to his God![11]

To their leaders, the patriotism of black Americans meant that they, too, should move into the center of American life, receiving equal treatment and equal recognition. These men stated quite clearly why they would cooperate in the war effort. W. E. B. DuBois, editor of the magazine of the National Association for the Advancement of Colored People, *Crisis*, wrote, "This war is an End, and, also, a Beginning. Never again will darker people of the world occupy just the place they have before." An African-American teacher taught his black audience, "when we have proved ourselves men, worthy to work and fight and die for our country, a grateful nation may gladly give us the recognition of real men, and the rights and privileges of true and loyal citizens of these United States."[12]

In almost every sense, however, black Americans were denied the "fair treatment and recompense accorded other soldiers." Of the 400,000 men in uniform that the pamphlet spoke of, only two divisions, the Ninety-second and the Ninety-third, or less than 40,000 men, were ever actually designated as combat troops. For the most part, African-American soldiers were used as labor battalions, unloading ships, building roads, digging graves, necessary work but not equal to combat in anyone's mind. And having been denied full participation as combat troops, they found themselves denied the recompense that should have come with that manifestation of their patriotism. While the crucible of patriotism and battle could melt away the differences between immigrant groups and different sections, black Americans remained separate. On the World War I Survey African-Americans sometimes recorded hopes they had held for their group upon entering the war, "I must do my best for my love ones and my country," wrote one veteran of the Ninety-second Division, implying a duty to family or perhaps to his race. A memory of disappointment appeared as well, "Drafted. Disgusting," wrote another member of the same division, the harshest response found to the questions about enlistment.[13]

Songs sung by black American labor battalions expressed with perfect irony their skepticism and pragmatism:

> Jined de army for to get free clothes
> Lordy, turn your face on me –
> What we're fight'n 'bout, nobody knows –
> Lord, turn your face on me

or

> Oh, you jined up for fightin' in a he man's war
> An' you're goin' to do your fightin' in a French freight car.
> Oh, mister French railroad man, whar you takin' us to –
> Please, mister French railroad man, whar you takin' us to?[14]

While many Americans joined the army hoping for some kind of advancement or inclusion, to join for new clothes was a humble ambition indeed. The second song here expresses complete disorientation: after the confirmation of virility and inclusion, the joining up for "fightin' in a he man's war" has been denied.

The unifying power of participation in war met its limits with black Americans, and the popular cultural context is clear. Many World War I soldiers first saw battle in D. W. Griffith's movie of 1915, "The Birth of a Nation," in which North and South were rejoined after the Civil War in the white man's defense against former slaves. The movie must have had an electrifying effect on American soldiers. Among the countless references in their diaries and letters to seeing movies, soldiers only *named* "The Birth of a Nation." The movie depicted Civil War battlefields filled with action and heroism, but ended demonstrating the post Civil War union of southern and northern white men to protect white domesticity from racial ravages inflicted by liberated slaves.[15] "The Birth of a Nation" promoted the idea that, when faced with a clear racial threat, normally peaceful and individualistic Americans should take up arms.

The preparedness propaganda of the two and a half years of neutrality that preceded American involvement in World War I also contained a message linking race, reproduction and willing belligerence. For example, the popular movie "The Battle Cry of Peace," released in September of 1915, warned that pacifism placed American women in sexual danger. In the movie, the hero's fiancée was shot by her own mother to protect her from rape by a gang of the unscrupulous, and German-looking, enemy. J. Stuart Blackton had made the film with the encouragement of his friend and Oyster Bay neighbor, Theodore Roosevelt. The film concluded with endorsements from Secretary of War Lindsay Garrison, General Leonard Wood and Admiral George Dewey.[16]

Roosevelt and the two military men had written frequently on the racial benefits of struggle in the context of American imperial ambitions before World War I.[17] Along with Captain Alfred T. Mahan, the promoter of American sea power, and General Homer Lea, they had created theories of American imperialism based on Darwinist notions. Wood had once been Army Chief of Staff. He had promoted the preparedness programs before the United States became involved and was early considered for the position of Commander in Chief of the American Expeditionary Forces (AEF). Having lost that position to General John J. Pershing, he nevertheless maintained considerable influence on training during the war. Wood's belief that war was as natural to human nature as "the general law which governs all things, namely the survival of the fittest,"[18] was certainly available to American soldiers.

Propaganda depicting Germans as racially alien, which might carry a Darwinist message, became part of the preparation for an American war effort. But Americans tended to be shown as racially and culturally homogeneous in a somewhat anti-social Darwinist manner. Germans as beasts became a staple of pro-war propaganda. But Wilson himself helped preparedness in speeches condemning "hyphenated Americanism," calling for a homogenizing end to the cultural differences between immigrant groups that might place barriers between white Americans.

The historian Richard Hofstadter has traced Darwinism, and the social Darwinist idea of survival of the fittest, in the thought of intellectuals up to the outbreak of World War I. He has found that the language that President Wilson used to conduct the war contained no overt references to the rhetoric of the benefits of struggle and, in fact, attacked such notions as typical of German thought.[19] At the same time, however, posters and songs, calculated to have a broad appeal, often depicted Germans as racially threatening. The image of Kaiser Wilhelm II, or of the Crown Prince, their features distorted beyond caricature into something less than human, enlivened much of the war's poster art.

Soldiers themselves adopted the language of propaganda, often calling the German enemy "Huns," or sometimes, in reference to the often recounted stories of atrocities committed by Germans, "baby killers." But the reasoning connecting race, reproduction and the benefits of struggle rarely found their way into letters. The fact that to enjoy any reproductive benefit that the war could confer on a man, he had first to survive a war of attrition, complicated this kind of thinking. "If the United States send troops over here I hope they will be the scum and not the finest for they'll all be killed or maimed for life,"[20] wrote one American ambulance volunteer to his parents just after America's declaration of war. In this case, the writer implied that no benefits of struggle went to those who participated in the fight.

On the US Army Military History Survey, veterans tried to give a personal, not racial, response to the question, "Why did you enlist?" Yet, any personal response had necessarily to be affected by the atmosphere of official and unofficial propaganda or the war discourse around the men. The individual and the mass were sometimes reflected even in the short responses on the questionnaire quoted above. When a man wrote that enlistment "Would be good for me and I would be helping my country," he moved, in a sentence, from an idea of personal development to a larger view. Another had written, "Desire to serve my country, and too, everybody who was anybody was doing it." Desire might be personal, but desire was influenced by the actions of people around this man. These soldiers expressed the difficult idea of individual development and desire in the face of a mass event. The two could exist side by side in soldier letters of World War I. Joining the army, at the beginning of the century, where a man submitted himself with thousands of others to authority and a uniform, did not necessarily reduce his idea of his individuality. The rigor of army life could in fact do him good.

Writing Americans at the time, not limited to the laconic style encouraged by a questionnaire, seem to have applied their talents to the same difficult question. The men whose words were published in books and magazines during and just after the war tend to come from among the college-educated, rather than the more random backgrounds of the men who answered the Survey, and their words can be read as more extended texts on the individual's place in a mass event. The Harvard-educated Alan Seeger who served and died in the French Foreign Legion, before the United States entered the war, explained his reasons for enlisting in a letter to a woman friend, dated February 26, 1916:

> My interest in life was passion, my object to experience it in all rare and refined, in all intense and violent forms. The war having broken out, then, it was natural that I should have staked my life on learning what it alone could teach me. How could I have let millions of other men know an emotion that I remained ignorant of?[21]

He started this passage in an entirely egotistical vein, looking for heightened experiences that would inform his poetry. But by the end of the passage, he has acknowledged that this war involved masses of people in the same experiences. The war experience he sought was both "rare and refined" and shared by millions.

In an article in *The New Republic*, he explained the motives of other Americans who joined the Legion at the beginning of the war. Like him, this unusual group, that included artistic aspirants and wealthy globetrotters, had found themselves in Paris in August of 1914.

> I have talked with so many of the young volunteers here. "Why did you enlist?" In every case the answer was the same. That memorable day in August came. Suddenly the old haunts were desolate, the boon companions had gone. It was unthinkable to leave the danger to them and accept only the pleasures oneself . . . Some day they would return, and with honor – not all, but some . . . "And where have you been all that time, and what have you been doing?" The very question would be a reproach.[22]

This contribution to *The New Republic* carried the reproachful question to Seeger's compatriots who had not yet come into the war. The tension between the individual and the mass is present.

Old haunts and boon companions were a matter of personal choices but those choices lead to peer pressure. Honor seems like an individual achievement. But the possibility of gaining it or not, according to Seeger, affected everyone who survived in the same way. Peer pressure may indeed always play a role in sending young men to war. Certainly it played a role in the choices of Civil War soldiers.[23] But Seeger, with his magazine articles and widely published poems, went beyond speaking of identity with a group of peers as a motivation.

Alan Seeger represented a quintessence of the warlike sensibility Samuel Eliot Morrison had noted at Harvard. Magazines held his model of patriotism aloft for the youth of America to emulate. During the last year of his life, "Seeger had become, in a sense, the mouthpiece of many Americans who in heart, at least, [were] anything but neutral . . . He has tasted that privilege, to him the highest, of death in a pure cause."[24] Seeger attempted to whip up American interest in the war, linking patriotism to a defense of racial and sexual superiority.

> You are virile, combative, stubborn, hard,
> but your honor ends with your own back-yard . . .
>
> What singly none would tolerate
> You let unpunished hit the state.
> Men of another race or hue
> Are men of a lesser breed to you . . .
>
> The neighbor at your southern gate
> You treat with the scorn that has bred his hate . . .
> He has jeering used for his bootblack's rag
>
> The stars and stripes of the gringo's flag . . .
> . . . greasers have taken their innocent lives
> And robbed their holdings and raped their wives[25]

In these inflammatory lines of his "Message to America," Seeger insulted American complacency over her border dispute with Mexico. He deliberately taunts his compatriots. Women have been raped and it is somehow their fault. But, at the same time, the poem does not accuse American men of permitting that dishonor individually. On the contrary, he says, they would not permit it individually. It is the state that has been dishonored. Without belligerent and collective action and sufficient identification between the individual and the state, American territory and sexuality were threatened by races white Americans scorned.

To maintain her status in the international realm, Seeger continued in this poem, America's men must learn, "the things that the individual / Must sacrifice for the good of all." Thus, Seeger disseminated a rhetoric of loyalty to the American state in the language of race and virility. And he put the tension between the good of the individual and the needs of the state explicitly in the balance. He illustrated the struggle between nations in terms of race and virility, but individual virility was never in question. If Americans could think collectively and allow themselves to accept training, and a place in a collective body, they could express the virility of the nation. Through identity with the collective state, the individual could survive the mass event with his honor intact and even increased.

He shared these solutions to the problem of individuality in the face of mass experience with others. It has two parts. First, a man must participate in the war – the act of an individual. Then, he must record that participation, making an individual contribution to the formation of a standard of participation. Early volunteers were determined to record their adventures, not losing one scrap of experience to forgetfulness, in case some aspect of their part in a foreign war be lost. In that way, they retained an identity as individuals while being organized into a vast modern organization.

Seeger was read and admired by many American volunteers. And some at least managed to maintain a jaunty individualism in the face of their war experience.

> At present I am lying in the crotch of a large elm tree which hangs way out over one of these picturesque French canals, my table is a volume of Alan Seeger's poems balanced precariously upon my knee and if I am not careful I shall tumble into water ... Have you read these poems of Seeger's? They are worth reading, especially the ones on the war. He expresses one's feelings under fire very well.[26]

This young volunteer had read Seeger's published letters and poems, and understood Seeger's message very well. In another letter he made this clear, reproducing in prose the point of Seeger's "Message to America."

There is no doubt that our national soul was rotting away, being undermined by selfishness, sloth and corruption ... A few Americans like Seeger and the aviators have given their lives as a protest and an example but what we need is to lose thousands, we need to suffer as a nation, not as a few individuals.[27]

His ideas about corruption and sloth seem to be echoes of Theodore Roosevelt's ideas about "the vigorous life." Such language had appeared in the context of the American military theorists of the end of the previous century. This transport service volunteer considered biological models, but finally preferred collective cultural models as motivation to war instead.

[The German] brand of civilization is so diametrically opposed to our brand that the two cannot exist on earth at the same time. One or the other has to be exterminated ...

As to whether either eugenics or birth control would do away with war I have my doubts. As I have tried to show this war may be one of commercial supremacy on the face of it, but opposing ideals are at the bottom of it.[28]

Much more common among this volunteer's contemporaries, however, was the notion that the suffering of individuals can add up to the suffering of a nation while bearing coherent meaning both for the individual and the collectivity.

Letters home carried the burden of individual experience and suffering back to the United States. And archives of soldier letters in repositories like university libraries and municipal historical societies serve to preserve a sense of nationhood. It might seem natural that a family would preserve a young person's letters from war. In case of a soldier's death, a letter might be his last communication and link with a loved one. But soldiers went beyond communication in their letter writing and participated in this preservation themselves. Often they numbered their letters so that lost parts of the sequence could be identified. Marine Lieutenant Clifton Cates described a system for preserving his communications in a letter to his mother as he crossed the Atlantic. The letter that contained his explanations of his precautions against loss also recorded an experience that he did not wish to lose, a successful test of bravery in which he became accustomed to climbing into the ship's crow's-nest during rough weather. He punctuated the description of his newfound physical courage with the expression, "It's a great life if you don't weaken," and then made the following explanation:

> I will number all of my letters from now on, so you may tell if any are lost. When I write on the typewriter I will make carbon copies and mail them in succeeding letters so that if one goes down, you will still get it.[29]

Both the sentence, "It's a great life if you don't weaken" and the systems for saving letters were common. Soldiers hoped to record their own progress, unweakened through the tests of war. Such experiences could be signs of individual development, even though the experience and the expression of the experience might be shared by many others.

To write about the war was a way both to participate in a mass event and to preserve individuality. A lady volunteer to the Red Cross recorded the self-consciousness of the early volunteers as she described the literary mood of a group of American volunteers in *The American Red Cross Magazine,* in an article called "The spirit of the young who could not wait for conscription and training but must needs volunteer at once as aviators and ambulance drivers in France." "They all write diaries and hundreds of letters," she reported. At least one of them intended to mimeograph his and circulate them through the state of Missouri, "where he has a large acquaintance." They had embarked on a great adventure and one of the attractions of that adventure was that they could record it and publish it at home. Collections of American soldier papers often contained letters published in hometown papers. Sometimes fond parents turned these communications, originally addressed to themselves, over to the local papers. Sometimes they were written for publication. Many small newspapers reserved columns for this first-hand reporting of the war from local boys.[30]

Towards the end of the war, the literary aspirations of soldiers had even become the butt of derision in *The Stars and Stripes.* The paper devoted one of its comic strips to "After the War Literature." The strip included likely titles of books by everyone from the army cook to the soldier court- martialed for drinking, Private Vin Blanc. The joke relies on the readers accepting the idea that some memories of the war – those of cooks and drunks – will not be worth a book. But then the strip made itself funnier by including "Helpful Hints, how to write a book," and the disclaimer that the advice might be misleading as the author, a mere newspaperman in uniform, after all not a warrior, wished to sell his own book too. The cartoonist returns to the World War I notion that all memoirs of participation contribute to the larger meaning.[31]

The volunteers "who must needs volunteer at once" had given reasons for enlisting in foreign services very like the reasons that Alan Seeger reported in *The New Republic.* "You see," said one volunteer to the reporter nurse, "the fellows in college got together and talked the thing out. College life seems to be over now, that is the fundamental thing that keeps a college together. Life seems to be working out on a different plane." For Seeger's group of expatriate artists and would-be artists, "the old haunts were desolate, the boon companions gone." Both these groups of young men had gone to war motivated by peer pressure, but with a consciousness of something larger than peer pressure too. Seeger wrote of not wishing to miss the experience of "millions." For the college boys who came to an agreement about their motives, "life" itself had moved to a different plane.

The way American men of the early twentieth century saw themselves moving into that new plane, putting on the uniform and submitting to military standards of behavior, did not necessarily erase their individuality. "The uniform was a beauty all blue, red and golden and you just knew there was a real *HE MAN* behind the smile," wrote one man who joined the Marine Corps.[32] Of course, this seems like the expression of the kind of cockiness that is often associated with military service, only in the idiom of 1917. But a "he man" was something of a nonconformist, an individual too. That a uniform could express this quality seems at least slightly contradictory. The relief and even gratitude at passing the physical examination before induction expressed by some soldiers shows the same impression of individual virility brought into relief by a standard. When Cliffton Cates passed his physical examination, he wrote to his mother:

> I went through with colors flying. They did not find any weak spots. I was scared to death they would. I sure do feel lots better since the marine doctors examined me and declared me to be perfect in every respect. It was an agreeable surprise.

Every other Tennessee man had some little defect that they considered before they would pass them.[33]

The physical examination for the Marine Corps declared Cates's perfection. But his new perfection only existed in the context of the service's standard test. His own body had triumphed, but that triumph only had meaning when compared with many other bodies. The "he-man" and perfection were both brought into relief rather than smothered by the uniform.

Women, too, could join up and prove themselves in relation to a standard. What they called patriotism included satisfaction at being part of a great enterprise. One Red Cross nurse wrote in her memoirs shortly after the war of what she had felt at belonging:

As I gazed at the pin, handling it affectionately, I admired its simple beauty and above all the symbol for which it stood. How lucky I am, I thought, to have had my training and to be able to join the coveted ranks of the Red Cross Nursing Service. Coveted indeed – for what real red-blooded woman in those days didn't want to be a Red Cross Nurse.[34]

Nurse Ethel D. Warner stressed the privileged position of the Red Cross nurse, the fact that they had not taken just anyone, but that everyone had wanted to participate. Her words of satisfaction echoed the marine officer who had been declared "perfect in every respect."

Theodore Roosevelt could give women an equal place with men in his thought about the need for Americans to merge their individuality into the national cause:

Never yet was a country worth living in unless its sons and daughters were of that stern stuff which bade them die for it at need; and never yet was a country worth dying for unless its sons and daughters thought of life not as something concerned only with the selfish evanescence of the individual, but as a link in the great chain of creation and causation, so that each person is seen in his true relations as an essential part of the whole, whose life must be made to serve the larger and continuing life of the whole.[35]

Historians have noted a gap that grew between men who had experienced battle and their women in World War I, but this gap has taken different dimensions for all the nationalities involved. In the American case, it hardly opened. Paul Fussell, writing for the most part about well-educated Englishmen, described this gap between men and women as part of a growing chasm between all civilian life and soldiers that some men never managed to cross.[36] Klaus Theweleit has described a pathological hatred of women, first taught to Germans in their nurseries, later taught as an informal but important part of the Imperial German Army's training, and then intensified by the essentially male experience of World War I.[37] Neither of these conditions described the relations between American men and women during the war.

If American men experienced an alienation from women in the early twentieth century, historians have explained it by pointing to the new place women held in commercial and leisure settings. The "new women" who worked outside the home as shop girls and stenographers, who could go shopping alone in the new great department stores, and who could take their pleasure at an amusement park, troubled American men. Independent and energetic and fresh though they were, they had escaped comfortable nineteenth-century domesticity to the harsh commercial and industrial world men inhabited, threatening the safe haven of the hearth. This "new woman" has left two images: one highly capable, respectable and chaste, the "Gibson Girl," and the equally capable but a-moral character of Theodore Dreiser's *Sister Carrie*. Beneath the capable, crisp, shirt-waisted, well-coiffed Gibson girl's exterior might lurk a prostitute.[38]

During the war, America seems only to have exported the "Gibson Girl" to France. She went as capable nurse, as YMCA hostess or as Salvation Army Lassy. She worked for the nation with the men, and this participation perhaps burned away the other negative image. Europeans were astounded at this military innovation. Respectable women following their country's army overseas kept up morale. The letters of American soldiers related gratitude, respect and love for these women. Prostitutes and loose women appeared in those letters, but once soldiers left the shores of the United States, these other women, perhaps conforming to a Gallic stereotype the Americans carried with them, were invariably French.

American women in France could share, to some degree, the soldiers' experience. In some cases, of course, a woman might have been closer to the front than a man. She could combine in her person the image of home and vulnerable domesticity with that of war. A Frenchman, while admiring the presence of American women with the American army, described such a situation. He had seen an American woman war worker, fresh from the front and the shelling, give a talk to groups of American soldiers. She gave the soldiers spirit and an immediate reason to fight far from their homes. First, she explained to them that the French fought so hard because they defended their homes and their women, but she understood that American women were too far off to motivate their men in that way. She spoke of the separation from American woman as the chief misfortune of the war for Americans.

> This war is hard for you in many ways, I know. If French soldiers fight with such a wonderful courage, it's because their country itself has suffered from the war, many of them have seen their homes destroyed and their families sent fleeing.
>
> And then French soldiers are supported by their women, their mothers, their girlfriends, who write to them every day, and from time to time see them. I know all this, I understand your problems, I know that letters are rare for you . . .[39]

She then explained the war to these men. This particular woman had talked about the war to a great many people in different places. Describing her technique was part of her technique. To farmers in Kansas, she said, she would show pictures of a farm that had been shelled with the beasts in the barn. The farmers were moved more fully by the useless destruction of dumb animals than by the destruction of soldiers. From animals, the woman war worker shifted to women and children. They, too, could be killed by war's senseless destruction.

Having first established that men fight best for their women and children, which is to say for their specific home, she had the difficult task of explaining to Americans that their own domestic life was at risk. War was total, she said, it killed animals in their stalls, it killed women and children at home. She said that if the Germans were to win the war in Europe, in ten years the war would have moved to the American continent. A general war that would thus envelop the world could thus touch them in particular.

She ended her talk by offering, upon her imminent return to the United States, to take messages to the girlfriends and mothers of these soldiers. If possible she would visit these female relatives. In her person, as in her rhetoric, she telescoped the distance from the American homes, whose defense provided the most pressing motive to fight, but that were not really threatened at all, to the front thousands of miles from those homes. Her French observer admired the effectiveness of her technique. She joined the highly individual emotion of attachment to family or farm – the specificity of dead animals in a barn, women and children dead in their homes – into the vast enterprise of this war that covered huge distances.

This unknown war-worker was not alone making the ties between soldiers, the war and their distant homes in order to motivate them for the task at hand. But she was better at it than some because she had found a way to move between the impersonal generality of the war and its destructive power and the individual soldiers. *The Stars and Stripes*, the AEF's own newspaper, started by and for American soldiers, specialized in this sort of connection. It printed, as a matter of course, the encouraging messages of American leaders to soldiers justifying the war, but more important was the special quality of its style: that of the soldier made skeptical by experience but who allows himself to be persuaded by reason, and can surprise himself with heartfelt enthusiasm. The editions of the paper that appeared around the July 4 and July 14 celebrations in Paris of 1918, while American soldiers were so dramatically helping stop the German advances, provided a good opportunity for the paper to make connections between France and the United States.

On July 5, *The Stars and Stripes* published General Pershing's message of July 4, 1918 on the front page.

> On this anniversary of our independence, the officers and men of the American Expeditionary Forces on the battlefields of France renew their pledges of fealty and devotion to our cause and country. The resolve of our forefathers that all men and peoples shall be free is their resolve. It is quickened by sympathy for an invaded people of kindred ideals and the war challenge of an arrogant enemy. It is fortified by the united support of the American people.[40]

Soldier-like, Pershing simply told the American people, to whom the message was addressed, that it supported the men in France, while reporting with utter assurance the feelings of his men. His men were motivated by the same feelings that had moved the founders of the United States. Pershing's message, formal and dignified though it was, took no trouble to persuade. It has nearly the style of a command.

The Stars and Stripes did more. It created in itself the same kind of bridge that the war-worker above had created. For example, on July 5, 1918, along with various news items about the war, the newspaper printed the kind of reverie in which it specialized: "The Second Summer."

> Could we have spent a year in a fairer land, under a fairer sky, be it in "le beau pays de la Touraine," or among the grass clad foothills of the Vosges?
>
> Yes, of course, in America. But in the days to be, when old familiar scenes greet us once more, when we return to find unchanged our own Berkshires, our Pocono Hills, our Ozarks, or our Sierra Nevada, who among us will not look back and reflect, with full heart that, for her ideals, for her people, for her very trees and rocks and soil, la France has won his love.[41]

The American soldiers' own newspaper told them that they loved France and made it seem convincing by telling them that "of course," they loved their own land better. The homely Pocono Hills, the Ozarks, and the dramatic Sierra Nevada, each representing home for some, and a vacation destination for different sections of the country, were loved because they were familiar. But because many American soldiers were now familiar with the Vosges and Touraine – many American units first saw action along the relatively quiet Vosges section of the line, and there were training camps in the Touraine, which is also a vacation destination – these French places too have become part of the lives of soldiers and must be loved. The newspaper invited its readers to look with a tourist's nostalgia at their time in service while the war still raged! Nothing could cover time and space like nostalgia, which can create, as here, a fond memory of a present event. *The Stars and Stripes* manipulated sentiment. It was an innovative paper with an innovative staff. Among the editors were Private Harold Ross and Sergeant Alexander Woollcott, the men who would create *The New Yorker* in 1925. *The New Yorker's* mascot, Eustance Tilley, the man in the top hat who carried a monocle, would take his dandified get-up and self-mocking disdain from an invented past of old New York into an ever more progressive and modern future. The future *New Yorker* editors were already perfecting their indirect approach to persuasion, persuading a skeptical young army audience that life in the army, the war, and France, would make part of a past, privileged to have been so full of adventure and sights.

By the edition of July 12, 1918, the weekly newspaper had had time to report on the patriotic celebrations of Independence Day a week earlier. President Wilson's July 4 message for the occasion interpreted the American Revolution, possibly a sore point with the British allies, as the descendent of the rebellion against King John that resulted in *Magna Carta*, and both those events as forerunners to the proposed League of Nations.

> Washington and his companions, like the barons at Runnymede, spoke and acted not for a class, but for a people. It falls to us, to watch over that of which it is understood they spoke and acted, not for a single people, but for all humanity.[42]

Wilson had telescoped history and geography in his speech at Washington's tomb at Mount Vernon, but his language did not reach out to soldiers. The complicated interpretive message strained even Wilson's rhetorical powers.

The editors of *The Stars and Stripes* from their semi-official position, dominated by enlisted men, could do better. Soldiers were asked to observe the French Bastille Day on July 14 with the same enthusiasm that the French had shown on July 4. The reporting of July 4 could not have pleased the French more.

> All in all, we counted ourselves luckiest who were in Paris that day, for Paris is the heart of France and France was the heart of the war . . . To begin with there were great goings on in the Place d'Iéna, where underneath the statue of Washington, they renamed the Avenue Tracadéro the Avenue du Président Wilson. And you knew for sure you were at the heart of the world when all unexpected and unannounced, a car drove up and out got the Premier of Britain and the Premier of Italy to sit them down beside the Premier of France and watch our boys march by.[43]

The paper had invented instant nostalgia that allowed the doughboy to remember himself at the center of the world, that happened to be in Paris. The well-orchestrated demonstration of international cooperation, a parade and a ceremony of naming an avenue for one head of state in the presence of three other heads of state, became a spontaneous, "unexpected and unannounced" event. A more official newspaper could not have described the event in that way. But *The Stars and Stripes*, existing between the enlisted men and authority, could interpret the simple soldier's feelings for him from his point of view. The newspaper performed, with consummate skill, the act of auto-persuasion in which soldiers were already engaged. The insignificant individual was placed in the heart of the great event, and his individual presence appeared to be what gave meaning to that event. War, a naming ceremony, a parade, while giving a soldier thrilling personal memories, took meaning from his presence. The paper told a story in which thousands participated marching along a Parisian avenue, but the point of view has been made personal. The technique is one from advertising that causes people to react to a product, but it functioned as well for Americans in World War I. Every man could feel what was deepest in him, yet every man "felt exactly the same thing," they had learned to express their feelings in a standard form.

2 "It's a great life if you don't weaken, but believe me there are few who don't:" The Meaning Americans Gave to Action at the Front in World War I

> Is there such a thing as "war" bravery?
> I would say yes.
> I witnessed many an incident, I must confess,
> Soldiers be they black or white, Americans all,
> Who had answered their country's call.[1]

The desire to probe the existence of "war" bravery in the trench combat of World War I concerned Joseph Shapiro, a private soldier and veteran of World War I all his adult life. He wrote the poem that heads this chapter in 1919, and reworked it in 1976 before sending his papers to Carlisle Barracks.

What concerned Shapiro was *not* the combination of feelings, the mixture of fear, resolution, desperation, faith, hopelessness, and strength that, in differing combinations, become either courage or cowardice in the eyes of a judgmental future. Shapiro used the "incidents" he witnessed, that in the context of the poem had the potential for portraying those feelings, as the foundation of something else: he translated what he saw into a national American standard behavior. In his poem, the incidental actions of American soldiers disappeared to become simply an indication of their Americaness, and proof that they had responded to the nation's needs appropriately.

Nationhood, stronger than race, and a standard of behavior are the subjects of this short poem. Shapiro translated what he saw of battlefields into this nugget of meaning. He and other Americans, on and near the battlefield of World War I, translated their personal sensations into a national experience submerging individual actions. The test of courage, so significant as individuals faced danger in previous wars, became modified by the conditions of World War I into a test of a man's ability to survive with his fellows.

During the Civil War, according to historian Gerald F. Linderman, the test of personal and conspicuous courage in battle gave officers ascendancy over their men and acted as the "cement of armies." Courage created the *esprit* and mutual respect necessary for military discipline and coordinated military action. The courage to stand in front of the enemy's fire could be interpreted as success in battles whose strategic outcome was uncertain, and the memory of courageous actions could compensate for the destruction of comrades. "In the Civil War soldiers at first were not much troubled by the discrepancy between their persistent idea of combat as an individualized endeavor and the reality of increasingly depersonalized mass warfare, because their notions of courage helped to conceal the gap."[2]

In the twentieth century, technology, the strength and wealth of the United States, and the rigor of the training that the Federal government could impose on men – removing them from the shelter and support of homes, families and communities to a degree unimaginable to Civil War soldiers – transformed the mobilization of armies, according to Linderman, into a "matter of persuading or compelling young men to accept a status of powerlessness." The gap between the idea of combat as an individualized or individualizing matter and its mechanical dehumanized reality had grown wider. Linderman cited Dwight D. Eisenhower to make his comparison with twentieth-century war, specifically World War II. "For Dwight Eisenhower, perseverance became courage; heroism, he declared, was 'the uncomplaining acceptance of unendurable conditions.' Here Eisenhower marked a transition from active to passive conceptions of courage." Of course, Eisenhower had first been close to combat in World War I. He had observed part of this transition of courage on the western front.[3]

The conspicuous acts of courage, so necessary for the functioning of armies in the Civil War, though threatened by rifled guns and exploding shells, had become impossible in the face of machine guns in World War I. But the idea of soldier bravery had not yet become restricted to expression in "group cohesion" or loyalty to the squad where courage became a private matter, well-guarded, for the appreciation of close companions. Though there was no notion of acts of bravery so exposed as in the Civil War, men still sought public recognition of the quality of bravery. Had Joseph Shapiro fought in the Civil War, he would not have had to ponder over the existence of "war bravery," he would have witnessed some outstanding examples that needed no interpretation. Had he fought in World War II, he would not have come to the conclusion that "war bravery" could translate into anything so vast as national identity.

Combining the emotional material of war literature with the technical details of what military men can relate of battle conditions, the Englishman John Keegan described not only what the soldiers felt subjectively but also such information as how many rounds of ammunition were thrown at them and what damage and wounds were inflicted around and on them to produce those feelings. Keegan made a bridge between the impersonal and mechanical forces of destruction at work and individual feelings. In Keegan's work, the soldier's training, expectations, confidence in his unit, and discipline helped him overcome fear and physical hardship in what we know, in retrospect, to have been the futile attack by the British starting on July 1, 1916 at the Somme.

Keegan called an important part of his inquiry "The Will to Combat." In it, he described the motivations that prompted those British soldiers to climb out of their trenches into the face of German fire. He found that training and the respect, leadership and example of officers were important. "Arguments can be found," he stated, "to suggest that leadership – conscious, principled, exemplary – was of higher quality and greater military significance in the First World War, at least in the British army, than before or since."[4] The coercion represented by armed military police, stationed behind advancing troops, and officers willing to use their firearms on unwilling soldiers, also motivated soldiers. And finally, fear, the fear of being taken prisoner, the fear of not acting aggressively enough for survival in the face of the enemy's aggression, kept soldiers moving forward in the face of terrible odds.

Eventually, the delicate balance between training, fear and leadership broke down. According to Keegan, this happened in World War I either as a function of the accumulation of casualties, or with the passage of time in the stressful conditions of World War I battle. The collapse of the Russian army, the mutinies in the French army, the disintegration of the Italian army, all in 1917, and the collapse of the British Fifth Army in March 1918, all took place when the number of casualties had reached the number of those armies' fighting strengths. The cases of failed discipline, with the exception of the German army's, happened within two and a half to three years from the date a particular army first encountered heavy losses.

Figures for the German army are more difficult to determine. But certainly it had suffered a greater proportion of casualties by the time of its collapse in the Fall of 1918 than the other armies had done. Keegan explained this anomaly by pointing out that the Germans had, unlike the other armies, enjoyed remarkable and some conclusive victories in the war.[5] They had forced the Russians to accept their terms for peace at the treaty of Brest-Litovsk in 1917. The victories in the East in 1917 were reason for optimism in the West in 1918, as the eastern divisions could be moved to the western front in 1918 for the last great German offensive there. When these offensives failed, the German army, too, showed signs of disintegration.

Significantly, the American Expeditionary Forces came into the war late and never came close to Keegan's critical proportion of casualties. And, like the Germans, the AEF achieved several notable victories during its comparatively brief time in battle. Their first active engagements, the defense of Seicheprey, April 20–1, 1918, and taking Cantigny, May 28–9, both isolated and comparatively minor affairs, were hailed as victories in the United States. Though the losses were heavy considering what ground was gained, these encounters gave confidence to American officers and men. At the end of May and in the beginning of June 1918, the American Third Division fought at Château-Thierry, stopping a flank of the great German advance of 1918. The Marine Brigade of the Second Division stopped a more important part of that advance at Belleau Wood between June 3 and June 13, with help from parts of the Third Division arriving to relieve them after June 14. The counter-attack at Soissons included the First and Second Divisions from July 18–22. They made an 11-kilometer advance, took 3,400 German prisoners and 75 guns at a cost of 7,317 casualties or 60 per cent of the officers and half the men of the infantry units involved.[6]

These early engagements after Cantigny, fought by Americans, differed from the great World War I engagements of 1915–17 in several ways. First of all, the success of the German Spring offensives had moved the front out of the system of trenches that had built up over years. Belleau Wood was intact when the fighting started. The Marines approaching it from one side came through fields of standing wheat. When they had gained positions in the wood, each man fought from a shallow depression he had made as best he could without a shovel. In the Soissons counter-attack that included tanks, movement played an important role. The second difference that set these battles apart was that the Germans were exhausted, and did not have the strength by August 1918 to reimpose the stalemating system of approximately equal power sheltered in trenches. And, finally, American units were not exhausted, and were arriving in great numbers in France throughout the Summer of 1918 – one million announced on July 4. After Soissons, the German General Ludendorff wrote of American soldiers, "Personnel must be called excellent. Spirit of troops is high. Moral effect of our fire does not materially check the advance of the infantry. Nerves of the Americans are still unshaken."[7]

Those American engagements left the enduring impression on American soldiers that, with their arrival at the front, conditions had changed. But the war could easily regain its old characteristics even with the presence of Americans. Through August 1918, eight American divisions participated in the Aisne-Marne campaign. Initially the front moved, but eventually the battle bogged down with Americans defending the low ground of the Vesle River. The situation resembled the kind of trench war European armies had been fighting for years. Any movement by day attracted shelling. Neither side could gain an advantage until, in September, French units made advances on German positions elsewhere.

In September, Americans again made striking advances when General Pershing had his first opportunity to command American divisions in an independent American army. He had struggled hard with French and British commanders who wanted American divisions to replace men in their own sectors, but, with the tide seemingly turning, Supreme Commander Ferdinand Foch became generous and the American First Army cast off for the St. Mihiel salient. This jagged westward projection of the German line had remained a quiet sector in German hands for years, but now with the lines moving, General Foch felt that the Germans would withdraw if attacked. When the First Army commenced its artillery bombardment in the early morning of September 12, German units were caught by surprise in the act of shifting men and material back. The American advance swiftly took the salient. By September 13, General Pershing greeted Allied and American dignitaries in St. Mihiel, and by September 16, the First Army was engaging the enemy in the newly-built line of defenses along the now straightened German front. Pershing's army had achieved its objective, capturing an important railroad line, many guns and supplies. His casualties – 7,000 in relation to the 2,300 German killed and wounded and 14,700 German prisoners – compared well with other World War I battles.[8]

Had the First Army continued to push through the new German lines in the direction of Metz, the strategic importance of their continued rapid advance would have magnified. Taking the German army off balance, they might have achieved the kind of significant victory so elusive in World War I.[9] Pershing had committed his army in another direction, however, against the Meuse-Argonne sector. There, American divisions fought from September 26 till the Armistice on November 11 against forty-seven German divisions in defensive positions twelve miles deep and in difficult terrain. Eventually, they captured 16,059 prisoners, and dominated another important railroad line. The cost, however, was 120,000 casualties, including nearly half the Americans killed in the war. This last offensive also proved the limits of American *élan* over mechanized war. Americans had broken the trap of the trench war model, but a short time later, it caught them just the same.

Americans then have a peculiar relationship to the battles of World War I. Though eventually Americans fought in trenches and faced the same German army and same machine-guns, walked through the same mud, experienced the same sensations, all with similar disheartening results, these experiences were sandwiched between the experience of more open battle, where objectives were achieved, and the Armistice.

The experience of battle is disproportionately memorialized in diaries and letters of Americans. It takes up far more room in their written records than the actual time spent in battle would suggest. This may seem natural. Though modern wars require much preparation, and though modern armies require more men in the rear than at the front, the dramatic climax of a war still appears to take place in battle. Soldier diaries can be seen as documents leading up to that climax and then retreating from it. Cultural innovations as diverse as modernist literary irony, cubism, and rising divorce rates have been variously related to the trench experience, and not the experience behind the lines.[10] Twice a year since 1978, as many as three hundred enthusiasts have gathered in rural Pennsylvania to "authentically recreate the experience of trench warfare in the First World War."[11] But given the comparatively brief period that most American soldiers spent at the front, and given the nature of the attritional victory eventually won, a victory in which the entire German nation collapsed from within, economically, politically, and then finally militarily, this insistence on battle as the central memory of World War I does not seem natural at all, but has been produced by an act of interpretation.

Focusing on battle could make sense of the destructive mass event for individuals because, though the death dealt out in modern war takes no heed of individual identity, any one man's possible death was an intensely individual experience for him. In battle, the mass destruction caused by some men could overlap with the possibility of the destruction of individuals, possibly at the same moment that they caused catastrophe elsewhere. Centering thoughts of war on the climactic moment of battle could preserve the notion of individual choices involved: the choice to act with courage or not, the choice to take initiative or not, even when confronted with a seemingly random hail of explosives. When the soldier worked behind the front, perhaps doing important responsible work, he was only conscious of working for the group effort, and as part of the team.

One officer in charge of repairing locomotives because of previous work with the Pennsylvania Railroad felt this keenly. He complained to his wife that others "seem to be just sailing by us and we've been over so long and I know they are thrilled and look down on us staying in the rear." His wife helped him overcome this difficulty. She clipped articles about the importance and extent of American railroad work in France. "After all," one clipping concluded, "this is to a very great extent an engineer's war. Applied science wearing the devil's livery is fighting applied science in the service of civilized ideals."[12] But never going to the front, this man never became convinced of his contribution to the war.

Military authority and doctrine have placed an ambivalent value on the individual. Studies of the choice between cowardice and bravery in World War I naturally attempted to describe training that leads men to choose bravery more often than not.[13] Training and military units have been designed to emphasize cohesion, loyalty to the group, and clear standards of behavior over reliance on an individual's fortitude. Since World War I, the size of the group and the reach of the standard with which a soldier identifies have become smaller than the cinematic abstractions of obedience envisaged by some progressives at the time of World War I. But this reduction in scale was based on the idea that the group closest to a man has the strongest influence on him. The existence of individual choice as a tool to stimulate effort under the most difficult circumstances has continued. Thus, part of the literature on motivating men into battle is the insistence on the importance of the soldier's will. At the same time, military authorities have attempted, through training and indoctrination, to make sure that soldiers have made only the right choice by the time they came into contact with the enemy.[14]

A man may originally have had some choice about whether or not he stood and fought. He could have resisted conscription, become a conscientious objector, arranged to participate in the war in some non-combatant role. But, at every step, at least for a very young man whose loyalties and habits of work and family life had not become fixed, to make the choice that led towards combat was easier than the choice away from combat.

When the moment came to climb out of the trench in the face of machine gun fire, hardly any choice still existed. A soldier's fellows depended on him, his training demanded that he do as he was told. To have refused would have separated him from the unit that contained the only familiar faces and organization in a disorganized and hostile landscape that offered no other means of sustenance. All alternative authority and structure had withdrawn or been sequestered. Religion, family, law, markets, even nature – in the case of World War I reduced to an infertile plane of mud – lay either too distant, behind the soldier, or in devastation around him, unable to offer any alternative to the sergeant or junior officer who stood beside him with a loaded firearm exhorting him to go over the top. The Military Police would follow shortly too. Having learned to think of himself as an individual unit operating inside the organism of the army, by resisting or escaping, he would have found himself without identity, in fact without individuality, in a landscape whose features had been obliterated by war.

The Chief British Medical Officer of World War I, Lord Moran, changed his thoughts on the subject of courage during the course of the war. Men might possess some form of courage innately, he wrote after the war, but no matter how much of that quality a man possessed, modern technological war could wear it down:

> There seemed to be four degrees of courage and four orders of men measured by that standard . . . Men who did not feel fear; men who felt fear but did not show it; men who felt fear and showed it but did their job; men who felt fear showed it and shirked. At Ypres [presumably the author refers to the Third Battle of Ypres fought by the British in Summer and Fall 1917] I was beginning to understand that few men spent their trench lives with their feet firmly planted on one rung of this ladder . . . The story of modern war is concerned with the striving of men eroded by fear, to maintain a precarious footing on the upper rungs of this ladder.[15]

Lord Moran made it clear that the two middle classes were preferable to the others in this scheme. The first group he said had not enough imagination or intelligence to feel fear. The last group had no use militarily. Men in the middle two classes had *chosen* to behave well under stress, and thus were the preferred soldiers.

By the time of the Third Battle of Ypres, in the Summer and Fall of 1917, Lord Moran realized that under sufficiently danger-ous and extended circumstances, men who had passed the test of courage before could break down. It took him time and much observation of break-downs to come to the conclusion. "The story of how courage was spent in France is a picture of sensitive men using up their will-power under discouraging circumstances while one by one their moral props were knocked down."[16] Most

American authorities were not in a position to make these observations, and they did not reach these conclusions. Even the comparatively brief engagements in which American soldiers fought could reduce very brave men to states of shock, but, for Americans, the fighting did not last long enough for this result of battle to become generally accepted. For Americans, the war's special dehumanizing conditions could still test an American identity.

American soldiers in World War I passed their test of bravery in great numbers. Facing death in company gave a man a standard by which to measure his individual performance against the performances of others in the larger society of the army. A test in isolation might have had less meaning to men trained to army standards and the standards of a growing American democratic mass culture. As Walter Benn Michaels has pointed out, the progressive era in America reacted to a tension in the meaning of individualism brought about by mass production and mass consumption. According to Michaels, figures as diverse as Frederick Winslow Taylor and Edward Bellamy found the independent individualism, of the time before mass production, to have become meaningless because each man's individualism had existed in isolation as he made his way alone. In a progressive setting, an individual could find his identity more truly against a standard, set by a scientifically organized industrial society.

The army before and during World War I became a testing ground for progressive organizational ideas in general and also for the ideas of both Taylor and Bellamy. In the Civil War, for example, the American clothing industry, as it manufactured millions of uniforms for the Union Army, developed a system of standardized sizes. For the first time, men who couldn't afford to have clothes specially made for them by a taylor, nonetheless had clothes that were intended to fit. Not every man had a uniform that did fit him, as Civil War photographs make clear. In this army setting, however, where some kinds of individuality had been erased as a soldier was trained to act with a mass of other men, each man had learned to regard his body as requiring clothes of a certain "size," that should fit.

The Civil War was the first American war to be photographed extensively. The famous portraits of soldiers taken by Matthew Brady, and others, created not only the record of individual appearances, but also created a standard of individual memorialization to which every soldier could aspire. Today's viewer, who can compare the photographs of different generals, knows, for example, just how eccentric General Grant's disheveled appearance was. Ulysses S. Grant must have known this too. The ubiquity of photographs allowed him to cultivate that unorthodox appearance. Soldiers sitting for the thousands of photographic portraits of the war had the same consciousness of creating a record of their individuality. Their aplomb might break down before the necessity of sitting still for the photographer, but their preparations, sometimes equipping themselves with strange weapons and props, give evidence of a conscious individuality.[17] The soldiers of the AEF bore themselves in a more uniform manner for photographic portraits. They buttonned up their coats, they turned their heads and showed their left ears. Individuality has become a matter of expression. The polished appearance of General Pershing and his staff projected an image of discipline that went beyond character differences between the commander of the AEF and the commander of the Union's armies fifty odd years before.

By the time of World War I, technological, industrial and market advances, along with over a decade of progressive politics, all aided army training and propaganda to spread the notion that individuality might appear best in relief before the standard of the mass. The progressive spirit of public service epitomized in the industrial army of Edward Bellamy's famous novel of 1888, *Looking Backward,* can be seen translated into the army, drafted by the United States in 1917 and indoctrinated with an official enthusiastic rhetoric.[18]

Frederick Winslow Taylor's disciple, Frank B. Gilbreth, applied time-motion studies to soldiers' drill, by means of movies, in order to make them more efficient while giving them an unchanging and cinematic standard by which to measure their progress. French military instructors, too, used film to train Americans when they arrived. Some French instructors complained that Americans preferred training films that provided a literal model to follow and refused to listen to more abstract instruction in principles.[19] Target practice, with rewards of promotion and medals, gave soldiers who had learned their marksmanship isolated in a rural setting, a sense of position in a national context. The army intended its intelligence tests to create a standard by which each soldier could be assigned to the task best suited to him. In these ways, the army could treat each man individually, and the man could recognize his own individuality against the background of the group. At the same time, each man had to learn to recognize himself as an individual occupying a very dependent place in the midst of the larger organism of the military.[20]

American soldiers reflected the tensions in the meaning of the individual in a mass event in the way they thought about battle and its meaning for them. A volunteer ambulance driver, who rejected biological causes of war in favor of cultural differences between the belligerent countries, expressed this tension, when he first found himself under fire.

> Well, I have something to write now – I have been under fire and in plain sight of the Boche trenches. You know I promised to tell you how it feels, so I suppose I shall have to try although I can't even quite explain it to myself. Yesterday we went over a hill and started down the road. Our guide said, "Gentlemen, that line where you see French shells bursting is the German trenches." Well, right then and there I experienced the most peculiar sensation I have ever felt. It wasn't fear, it wasn't excitement, it wasn't curiosity, it wasn't battle-lust, it wasn't anything I ever heard of or imagined, just this: over there in plain sight were men who by pressing their buttons could blow you into kingdom-come and refrained for no reason at all, just the stupendousness of the whole thing, your absolute im- potence and littleness, and the invincibility of fate – oh Hell! there is not any use trying, it just simply can't be described, like the advertisements say it must be "experienced to be appreciated." Sorry this explanation is so inadequate, but you can't explain the beauty of moonlight or of a sunset, you can't explain the mystery of the sea, or the exhileration of rain in your face – no more in fact far less, can you explain the thrill of modern warfare. Every other fellow felt exactly the same thing.[21]

He wrote a letter bursting with the power of a great experience and his desire to describe his feelings even in their state of almost systematic contradiction. His difficulty lay in the difference in what the experience might mean to himself and what it meant in broader terms: between the human and mechanical qualities of the confrontation.

He had experienced closeness to death as a great inexpressible mystery, corresponding to what was deepest in him and in nature. This confrontation with the inexpressible might have left him isolated in his enlightenment. But he went on to translate the ineffable by means of a simile taken from modern marketing into something anyone could understand. He even assured his reader of the reliability of his reactions because those reactions could be reproduced in anyone and were. He wrote, "Like the advertisements say it must be 'experienced to be appreciated.' . . . Every other fellow felt exactly the same thing." And the German enemy produced this ineffable, yet standard feeling in him, and in everyone around him, in an entirely mechanical way, by either pressing or not pressing "their buttons." Everyone felt exhilerated, and also felt "impotence and littleness."

A month after his first encounter with battle, he wrote that the deeper considerations did not matter because war would make him see who he was in the context of many other men:

> What is the sense of asking oneself what one is here for? Go out and do something and one will soon find out something one can do or else one will realize that one does not cut so very much ice after all and there are other pebbles on the beach . . .[22]

During his earliest exposures to battle, the importance of the older individualism that could exist in the isolation that comes with a mystical experience was replaced, first by a comparison with the feelings of other members of his unit, and later by a more general comparison with men as numerous as "pebbles on the beach."

The tension between individual accomplishment and determining a standard of bravery made its appearance in the letters of Lieutenant Joseph Brown describing his part in Belleau Wood. He emphasized exploits that he had carried out single-handedly. In a letter of June 23, 1918, he described rescuing a wounded man from a position in front of his own lines and under German fire – an exploit, he reported, for which fellow officers recommended him for a Medal of Honor. The fighting of World War I has often been characterized as the passive, dehumanizing waiting in trenches for destruction, but for Lieutenant Brown at Belleau Wood, fighting remained active, effective and even life-affirming.

I wouldn't have missed it for anything but Oh my! 4 yrs of war crowded into one. Our experience was the freak of the whole war. Our whole position was the worst and hottest in all France, and Hell's Half Acre – my stronghold – was the worst spot in our whole position. Every man there had vital experiences one after the other more fantastic than any movie. People back here won't believe we occupied such a position with Germans on 3 sides not more than 30 yds. away at all times.[23]

With a good deal of pride, he informed his wife that he had survived very difficult fighting with few ill effects. "Tell my good brothers, who thought I was too frail to endure the hardships of war, that I have outlasted all the huskies and seem to bear the strain better than anyone in the regiment thus far," he wrote on July 31, 1918. He had participated in the fighting at both Belleau Wood and Soissons and his fortitude was a great source of satisfaction to him.

But in addition to his satisfaction in his own exploits, and his passing a test of physical endurance, his reactions included a collective satisfaction. "Every man there had vital experiences one after the other more fantastic than any movie," he had written. Not only had he proved himself fitter than others, but everyone around him had passed the same test. They had come up to, and even surpassed, the standard set by movies. Frank B. Gilbreth had attempted to instill a standard of drill into the minds of soldiers, using film. But the power of film viewed by mass audiences had established a standard of bravery already, to which soldiers could compare themselves.

In the thought he expressed in his letters, Joseph Brown placed individual worth and adherence to a standard, which are not the same, so close together that they could become indistinguishable. In his letter of June 28, he repeated his comparison of war experience to film, writing, "every moment of the existence of every man there, was as fantastical and more so than any moving picture." The beginning of the sentence implies extraordinary specificity and variety, but by the end, all men compare to movies. On June 23, just after the battle, he had written making the bridge between individual self-discovery and the formation of general standard: "It's all over and I wouldn't have missed it for anything. It was a tremendous experience and one in which each found what he truly was." Every man found out what he truly was, but Brown left the impression of uniform courage.[24]

In fact, Lieutenant Brown did not experience the excitement of a four years' war in one year, but in one week of fighting at Belleau Wood in conditions unlike those elsewhere on the front. After this action and another week of battle around Soissons, Brown thought of going home. "I would give anything to be sent home as an instructor for about 17 weeks ... Far more than being a major I want to get back and see those dear babies of mine before the next show. We who came through thus far are temporarily tired of the game and talk of the great wisdom of 'swivelers.' "[25] By "swiveler," he referred to all those officers occupied in rear sections on swivel chairs at desks.

Part of Brown's conception of a standard of behavior set by men in battle came from his growing awareness of the suffering around him, and of the limits of his own endurance. Though he filled his letters immediately after battle with descriptions of his fortitude, his superior resistence, upon reflection, turned out to be a matter of comparative degree, rather than of kind. "My men were on edge all the time, and I've no doubt many would have developed shell-shock if they had known how to get it or what it was," he wrote on June 23, after Belleau Wood. He suggested that other officers had not set their men such a good example: "Kennedy got shell-shock the first night in, and poor Monty went crazy soon after – he's still nutty."[26] On June 28, 1918, he admitted that he too had been "nutty," while under fire in Belleau Wood. By July 24, after his second period in battle, he wrote, "It is a great life if you don't weaken, but believe me there are few who don't." He used the standard, optimistic phrase of the young army, but he modified it. He implied that there was a standard breaking point, as well as a standard of strength.

Brown's experiences at Belleau Wood and Soissons were fought in unusual conditions for World War I. At Belleau Wood, there was no system of trenches, and in the offensive towards Soissons the units covered considerable distances. But in spite of how much men differ from Brown in the recounted events of their experience of battle, they constructed meaning out of it in the same way. Brown described moments of active bravery, his own and of others, where men made conscious decisions to move in the face of enemy fire. Much more common were descriptions of passive survival of terrible shelling. But, in either case, American men expressed relief at finding themselves to have passed the test of courage. In either case, they had acted as part of the larger organization of the army and to survive in that organization was to live up to its standard. Bravery acted as a subjective self-judgment that could give personal meaning to conformity to the collective standard.

Lieutenant Clyde A. Hunsucker wrote a letter to his mother exactly a month after the Armistice, describing his first and last military engagement. He described confusion and terrible casualties: "Fully 50 per cent of the officers of our regiment were either wounded or killed." The letter described the dangers of the battle from a very personal point of view. "They threw at least 200 big high explosive shells right around my position trying to blow up my headquarters. They threw one in from the flank which hit within at least 3 feet of where I was hugging the bank. I thought my legs were torn off." Of this terrible experience, he wrote: "My military ambition has been realized. I wanted to be in command of Company M. in battle and I was. Now that the war is over I want to go home." Yet nowhere did he mention any command or encouragement he gave his men. Nowhere did he describe any active part he played in the battle. He simply survived it. His report of his survival was such a source of pride to both himself and his mother that they caused it to be published in their local newspaper in Texas.[27] The letter demonstrated not that he had been an effective soldier, but that he had participated with others and survived.

Though he cannot have imagined that commanding Company M. in battle would consist of clinging to a collapsing canal bank while under fire for days, the reality did nothing to alter his idea of military ambition. Nor did the cost in lives alter his way of expressing himself from pre-war literary formulas. In the same letter, he wrote: "I saw many of my old friends slain upon the field of battle." He used the old turn of phrase for the honour of the dead around him. The phrase lent gravity to his own experience without leading to speculation about his good luck or the randomness of destruction.

Lieutenant Robert Sawyer, another Texan, used a romantic idiom about the dead he saw too. "For the first time in my military career I had gazed upon the gory fields of human carnage." And the presence of the dead did not alter his generally positive interpretation of his battle experience either. As with Hunsucker, surviving the battle counted for more than anything he recounted having done in the battle:

> I had for the first time been able to find myself out – whether or not I was equal to the great trust given to me as an officer and soldier of the American Army.
>
> I do not hesitate to say that during that night I felt a physical weakness. The man who can stand under such fire without dread creeping in must surely be made up of iron. I may have been frightened at times but my best thought was that I would be a dead one before I would show it. And that is the American soldier in general.[28]

He went on to say that men existed in the AEF who would rather "fight than eat," corresponding to Lord Moran's first level of bravery. His comment that these men gained "posthumous decorations" may be a judgment, similar to Lord Moran's on their military utility. Battle had allowed him to "find himself out." But he had not found some individual self. The qualities he discovered were the qualities of Americans in general. His description of his degree of bravery, which he shared with so many others, corresponded to one of the degrees Lord Moran described above: those who chose not to show their fear. For him, this was the standard of American courage. Apparently, he saw no contradiction between the language he used that came from a romantic past, and what he described: courage made relative by modern technology.

In fact, he had taken shelter for a night in a shell hole after getting lost. He had become lost because he wished to avoid shelling in daylight along the route, "I desired to delay that 'joy ride' as long as possible," he said of his delayed trip up to his men. Like Hunsucker, he submitted to shelling during this trial. He never wrote that he took action or gave orders. This survival was enough to identify him with "the American soldier in general."

Sawyer knew great personal loss during his brief time at war. His brother Joe was killed at Soissons in August, 1918. And he saw the ghastly human wreckage that the war left behind. But he never abandoned the optimism that he coupled with a heroic rhetoric. After hearing the news of his brother, he wrote:

That was a glorious fight – a standard of service was set that thrilled all Americans with pride and every soldier will fight from now on to emulate and preserve that blood caste standard. I am proud of my brother. I am proud of my name and though I may make the same sacrifice – I feel that my wife and baby can look upon the pages of history and feel proud of my efforts. The tide has turned.[29]

Again this soldier's rhetoric owes more to the nineteenth century than to the twentieth, but he has adapted this style to a message about setting standards, in which no individual's action remains. It had been a glorious fight, his own brother contributed, but he contributed as one of a collectivity of the dead to be evaluated, rather than because he died in any particular way. For this man, romantic conceptions of battle from the nineteenth century could meet the destructive capacity of the twentieth century and survive in a positive, if sanguine, interpretation.

The American dead, in Sawyer's letter, helped to set, or meet, the standard of American pride. Of the battlefield where he had spent his night of trial, he wrote:

We came to the spot where the fellow was hit during the night – he had one boot and leg blown off. We were now on the old battlefield, where the 8th and 71st Brigades had made a glorious page in history – the dead seemed to be in hundreds, though I am quite sure it was my imagination. I saw some of my old comrades of the border service who had made good, but had paid the great price.[30]

Sawyer's high-flown rhetoric about standards of bravery, or "making good," became the war itself. The hundreds of dead he saw, part of the 30,000 very real Americans killed in the Meuse-Argonne offensive in the last weeks of the war, melted into his imagination, while the abstractions they called up to him, the "glorious page in history," became concrete in his mind.

That "glorious page in history" could take form under these terrible circumstances because the tide of the war did turn during those battles of the Summer of 1918 in which American soldiers first distinguished themselves. The purposefulness of the American engagements was apparent to soldiers from the first. "Had we not made this attack first, there is little doubt in the minds of most historians that Paris would have fallen,"[31] wrote one soldier of the American counter-attack at Soissons, of July of 1918. The German armies had made their last great attempt on Paris in the Summer of 1918 with the divisions they had recalled from the Russian front. Their advances failed and the German army never regained an offensive position. The collapse of the entire German empire coincided with the first American counter-attack. It is hardly surprising that American participants remembered their own success and sense of purpose.

American participants in the war seem to have been able to share the optimism of successful and brief engagement regardless of their race. If any Americans had been excluded from a sense of progress and fulfillment from involvement in the war, it was black Americans who, for the most part, were kept away from battle in labor battalions. But those black soldiers of the Ninety-second and Ninety-third Divisions who did participate in battle could express some of the same personal optimism as white Americans. John F. Dixon, an African-American man from New York, wrote home to the women of his family, after he had first seen battle, in very optimistic terms.

> We are real soldiers now and not afread of Germans. Give my love to Claypool, Mary, June, and Grace. Tell them I say war is more than a notion. Our boys went on the battlefield last night singing, you can't beat them, they are surely game and happy bunch. It is not time to be sad. We'll get that Kaiser yet we are making good you know we can't come home until we get the Kaiser.[32]

Having been in battle, he knew not so much that his unit had no fear of the Germans as that it could stand up under that fear. They had been able to choose bravery when faced with danger. Dixon's experience reassured him about his worth in a segregated army where Blacks were usually relegated to menial jobs along with penal units. This reassurance comes from experience along with the special, if undefined, knowledge that "war is more than a notion." Perhaps because of this knowledge, "It is no time to be sad." War and the experience of battle have, Dixon thought at the time of writing, made him and other members of his segregated unit into men as good as any other men, "You can't beat them." For the time being, he had possibly been caught up in the uplift that the progressive era promised, and that black leaders thought would be the reward for Blacks in return for their participation in the war. Dixon did not say that his unit had been militarily successful nor that they had done anything more than survive with their spirits intact. He mentioned no individual acts of bravery or initiative. Yet, for these black men participation with the mass of the American army was occasion for optimism.

Years later, when men from the segregated divisions of the AEF responded to the US Army Military History Institute Survey, the most negative thing any of them wrote about battle was, "Thought we were underpaid for what us had to go through."[33] Like white veterans answering the survey many years after the war, they seemed at ease with admitting fear, but most commonly they expressed fear coupled with enthusiasm, "Let's get at the enemy and get it over with fast,"[34] said Austin Roberts of the Ninety-second Division. Leonard Bogart, a white man of the Thirty-sixth Division, said almost the same thing, "I was thinking about doing what we were sent over to do and get it over with."[35] These words seem like common sense. They had an unpleasant job to do, they wished to get it over with. There is an active spirit behind the words, "let's get at the enemy." They created a pattern and set a standard for optimism that colored the battle memories of these men.

When answering the final questions of the US Army Military History Institute World War I Survey that asked what lessons soldiers had taken away from the war, black veterans of the two black combat divisions wrote quite negative responses. Sergeant Roman Cooper, who had found being drafted "disgusting," wrote that his war experience was a detriment to his progress in life. Others wrote that they were offered no school, no benefits and no career opportunities. "America needed to fight discrimination," wrote Henry I. Craven who had entered the army with enthusiasm. Corporal Roscoe Brewer wrote, cryptically, that "America was good and bad."[36] Though they had entered the army with hope, and though they reported performing their duty with an optimistic pragmatic spirit, their overall impressions of the war, filtered through decades of disappointed hopes for progress, left an ambiguous message.

Lieutenant Lawrence, a white officer with some of these men, had only positive things to say about his war experience. He had learned the "psychology of leadership." The war "made me appreciate U.S.A. more," it gave him a "broadened outlook," and "my experience served me well in my profession; in knowledge, skill and attitudes. Yes, in ideals of our democracy." The war could leave a very different impression on men who had served together.[37]

Though important African-American units served with the French army, it is very difficult to find reactions to the French in the context of combat. Of course, the senior officers of those units, the men who actually came into contact with their French counterparts, were white. Only a few African-American junior officers served in France, and they would have had very limited contact with the French.

The integration of Native Americans, another American minority group, into the war effort, took a different form. The familiar scenario of passive trench warfare became re-written during periods in the Summer and Fall of 1918 when Americans advanced. General Pershing and other American commanders had always favored open warfare, rather than trenches, on the principle that the better possibilities for individualistic action and initiative suited an American spirit and appetite for action. Fighting on the western front, usually characterized by terrifying, monotonous, impersonal bombardments and machine-gunning, took on a symbolically American air of improvisation and individualism when described in terms of the American frontier.

> It is not difficult to imagine the consternation of the Prussian Guard when the redskins, with war whoops, came out of the forest in true woodman style, reverting to the typical Indian fighting tactics, disregarding rules of modern warfare, disregarding also the withering enemy machine gun fire, and proceded to clean out the nest of machine guns. Reports from France indicate that the Indian was one of the staunchest, coolest men under fire that faced the Germans in the Great War; that the Indian never knew fatigue, never knew fear, smiled in the face of death.[38]

The individualistic frontier qualities of the "Indian," and by extension all Americans, had proven their worth, and indeed had transformed this mechanized, brutal and modern war. In this kind of reporting, the romantic images of the previous century waged a unifying and winning campaign in the mechanized world of our own century.

The letter of a wounded Indian, Robert Big-Thunder of Wittenberg, Wisconsin, also quoted in a pamphlet for propagan-

da purposes with the battle description above, did nothing to bear
out this image of successful "indian fighting tactics" in France,
even if the men reached their objective.

> Our raid was very successful. A piece of bursting shrapnel shell
> hit me below my left eye, cutting my skin, and went through
> my nose. I shall be well again, but am afraid my left eye will
> be very weak. After being wounded, I ran all the way from the
> front to the first-aid dressing station under heavy artillery fire.
> . . . Thank god, I was not killed. I wish I was home working on
> the farm, but this is our duty and we must fight it to a finish;
> then we can go home safe.

Big-Thunder described all the confusion one would expect from
a man fighting for the first time against heavy artillery and
machine-gun fire. He demonstrated no particular "woodman
tactic," though at one point he sheltered behind some trees. He
certainly did not ignore the enemy fire. He showed no particular
enthusiasm for war. He just wished he were home working on the
farm. He had, however, learned to think, or at least write home,
in terms of duty to his country. That expression of duty connected with his Native American name proved the point for
propagandists. Native Americans had become absorbed into the
American state. As a symbol, they were an important part of any
American standard of bravery.

Success in battle amplified the patriotic and enthusiastic
rhetoric of soldiers. "We are driving the Huns back so fast we can
hardly keep up with them," wrote Samuel Kent of the Thirty-
second Division in July, 1918.[39] Success could allow the integration of propaganda that men heard in speeches from every side
into their own enthusiastic language. Just before going into action
again on August 26, 1918, this man entered the unambiguously
patriotic and blood-stirring message, "We have only one life to
give and we are willing to give that one if necessary, to beat those
'baby killers.' Let's Go!" Nathan Hale's famous phrase, learned
by Americans at school, and relearned in the AEF, has been
joined to the images of the anti-German propaganda campaigns
and the cheer, "Let's Go," that was the slogan of the Thirty-second Division. The unlikely positive combinations were all made
possible by the apparent success of Americans and the collapse of
the German lines.

Men expressed pride in their more active skills, when military successes moved the war temporarily out of trenches.

> We had changed from the stereotyped trench warfare to a warfare of maneuver, a warfare which requires a great deal more military knowledge and ability to carry on properly than it does to "sit tight" "holding a sector."[40]

The man who wrote this to his mother directed the fire of an artillery piece. Stationary positions behind the front lines posed fewer technical problems for the artillery man than positions that moved forward.

In the same letter to his mother, this artillery officer described moving forward with the American infantry into the face of German artillery fire. Not only did movement require quicker wits for an artillery officer, but it required bravery as well.

> It was just a normal steady walk forward, hesitating for a few moments at enemy trenches while their bayonets struck downward, and then the march continued up and over a ridge, beyond which few came who went in.
>
> I have never seen so many dead so close together, but there were easily three dead Germans for every American.
>
> It was a very long line, massed more than I have usually seen our infantry. The German batteries quickly opened on them as they appeared in the open and "got into them" with some effect, but they came right on, most of them smoking cigarettes, all calm, but not talking much. It was interesting to be in the line with them and to get a really close up view of the [battle].[41]

This officer included rough casualty statistics – three Germans for every American – perhaps to reassure his mother that what seems, from the description, to have been a very wasteful maneuver, had in fact met with success. The detail of the cigarette smoking placed him, as observer, right among the massed stoic Americans. For a while at least, as they moved forward, the artillery officer shared their danger and fortitude. They were close enough to recognize as individuals, and most of them smoked, a sign of individual choice outside the rules of marching and uniforms. But their individuality fades quickly. They were "all calm," they were all stoic. The description of bayonets striking down as their march to death hesitated at a

German trench seems like the mechanical action of a harvesting machine tilting into a depression in the landscape before continuing. Austin has witnessed and been part of the mechanical American standard of bravery in action.

American units lost much of their momentum on the banks of the Vesle in the Aisne-Marne offensive of August 1918, and in the Meuse-Argonne offensive of October and early November. They became bogged down in much the way French and British attacks had in earlier offensives. Their last battle marked the moment when the experience of American armies most closely resembled that of the European armies. General William Mitchell of the American Army Air Service wrote later: "The art of war had departed. Attrition, or the gradual killing off of the enemy, was all the ground armies were capable of."[42] This last American offensive at the end of four years lessons of war dominated by machine-guns justified Mitchell. But, however costly this last battle, and however much its tactics repeated the failed formula of the French and British armies, because it was the final offensive and because it was the only battle for many Americans, many connected it in memory with their baptism of fire and with victory.

> It was between the dates of November 1 and 11 that [we] received an education in life and death. Our company moved to the front lines under cover of darkness the night of October 31 and was instructed to dig deep with our trench shovels, since our artillery would be laying down a heavy barrage ... Shortly before daybreak it all happened and this rookie combat marine must admit that he was frightened when high explosive shells showered dirt into our hole and rocked the earth.[43]

This Marine private went on to describe the death of two company sergeants by a direct hit, and other casualties on that day that reduced a company of 150 men to 37. During his company's engagement with the enemy, 1,000 men passed through its ranks, killed, wounded or victims of flu. His letter home of November 16, 1918, connected some satisfaction at having experienced war along with his relief that the war had ended: "I was over the top in this last big drive and saw it all." He asserted: "I was on the line when the cannon stopped and hostilities ceased and oh! what a wonderful feeling that silence was."[44]

Certainly, this man had every right to describe his experience in the exalted terms he gave: "an education in life and death." But his eleven days of combat that ended in allied victory provided a very different education from that given by the four years through which members of European armies struggled. A soldier who had had a longer experience in the trenches would have expressed relief certainly at the silence after the Armistice, but he would not have needed to assure his family that he had seen it all. His family would have already become aware of the disturbing evidence that he had "seen it all," and that he had encountered something very alien to their own lives over the four years of the war.

The great mass of American soldiers who engaged the enemy for a much shorter period than Europeans seem to have fought when and how they were asked. They did, however, desert, hang back, and shirk in significant numbers during advances. This was common knowledge among them. Men reported that comrades who had vanished during the advance turned up again at the portable kitchens in time for a meal. "While we had lost quite a few in killed and wounded, yet we found some back at the 'chow wagon' who had gotten lost? Seems strange they could always find the kitchen – but not the company especially while at the front."[45] Though, officially, the army considered desertion an offense punishable by death, nothing so dire happened to these rather common casual shirkers. Certainly, no one was ever recorded as executed for desertion in the AEF, as they were in the German and English armies. General Pershing, as Commander-in-Chief of an army in the field acted personally on all death sentences from courts-martial. He wrote that "of purely military offenses there were only four in which execution was recommended to the President, and none of these were approved by him."[46]

Rather than mete out severe punishment for stragglers, the Military Police took on the task of following behind the advancing infantry in battle, apprehending deserters or stragglers and sending them up with their units. An MP who wished to explain his function in battle to a woman friend called units devoted to rounding up stragglers "proving platoons." He wrote to his friend that the MP's followed the "doughboys giving them the moral support that a barrage gives."[47] He likened their activities to the curtains of artillery fire intended to either trap enemy infantry (a box barrage), or to precede friendly infantry, sweeping obstacles from the path of attack (a walking barrage). Infantrymen feared advancing beyond a walking barrage and finding themselves trapped between the enemy and the falling shells of their own artillery. Though MP units must have chased soldiers forward, like the much feared following barrage, in an MP's letter, his men aid, rather than force, the regular soldiers' advance.

This MP probably exaggerated the effectiveness of their units by comparing their persuasive power to that of concentrated shelling. His words put the whole question of choice-making, and test-passing, however, in a different light from that implied by infantrymen who wrote of finding some essence of themselves in the experience of battle and their survival of it. After all, if the MP's acted like a walking barrage, then the men had no choice but to advance. If these "proving platoons" tested the quality of the American troops, they did so by forcing men to advance mechanically in large numbers, not as willing individuals. He used the expression "moral support" ironically. Some men had advanced of their own will, and in obedience to their training. Others could be forced. But everyone would pass the test.

It is difficult to judge just how many American soldiers became stragglers during engagements. The study of desertion in World War I, written at the Army War College in preparation for World War II, noted the problem but emphasized solutions – morale building and Military Police enforcement platoons – rather than descriptions and statistics. Few records exist because the Military Police, like so much of the AEF, was still in the process of formation long after the Armistice. "During the fighting [it] had been found quite impossible to handle the questions of traffic and of stragglers with the divisional units only,"[48] the study had reported, giving the impression that far more men had fallen behind units than had been anticipated.

The official history of the Provost Marshall, under whom the Military Police acted, attempted to paint a very positive picture of their activities and of the war in general. Hence, the history described the growth of the MP's in the light of a successfully expanding corporation. Originally, the army desired no more than 150 MP's for every Division of approximately 20,000 men, or 0.7 per cent of the AEF. By the spring of 1919, the MP's had grown to three times that proportion. The Provost Marshall's history reported this growth as a triumphant achievement, not as an indication that criminality, absenteeism and desertion were greater problems in the AEF than had been expected.[49]

Members of the Military Police had to endure the taunt: "Who won the War?" with its sarcastic answer, "The brave MP's."[50] If battle were a proof of bravery, theirs was an ambiguous position. The member of the MP unit who likened the MP's to a barrage gave a description of a battle in which his unit and the artillery units they disciplined, all shared the danger and no animosity existed between MP's and the other men. "Give 'em beaucoup of Hell for me," doughboys told his unit as they went forward. And he wrote of the artillerymen in affectionate terms:

> Lads behaved extremely well. Section chief kept men well in hand. The gunners sat non-chalantly at their posts. There [missing word] no doubt bursting shells of all descriptions formed a beautiful picture and will remain emblassened in all our minds. This is what proved the boys had "guts" when it was discovered they were between the German lines and our own, marooned without a single round of amunition. The boys were left to wriggle under the trail [that part of a cannon that rests on the ground] the best they could.

He then switched the point of view to his MP's:

> Moving slowly forward, never heeding the bursting shells, nor gas, we followed a road forking to the left . . . into "no man's land." It was soon noticed however that we were in the bracket of a German barrage. The same which the peices [American artillery] had to stand up under. The barrage had the ear marks of a good American cocktail, the mixture of shells being so great. But this was only one of many incidents.[51]

This MP wrote of these adventures shortly after the Armistice. It is safe to assume that he wrote of one of the final battles of the war. This experience resembled that of infantrymen, for his men were caught in the brackets of a German barrage that simulated the position of infantrymen caught between the curtain of a walking barrage that preceded them and the MP's who followed. His story has turned the tables on the Military Police. From being a "proving platoon," a position in which strict attention to duty removed the possibility of shirking from others, they found *themselves* caught in the barrage they were supposed to emulate.

He and his men moved from being part of the mechanical proving mechanism of the army to being proved themselves.

The proof of bravery for men caught between barrages became a question of surviving devastation with no recourse. Even though the men had moved out of the trenches in this soldier's description, they, and the units around them, must submit passively to the shelling from an invisible foe. In spite of this enforced passivity, this man's memory of danger would remain connected in his mind to the successful finish of the war, to be told in this jaunty style. No subsequent conflict between his unit and shirkers would act to lessen his memory of this unifying experience of survival that proved men's bravery: his unit sharing their entrapment between barrages with the stranded artillery.

The MP described a proof of war bravery that paradoxically depended on the removal of individual choice, and yet left men with a positive impression of war. Europeans had experienced combat in World War I as a removal of individuality, but certainly did not emerge with the same positive memory. Eric Leed, in his work *No Man's Land*, described what happened to European soldiers, especially Germans, in World War I, when they became aware that the choice of heroic action did not exist in the trenches. Combat in the trenches only consisted of work, not unlike labor in industrial settings, Leed pointed out. Men lived in the trenches according to rigid time schedules for work, eating and repose. They lived according to a strict hierarchy of privileges and authority. Only the greater possibility of explosions and cave-ins differentiated trench life from life in any industrial or mining work environment.

Men found themselves trapped in the choiceless, narrow and brutal actuality of war, that had become so divorced from any meaning commensurate with the suffering it caused that they formed new paradigms for meaning and for power. New myths and states of mind emerged from the war such as the compensatory myth that from the air the war made sense, and that flyers could maintain the chivalric choices of heroism. The neurosis of shell-shock can be seen as a new state of mind linked with this new kind of war. Ernst Jünger, the German storm-trooper, developed his revolutionary notions of a new man who might emerge from the war empowered by his recognition of his place in the mechanism of war and freed from pre-war cultural authorities.[52]

Working-class Germans, who tended to be conscripted into the army, according to Leed, moved from an industrial setting to the war setting with the worst expectations, understanding full well the violent side of their machine-dominated world. Educated bourgeois men expected to find the possibility of heroic action in combat as they shed the constraints of disciplined industrial society. They were appalled when war reduced them, along with more proletarian soldiers, to the troglodyte existence of the trenches. Ernst Jünger took their ensuing disillusion a step further. By identifying the veteran as the child of the machine war, the veteran became a revolutionary prepared to overthrow bourgeois authority and replace it with the authority of technology.

The testimony of young men from the Ivy League in America, privileged in privately published volumes of letters and memorials, has left the strongest impression of American enthusiasm for war. Enough farmers and laborers, however, volunteered to bury the more privileged statistically. The thoughts of men off farms, or out of factories, or members of immigrant and racial minorities made no such unified chorus as the better educated. These men, however, often draftees, still recounted patriotic motivations. They sometimes said that they owed allegiance to the state or to the president. And though it is unlikely that men who already knew first-hand the dangers of industrial life, of steel mills, mines, or even the dangers of farm machinery, entertained illusions about war as the unique locus for proving a man's physical courage, they could still find in war the materials for a positive standard of identification. None of these Americans expected the degradation and passivity of the trenches to be part of their proof. When faced with those famous conditions, however, the brevity of the experience, coupled to their familiarity with mass democratic culture and the collapse of the enemy, allowed their survival in the war to enhance the values they came with, or to learn the values disseminated by the army. Americans found meaning in surviving the most wretched situations, and found meaning in the diminution of difference between individual Americans that the war caused.

Men who suffered the loss of limbs in the war were one group of Americans who interpreted their war experience as unambiguously negative. But as a result of the war, these men found themselves excluded from the forward moving American procession. Amputees interviewed in a New York hospital in 1919 had an understandably bitter view of the war and an undisguised hostility towards authority. Of American voices from the war theirs were among the few to emphasize the army's undemocratic hierarchy, and certainly they were the most hostile to it. "It did not seem to be anything for an officer to send a man a mile through shell fire at midnight to carry a newspaper to another officer," said one man who lost a leg during the war.[53] Another man suffered a second amputation because of a fall down a companionway into the hold of his transport on the way home. He blamed his fall on his accommodations, maintaining that a first class cabin, available but reserved for officers, would not have necessitated his climb on a steep ladder. His story of the war contained senseless accidental deaths, the destruction of a Frenchman's barn for fuel, and a major who advised his men to kill prisoners because "every prisoner you capture is taking a potato out of your mouth." Few amputees had anything positive to say about their doctors. They sometimes cited conditions that surpassed negligence, approaching sadism.

Their reaction to amputation went far beyond dislike of the doctors. These men rejected a whole vocabulary of progress, democracy, and optimism that other men were learning. Of course, after an amputation, in the early part of this century, a man could hardly participate in a culture that celebrated limitless possibility. He could hardly belong to a democratic throng joined together by prosperity. One man complained that the artificial leg he had been given by the army was constructed of iron and plaster of Paris weighing twenty-six pounds, quite a burden in an age of uplift. Loss of limb marked a man individually, he could not possibly conform to any standard of movement or identity.[54]

If a man thought he could recover from his wounds, however, he could still speak positively about the war. After the Armistice, men recovering from wounds seem to have used a positive interpretation to help their re-integration into American society. One patient, who listed his occupation as "salesman," managed to get enough stock positive phrases into a brief interview to have become a Sinclair Lewis "booster" of the 1920s: "When Uncle Sam decided to get into the big noise . . . I had a strong itching to get in the swim."[55] Another convalescent postwar salesman had a less clear message to give when interviewed about his war experience. His lessons were self-sufficiency: "every man must look after himself and carry his own burden", and brutality: "[one of] the German flyers came down to the ground in flames, but the boys finished him." But he balanced these opinions with a direct quote from a general's inspiring speech on the nature of battle: "Americans never retreat . . . Americans who were defending democracy had successfully withstood the foe . . ."[56] Even wounded men could find a way to interpret the war in a positive fashion. As products of a business culture, these salesmen knew the value of accentuating the positive.

The Armistice, at 11 o'clock on November 11, 1918, like other great historical moments since the mass diffusion of accurate time pieces and mass communication, became an instant major event in lives of people who had lived through it. American soldiers remembered what they were doing at that moment as a sign of their joint participation in the great event of the war, regardless of what action an individual had actually taken. "To be killed the last day of the war, never!" wrote an officer of the Ninety- second division. "Fear was in my mind for the first time. I would not leave the shelter of that basement until noon the next day."[57] This man acknowledged the uselessness of one junior officer's actions, at least on the last day of the war, while his overall impressions of the war were positive and even triumphant. He told his part in the Armistice to connect himself with the moment of victory provided by the entire American organism. He shared in that victory by survival in the organization and according to organizational standards, not by individual action.

Some American units refused to quit until the last possible moment. "Oh, man, everyone in my outfit wanted to fire the last shot. We decided each of us would put a hand on the lanyard and pull at the same time. And that's what we did, at 10:59," recalled Harry Croft of the Third Division.[58] Frank Sibley with the Twenty-sixth Division also described a widespread desire to have a hand in the final round. "In one battery, each man took a shell and waited in line for his turn to fire the gun. In another battery, five officers took hold of the lanyard, and all fired the last shot together. In still another, a long rope was made fast to the lanyard of each of the four guns. Some two hundred men got hands on each rope, and one man, with a watch, went out forward. At the hour, he dropped a handkerchief."[59]

Men who desired the distinction of having fired the final shot in a terribly destructive war wished to link some individual contribution of their own to the historical signpost the moment of Armistice became in their imaginations. This desire was widespread, in the American army, and accommodations were made so that as many men as possible might hold the honor of making that final destructive gesture. Thus, what on the surface seems an act distinguishing an individual – firing the last shot – became a mass act. The near ceremonial quality of these final shots provided soldiers with a memory whose importance lay in the specificity of time and place, rather than in the contribution made by any one soldier. An exact memory of the moment thus became the measure of participation in the Armistice as an American cultural event to be treasured. Memories of the announcement of the Pearl Harbor bombing, the assassination of President Kennedy, and the first moon landing would serve to join later generations of Americans together by means of the specificity of moment provided by mass communication.

Even after the Armistice, some Americans did not wish to give up hostilities. "Today the [German soldiers] have come over and asked for some eats and to talk to our boys – so many of them speak German. General Hahn doesn't approve. Drive them back with bayonettes. He's a fighting fool and greatly liked by all,"[60] wrote one soldier on November 12. Whether or not he felt keeping the former enemy away from American rations warranted the use of bayonets, he certainly approved of his general's fighting competitive spirit that had promoted a situation on November 11 in which "Each side tried to see which could do the more damage in the short time left."[61]

The Stars and Stripes described the end of the war as if the hardest fighting had occurred right at the end, "It was no mild thing, that last flare of the battle, and the order to cease firing did not reach the men in the front line until the last moment, when runners sped with it from fox hole to fox hole." The newspaper of American soldiers also reported the disappointed words of a draftee replacement who arrived at the front to hear that the war had ended, "Hell, I just got here," he said. French, German and British soldiers sometimes fought to the very end of the war but seemingly with caution in those last few hours. They wished to reach the end once they could see it.[62]

European soldiers had had enough of the fighting years before. Men of the French army during and after the pointless slaughter of the French 1917 offensives refused to advance. Whole French divisions mutinied. Historian Tony Ashworth has seen these mutinies as an extreme expression of an informal "live and let live" convention that had grown up among front-line infantry on both sides of no man's land.[63] In the American army, however, no resistance on such a scale took place, nor did any evidence suggest that Americans by careful inaction in the trenches maintained the relatively safe passivity of "live and let live." On the contrary, American junior officers were under orders to liven up quiet sectors, and to attempt to control no man's land as a general principle. But even when the conditions of mechanized war reduced them to passivity, Americans could find their way to a positive interpretation.

3 "From a hayloft to a hotel where kings have spent their summers:" Americans' Encounter with French Culture

> One goes off really light-headed. One laughs at everything, laughs when the train stops, laughs when it moves off again, enjoys an unburdened flow, almost a nervous seizure, when at last one pushes with hundreds of others through station gates into the vast shimmering Paris background outside.[1]

In World War I, American soldiers arrived in France in the greatest numbers during the summer of 1918. They fought briefly and successfully until the Armistice, November 11, 1918, and after that experience – combat for some and being part of such a successful army for others – soldiers were ready to go home. Volunteers and draftees alike, they had accomplished what they had set out to do. For the moment it seemed that they, their country, and possibly Europe had been uplifted to the democratic possibilities that Woodrow Wilson had spoken of in his speeches at the opening of America's involvement in the war.

Only a very few could return home immediately. The allied shipping that had so urgently transported American soldiers to France to fight was employed re-establishing trade afterwards. Just 26,000 of the two million American soldiers in France went home in November of 1918. The greater part of the American army stayed in France till the summer of 1919 when the largest concentrations of soldiers sailed for America. By August, 1919, 40,000 soldiers still remained in France. And an army of occupation 240,000 strong had moved to the American sector of Germany around Coblenz where they stayed in diminishing numbers until 1923.

Americans stayed in Europe in very large numbers for the six months following the war with very little to do. The army offered

what it had always offered soldiers with time on their hands: drill.
But, during and after this war, the army offered something else
too, tourism. Soldiers became tourists, but tourists in a very
tourism special sense. They were involuntary tourists, their hotels and
meals paid for and destinations ordered by the United States
Army. New to tourism, they needed sometimes training in the
tourist's passive enjoyment of the surrounding culture and sometimes restraints from imposing their own desires on the foreign
culture. And they toured in the context of the war they had
recently fought, so they started their touring with a connection to
the place they toured that was profound. After all, some had shed
blood for the France they toured, and when soldiers toured with
the Army of Occupation in Germany, they were very aware of
the country as their recent enemy. Most tourists travel with a
more detached curiosity.

Some Americans resisted a tourist's interpretation of France
and a tourist's restraints on what they did while away from the
strict control of the army. But others seem to have taken to
tourism easily. Having accepted a standard definition of participation in the AEF as a mark of war bravery or military ambition,
accepting a touristic definition of suitable contact with a foreign
culture, promulgated by the YMCA, was another step in becoming members of a mass culture. In the face of mechanized battle,
soldiers sometimes wrote that all men felt "exactly the same
thing." The essence of touring certain cultural sites is that those
sites produce similar reactions in people. Battle and tourism could
have connected meanings for Americans in World War I. For
logistical reasons, battle and tourism had become experiential
neighbors. Later, in peace time during the 1920s, when American
civilians toured France in unprecedented numbers, the battlefields where American men had fought, and the graveyards where
Americans were buried, had joined the older French touristic
sights as places requiring a tourist's attention.

To Alden Brooks, who wrote the passage that opens this
chapter, a soldier's own excitement seems to make Paris shimmer
with the meaning of the promised land. To share that excitement
with "hundreds of others" did nothing to diminish the pleasure
or reduce the meaning or authenticity of the touristic experience.
In fact, to tour France in the company of the same army with
which a soldier had fought or served enhanced the value, the
authenticity, the Frenchness, the high-brow quality of what they

saw. Each fellow soldier/tourist added to the numinous glow of the site, where more usually flocks of tourists might be seen as bothersome competitors in the rush for a limited commodity. The context Brooks described included the war. "One goes off," with all those others on leave from military duty, perhaps from battle. Participation in one experience has influenced the quality of the other.

The connection between battle and tourism could work in the opposite direction as well. During the Summer of 1918, Samuel Kent returned to the front after recovering from a wound and a brief leave. He was happy to be with his unit on their way to "give 'em hell." In a diary entry written during this trip he had this to say about the destruction he saw on the way back to battle:

> We passed thru several towns which were completely wrecked and ruined. Churches and all public buildings are special targets and they are generally demolished. It certainly is a crime – wonderful and beautiful works of architecture, destroyed beyond all hopes of repairs.[2]

His upbeat confidence in the American army's purpose and his own part in that army was placed alongside this more somber description of destruction. As they trained and fought, common American soldiers became aware of the rich European culture around them. Conscious efforts were made to teach them about French history and culture as something to defend against German Kultur. Kent's prose, "wonderful and beautiful works of architecture," stiff for an enthusiastic young man of seventeen or eighteen years, may echo the words of an officer or YMCA tour guide giving one of their ubiquitous lectures on American motivations for war. Kent absorbed them sufficiently to write them into his diary, connecting French cultural sights, battle, and his memory and identity.

Jonathan Culler has analized tourism, naming it, along with cinema and other aspects of popular culture, as one of the forming experiences of modern society.[3] Tourism, according to Culler, has united large segments of the world population by a systematized and shared knowledge of what is significant, and disseminated a set of moral imperatives – for example, all tourists know what one ought to see in Paris, or that it is important to visit Rome. By bringing an American army of draftees and volunteers to Europe, World War I vastly broadened the segment of American society that participated in this system of knowledge. At the same time, these first-time tourists added to these signs. After World War I, American tourists knew they should visit the battlefields around Verdun and Rheims where Americans had fought. Perhaps because of this contribution as sight-makers as well as sight-seers, these new soldier tourists did not feel the antipathy for their fellows that Culler found to be the defining characteristic of tourists as they seek to find some site unspoiled by the presence of site-seekers. They had set a new standard for contact with a foreign culture. They were not in the more usual tourist's condition of having to meet or surpass a standard set by other tourists.

Not all soldiers came to accept the limits of a cultural connection to a foreign place according to the standard of touristic terms. Lacking an education that would have offered alternatives to the touristic authority of the YMCA guides and would have allowed soldiers to explore famous French sights on their own, while remaining within the conventions of tourism − "getting off the beaten track," is after all an accepted touristic move, but implies a certain knowledge of the beaten track to start with − soldiers left evidence of having taken one of two alternatives. Some accepted, and repeated in letters home, the words of the guides and presumably learned, at least rhetorically, to be good tourists. Others, however, established a more participatory relationship with the French and with France. Each member of the AEF, after all, could claim participation in French culture in the most dramatic terms, for they had helped fight for the preservation of the culture of a country they also found themselves obliged to tour. If they did not wish to accept the detached status of tourist, their numbers and role in France gave them a certain cultural weight while establishing their own terms of contact.

These two alternatives suggest an aspect of modernity forced on American soldiers as they moved back and forth between obedience to the cultural authority of the army and the YMCA and cutting themselves off from that authority and from the support system that belonging to the army entailed. Dean Mac-Cannell, in his analysis of tourism and leisure in the late twentieth century, has pointed out the blurrings of class oppositions and the distinction between work and leisure that our culture has produced.

The "class struggle," instead of operating at the level of history, is operating at the level of workaday life and its opposition to culture. In the place of the division Marx foresaw is an arrangement wherein workers are displayed, and other workers on the other side of the culture barrier watch them for their enjoyment. Modernity is breaking up the "leisure class," capturing its fragments and distributing them to everyone. Work in the modern world does not turn class against class so much as it turns man against himself, fundamentally dividing his existence. The modern individual, if he is to appear to be human, is forced to forge his own synthesis between his work and his culture.[4]

American World War I soldiers fought for France and then toured France. They could find themselves spectators at a parade watching men like themselves, wearing the same uniform, marching past. Men who at one moment might observe French culture at the proper touristic distance might find themselves breaking rules the next, and appropriating artifacts, or participating in acts of destruction the next as the opportunity or necessity presented itself. The blurrings, including blurrings of class, that MacCannell found so characteristic late in our century, had been forced quite consciously on American soldiers at its beginning.

This blurring took place as soldiers' leaves, in the hands of progressive politicians, took on greater positive possibilities than keeping up the spirits of men for military purposes. A characteristically combined desire to promote uplift and control soldiers prompted the army, and the welfare organizations that organized soldier tourism, to action. From the earliest stages of the war, the Commission on Training Camp Activities (CTCA), a powerful group of progressive reformers, had attempted to channel soldier energies into improving activities during the time they were not receiving military training.

Enlisting the help of the YMCA, Knights of Columbus, Jewish Welfare Board, Salvation Army and other social welfare organizations, the CTCA had controled the leisure time of soldiers in the United States promoting sports, singing, educational programs, well-chaperoned dances and many other activities. The CTCA had discouraged the uncontroled leisure of soldiers, for example drinking and unsupervised contact with women, especially working-class women.[5] The tourism of soldiers in France was an extension of the CTCA's attempts to improve American men in training camps in the States. At the same time, some sort of control of American soldiers while on leave would reduce friction between them and the French.

Newton Diehl Baker, America's Secretary of War and a progressive politician, believed that the war could be turned to good on every level, from the international, where imperialism would succumb to democracy, to the personal, where it would improve individual Americans. Baker proposed that the war could be won at a low moral cost and could be progressive. Moral leave that heightened morale attracted his attention. Of leave and recreation, Newton Diehl Baker had written to Woodrow Wilson before America joined the war:

> My experience with the Mexican mobilization was that our young soldiers had a good deal of time hanging rather heavily on their hands with two unfortunate results. 1. They became homesick. 2. They were easily led aside into unwholesonme diversions and recreations, patronizing cheap picture shows, saloons, dance halls and houses of prostitution. I immediately began to consider whether a part of the discipline of the army ought not to be the regular provision of wholesome recreation, so as pleasantly, if possible, profitably to occupy the leisure hours in camp. No comprehensive program on the subject has ever been regarded as a part of the regular provision for soldiers in camp.[6]

The words "wholesome" and "profitably" here marked Baker's rhetoric of personal improvement, a staple of progressive social thought. He knew that in organizing the leisure time of soldiers he took charge of a part of soldiers' life that previous army administrators had left to the discretion of individuals. But, of the diversity of the new recruits, the army would make an improved American society. For Baker as for many other progressives, the war was an opportunity not to be lost.[7] He felt soldiers could use the war experience for their personal progress that certainly did not mean contamination to things foreign. Tourism, non-participating observation of the foreign, suited his educational purposes very well.

He first made the effort to keep the soldiers away from traditional sources of immorality – drink and women. But plans for the rest and recreation of American soldiers went beyond

traditional prohibitions and included positive measures as well.
Baker took institutions of higher education as his model for
providing recreation.

> I have the feeling that as our young soldiers are substantially
> men of college age, the experience of our colleges in recreation
> will go a long way by analogy to aid us. Ultimately I hope to
> have at West Point a course in recreation, so that young
> officers will be taught systematically both the importance and
> the mechanics of group recreation.[8]

Secretary Baker's words expressed the intention of a new uplifting
form of recreation to be incorporated in the fabric of the army.[9]
Men have often seen their time in the military as wasted, a delay
in the pursuit of their life's goals, but Baker planned to make each
man's stint in the army a part of his education. The model Baker
would take for this transformation would be the college-educated
man. Soldiers would spend their time away from military duties
not in the disruptive activities usual to soldiers, but in the more
passive role of receiving education. Sometimes, they would find
themselves on one side of Dean MacCannell's "culture barrier"
as actors in a mortal struggle often characterized as a fight
between cultures. Sometimes, they would find themselves on the
other side of that barrier, where they would observe the culture
practiced by people they had recently either protected or fought.

Some military men caught the progressive current. In writing
about training, recreation and morality in the American Expeditionary Force, General Pershing emphasized the wholesomeness
of the AEF. In his memoirs, he defended the moral reputation of
his men while pointing to the ways in which moral soldiers make
more effective fighters.

> There has never been a similar body of men to lead as clean
> lives as our American soldiers in France. A rigid program of
> instruction is carried out daily with traditional American
> enthusiasm. Engaged in healthy, interesting exercises in the
> open air, with simple diet, officers and men like trained
> athletes are ready for their task. Forbidden the use of strong
> drink and protected by stringent regulations against sexual
> evils and supported by their own moral courage, their good
> behaviour is the subject of most favorable comment, especially
> by our Allies. American mothers may rest assured that their

sons are a credit to them and the nation, and they may well look forward to the proud day when on the battlefield these splendid men will shed a new luster on American manhood.[10]

Pershing left little doubt that an improved American manhood's purpose was to fight more vigorously. But he also believed in the improvability of men, and in the army as a place to do it. The rhetoric of progressive reform had penetrated Pershing's thinking on the subject of the soldiers' welfare even if he never strayed too far from military purposes. While the war continued, the army quite naturally focused on soldier welfare as a means to good morale that in turn would make a more effective army. As the commander of the army's Leave Area Bureau put it, "leave of a few days every four months was necessary as a measure of preserving the health and the morale of the soldier, to provide a period of rest and relaxation after the tension and exhaustion of war conditions and to restore him to his normal point of view with renewed determination and capacity to carry on."[11] The military in general put the military aspects of leave, rest and recuperation in first place. But the progressive laboratory of the war had allowed military authorities to determine a standard of recreation necessary to maintain military competence. Why should the progressive spirit of improvement stop there?

A program was eventually developed for soldiers' leave time that included channeling the recreational tastes of Americans in directions away from participation in French culture and towards consumer tourism. American tastes in recreation initially disrupted French society and very quickly became a cause for complaint. Difficulties arose very shortly after the first Americans arrived in France. An army historian described these difficulties laconically:

> Unit commanders had issued weekend passes permitting their men to visit towns and localities in their vicinity, but the lack of knowledge on the part of the soldiers of the French language, ways and customs, and perhaps a difference in the ideas as to ways of having a good time, led to misunderstandings and in some cases to more serious disturbances.[12]

The complaints received by American liaison officers stationed all over France tell a more vivid story of mayhem inflicted on French communities, requiring some system of restraint. The Provost

Marshal left long lists of assaults against French people and damage to French property – café windows seem to have been especially vulnerable – that reached a peak in the early months of 1919 and then trailed off indicating that first a restraining hand did indeed take effect and eventually that the problem receded as American soldiers left France.[13]

That American drinking habits differed from those of the French was a truism of the literature that came out of the war. The stereotypical American usually drank nothing alcoholic, but when he did drink, he did so to become drunk.[14] When charges were brought, either their superiors accepted the pattern of soldiers' binge drinking or drunkeness was forgotten in the presence of more serious crimes like vandalism and assault. While the Provost Marshal recorded numerous incidents involving damage done to French property, especially to cafés, and assaults whose circumstances suggested drunkeness, the crime of drunkeness was almost never recorded. Americans preferred hard liquor to wine and seem to have made American cocktails, especially the gin martini, fashionable among the faster French.[15] Also, American soldiers, paid eight or ten times more than French soldiers, seemed to French soldiers to have had an almost limitless purchasing power.[16] The lack of control on this purchasing power gave rise to an overwhelming proportion of the complaints of the French against American soldiers. The earliest mention of American soldiers in the French undercover police reports of rumors and disturbances throughout Paris, the *Physionomie de Paris*, recorded some of the negative effects of mixing Americans and French when Americans had too much money.

> These American troops are recognizable by their sloppy deportment and their lack of respect for the inhabitants of these places. The detachments are made up of regulars of which a large proportion represents the dregs of the American population. Some of them, because of their pay – 8 francs a day – lead a carefree life. They allow themselves extreme license with women who they accost even when they are accompanied by their husbands. This attitude has already caused fights between American and French soldiers.[17]

Apparently, the power to purchase led Americans first to abuse alcohol, then to abuse women.[18] From the French point of view, Americans turned the local culture towards drink and prostitution with their money and presence like a natural force. As the French police reported: "It is said that the first American contingents to debark in France have caused an outbreak of prostitution. The government has been obliged to take the decision to keep these troops away from Paris."[19] Teaching American soldiers how to be more sophisticated consumers was obviously in the interest of both the French and American authorities.

Even when Americans were more restrained, pressure on Franco-American relations followed the arrival of American soldiers all over France.[20] The price of edible produce especially would rise quickly beyond the reach of the French and then, as soldiers literally ate the area around camps into deserts, would rise beyond the reach of most soldiers. Typically, a soldier would remember most fondly a billet where no other Americans had preceded his unit. Lieutenant John Kress wrote of La Chapelle du Genet: "Our most pleasant experience in France. We were the first Americans to be quartered there, and therefore, we were given the opportunity to see the Frenchman as he was before the Americans spoiled him."[21] Kress's word "spoiled" suggests the kind of supply and demand pressure on prices so commonly experienced. But it also suggests the adulteration of Frenchness brought about in a small village by the presence of too many foreigners, the kind of "spoiling" described in Jonathan Culler's analysis of tourism.

A private in the same outfit offered an explanation of the mechanics of rising prices somewhat differently. He, too, reported a deterioration in Franco-American relations, but he blamed army regulations, and the progressive army's abhorence of drink.

> The little town had never seen American soldiers before, so for about a week they treated us like kings. Everytime we went to the café the French people bowed to us. Nothing was too good for us. For about one franc (20 cents) we could get a good sized drink, but that didn't last for long. Our M.P. went around and told the café owners to charge more for the drinks.[22]

For the officers, who were usually better educated than their men, and, in many cases, had already had the experience of tourism, the French became "spoiled" in any sector by a natural process of contact with Americans. For the private, spoilage of relations occurred when puritanical army authorities stepped in to control relations between soldiers and the French.

In all cases, Americans disrupted French life. Americans outside the absolute authority of the AEF participated in French life and altered it. Often enough, American soldiers introduced new drinking habits and offered temptations to French women. Some soldiers deserted, escaping army authority entirely into uncontrolled contact with the French. Americans created communities of deserters outside important centers of AEF activity. Men, sometimes living in hobo jungles of deserters, acted as important go-betweens on the black market between Frenchmen involved in distribution of goods and American soldiers attached to camps who would procure American supplies for the market.[23] Sequestering American soldiers from the French or turning them into tourists who respect certain rules of consumption would solve all these problems.

When at the front, the United States Army took complete charge of a soldier's life. Contact with the French dropped off. Problems of morale dropped too. But an army needed rest and training. Away from the front, control lessened, contact with the French increased and, for the army, problems started. The AEF, in conjunction with the welfare organizations that took care of its morals, developed a leave plan that would provide tourism to Americans and channel their energies away from tendencies so objectionable to the French and their own officers.

For the United States Army and General Pershing, the problem presented itself as one of morale. Morale ranked high because the army had learned to equate a high desertion rate with low morale. In a report on desertion in the AEF written in 1942, when the army collated all it had learned in World War I for another massive overseas effort, the army remembered leaves as its first remedial action. "The Leave Area system was created with a view to promoting morale, health, and efficiency, and to diminish the temptation to be absent without leave and to desert." Between the wars, officers were taught this lesson of World War I: that "Leaves should be granted as a means of raising morale and reducing unauthorized absences."[24]

Control of soldiers certainly lay in the interest of French and American authorities, but plans for an elaborate system of leaves needed time to evolve. Mr Tener of the YMCA designed the first leave system for American soldiers: an energetic scheme of showing as much of France as possible to the soldiers in the quickest time. Basically, it was a tourist's travel plan, involving

brief leaves to different places. Army authorities rejected it, not
because they disagreed with its educational purpose, but because
it would have strained the overburdened French transportation
system and because it did not leave the men in any one place for
a sufficient time to recuperate from the strain of battle. Though
it might have eventually resulted in teaching soldiers to be
tourists, that first plan also lacked any more immediate means of
controlling soldiers. The plans adopted, starting with General
Order No. 6, issued January 6, 1918, toned down Tener's
ambitions. They provided for a seven-day leave for each soldier
every four months, if military conditions permitted. Soldiers were
restricted to the geographic limits of one Leave Area, centered on
a resort town, for the duration of their leave.

General Order No. 6 instituted leaves at resorts but only at the
individual soldier's expense. Thus very few men could take
advantage of the order. The US Army provided transportation to
the Leave Area, but the soldier had to pay for his own room and
board. The YMCA noted this inadequacy first. Franklin S.
Edmonds, YMCA Divisional Secretary for Savoie, figured that
each soldier would need from 125 to 250 francs, or between
twenty-five and fifty dollars during his stay. He stated that "based
upon an experience in America, where I had been serving as one
of the special assistants of the Treasury Department in organizing
War Risk Insurance, that with allotments for insurance, support
of relatives, Liberty Bonds, etc., but few soldiers were in a
position to take advantage of the terms of G.O. No. 6, unless the
army could make some provision for paying their board."[25] The
army had not yet accustomed itself to giving soldiers a vacation
at government expense. The YMCA would undertake its education.

The testimony of soldiers tends to agree with Edmonds.
Though the AEF was well paid by comparison with the other
allied armies, most men would have been hard put to find money
to eat for a week in a resort town's restaurants. Sixty years later,
Andrew J. Kuchick remembered that out of his $30 a month
came $15 to his wife and $6.60 for insurance, leaving him with
$8.40. He recalled that it was not sufficient to buy meals from the
French.[26] Many veterans responded to the army's World War I
Survey questionnaire's item on off-base activities by saying that
they simply had not the funds to do anything. An American
soldier's pay may have seemed princely while he lived in camp

with all his expenses paid, but vacation in a resort town was another matter.

Army authorities did not seem overly eager to help their men. At first, they only made an allowance to each soldier of one dollar a day. YMCA officials canvassed various army departments before their requests eventually found their way to G-1 General Headquarters and received this minimal response. The army's reluctance to take responsibility for this aspect of the social welfare of its soldiers left soldiers' leaves open to the improving influence of the YMCA and other institutions. Only after the war did the US Army completely formulate a position on leaves.

With just this small subsidy, one dollar per day per man, the leave area at Aix-les-Bains commenced operations. On Saturday February 16, 1918, a contingent of 500 men was met with a band and the dignitaries of the town. No man could be permitted to stay who could not produce at least ten dollars and many of the newly arrived men could not. A collection, taken among the vacationing men and the attendant YMCA personnel, produced the needed cash and the first group commenced its enriching experience in one of the beauty spots of France.[27]

By March, 1918, Karl Cate, the YMCA secretary who had negotiated with French hotel keepers and made the original arrangements at Aix-les-Bains, had taken the matter of funds for leave back to GHQ and had secured G.O. 38, which placed soldiers on a "duty status" while on leave. Thus, the Quartermaster General became responsible for the men's room and board at the leave areas. It had taken the army several months to adapt to the idea that it had this responsibility for the recreation of its men in an overseas theatre of war. It was becoming a progressive institution concerned with the welfare and even improvement of its members. In his final report, the Chief of the Leave Area Bureau, an army officer, had the following to say upon the subject of the beneficial effect and value of the duty-status leave to the soldier:

> The current and immediate benefit was the improvement of his morale and of the good which arises from a vacation spent in a healthy place under comfortable conditions and with an abundance of healthful amusement.[28]

The Chief of the Leave Area Bureau listed improved morale first, with all its important strictly military implications. But during the course of the war, the US Army had gone beyond leave for the sake of maintaining morale. The military head of the Leave Area Bureau concluded his report saying:

> The benefit in the future remains to be demonstrated, but it is my belief that the educational and broadening influences of sending men for a week to one of the seventeen beautiful places in France where the Areas were located, at the expense of the Government, will not only have an influence which he will remember upon his return to civilian life, but also give him a correct conception of the interest which the Army as a body and the Government as a whole takes in him.[29]

During the war, the army itself had learned three valuable applications for the rhetoric of uplift as it pertained to the Leave Area System. For military purposes, uplift boosted morale. From a less military standpoint, the time the men spent in the army could be useful for their self-improvement. And finally, by speaking in terms of broadening influences and educational opportunities and uplift, the army could improve its public relations and maintain the loyalty of its veterans.

The description of what the AEF offered soldiers in France went beyond the military necessities of good morale. It often seemed that the army had helped soldiers to a taste of the lifestyle of the upper-class, if it had not actually managed to engineer the social changes necessary to maintain people in that position. The army offered a tour of social mobility:

> Soldiers were lodged in the luxurious hotels frequented in ordinary times by wealthy vacationists from all over the world; were furnished the best food and services; were provided with free access to the large casinos which had all the usual conveniences and facilities of an expensive country club, in settings of great natural beauty...[30]

Tourism attached soldiers to values and goals that might have seemed beyond their means before.

Pershing himself had very much a tourist's sense of France. He punctuated his memoir of the war with travelogue accounts of his trips through the countryside, descriptions of sights he had seen, and the historic and beautiful accommodations he used. Where possible, Pershing felt that the men under his charge should profit too from their time in Europe as tourists would. He made this clear in his plans for the men's recreation once the war ended. In the discussions around the liberalizing of the leave policy right after the Armistice, Pershing had "announced that he wanted a plan worked out whereby all men of the AEF might have an opportunity to visit Paris before leaving France. [He felt] that the leave system should be utilized to capacity and the opportunity made available to every soldier that had become entitled to it to enjoy the privilege of the duty-status leave as something earned and something of value."[31] A few days of pleasure in Paris after fighting for their country might be considered a simple reward for men after a successful campaign. Yet the word "value" used here, indicating a whole realm of possible improvements to the soldier's cultural life, suggested the extent to which General Pershing shared the progressivism of Secretary Baker.

Changes in the leave orders, issued on December 9, 1918, about a month after the Armistice, liberalized the system. Leaves could be longer and could be accumulated more rapidly; soldiers could visit Italy and Britain. Pershing's desire, however, that deserving members of the AEF would spend several improving days in Paris, became part of the program for comparatively few soldiers. Again, reports on the leave system cited the limitations of French rail transportation, but discipline problems certainly figured in the reasoning.

The French trains adapted to carrying American soldiers to leave destinations all over France. The daily "Permissionnaire Americain" carried Americans going south from Is-sur-Tyle to Menton. The "American Express" carried them from Paris to the Riviera. By the middle of June, 1919, when the leave areas closed and the special trains stopped, between four and six hundred thousand of the two million American soldiers in France had benefited from the program.

The AEF's plans for the rest and recuperation of soldiers demonstrated that, even in a military context, Americans thought of France readily in touristic terms. These plans had their origins among YMCA and other welfare organization personnel, but the military authorities eventually approved them and approved of the educational and broadening spirit behind the plans. The plan eventually adopted – seven nights at a leave area and travel time to and from the area earned for every four months of active service – provided the needed time of rest. It included, however, aspects of the original Baedeker-like touring plan as well. Destinations were to be rotated to insure that every member of the AEF might see as much of France as was possible.[32]

If army authorities included the culturally beneficial aspects of the war experience in their plans for leave only after military considerations, the welfare organization workers who actually executed the system wrote in effusive terms of these cultural effects. The General Report of the Soldiers' Leave Department of the YMCA stated the problem of leaves as follows:

> The American soldier was in a foreign country, with whose language and customs he was not familiar; living under conditions of great physical hardship and nervous strain, accustomed by the experience of the race to ample recreational facilities and yet without opportunity to indulge in American recreation unless special facilities should be provided.[33]

They proposed a "profitable and pleasant vacation for the men." The first agency they contacted for aid was the Bureau National du Tourisme of France. This French agency suggested Aix-les-Bains, the watering resort, as a suitable location. The YMCA achieved its desired educational ends:

> One of the unique features of the Leave Area experiment was the securing of the most beautiful and elaborate places in France, such as the famous casinos, for their entertainment and accommodation. It is to be noted that without exception the men responded admirably to this kind of hospitality. Not only did they exercise the greatest care in the use of the casinos, but also their interest in the buildings, their structure, the mosaics, the ornamentations, the system of lighting, etc., all contributed indirectly to the general educational effect.[34]

The merchants and hoteliers of Aix-les-Bains had the opportunity and desire to educate the approaching American soldiers as commercial prospects. *L'Avenir,* the local newspaper, stated that between January, 1918, and May, 1919, 113,000 American soldiers spent seven days at Aix "to amuse themselves and to give them the best idea of gay and cultivated France." It went on to quote Docteur Françon on the manner in which Aix should accept Americans. Françon, a respected member of the watering cure community of Aix, had had the first contact with the YMCA. "We will greet these brave boys as we would wish our own to be greeted in similar circumstances, and we will do our best that they may find a familial atmosphere here that will soften the sorrow of separation from their families, and rest them from the fatigue of war."[35] Aix had been a watering place for the very wealthy of the world. Apparently, its hoteliers needed instruction in accepting and handling large numbers of American enlisted men.

In fact, the American presence revived an hotel business that had sagged badly since 1914. The great casino had closed after the start of hostilities. The hotels had struggled along, sometimes receiving convalescents from distant and impecunious countries. According to the leading newspaper of Aix, the arrival of the Americans would change the fortunes of the city.

> The American pays well – that can been seen already by the correct rate he will pay upon arrival at the hotel; this is not at all a question of those unhappy Serbs and war time prices suitable for refugees.[36]

Karl Cate, of the YMCA, and the hoteliers' association had come to agreements quickly. On January 5, 1918, the newspaper of Aix invited owners of private villas to register with the mayor in order that these be rented to the Americans. By January 12, the meeting had taken place between Karl Cate of the YMCA and Dr Françon. 1,600 beds were promised. On January 19, a long article explained the YMCA and its relation to the U.S. Army. On January 26, negotiations had reached page one and become the subject of huge headlines for the little resort city. 2,000 beds permanently reserved till six months after the end of the war would mean a cash flow of twenty to twenty-five million Francs.

L'Avenir restrained its commercial readers against taking advantage of the AEF. Americans would pay handsomely, but they must not be abused.

> Americans pay well but hate being taken. This side of the American psychology should be kept in mind. The people of Aix do not have to be reminded that they come from a nation with a world-wide reputation for honesty. Simply do not dry up the spring by a jump in prices.[37]

The authorities in Aix wished to prevent deterioration of relations partly because they took a long view of their town's future:

Such acts would result in the most awful ruin of the development that by rights we can expect, in our popularity in the United States. Publicity by postal cards, sent in the hundreds of thousands, will carry the most seductive views of our splendid countryside across the Union from the shores of the Atlantic to those of the Pacific.[38]

Whether they would succeed or not, the hoteliers of Aix-les-Bains saw it as in their best interest to turn American soldiers into habitual globe-trotting tourists, and wittingly or not, into promoters of tourism. From acting as saviors of France they had become temporarily consumers of France and perhaps would become promoters of France.[39]

For some other Frenchmen too, the American presence presented as much a marketing problem as it did a cultural problem. For Galeries Lafayette, teaching Americans to appreciate things French meant teaching them to buy things French. The great department store printed a little booklet called "Paris for Englishmen and for Americans." Combining military and commercial etiquette, the book told how and where purchases could be made: "Once you obtain the required information you say: 'Merci' (pronounced Mare-see). You can make a sort of military salute when asking or thanking." Galeries Lafayette was a good place to start looking for most things. Le Printemps, another department store, printed in English "My Little Diary," in which soldiers could keep a record of their time in service. The booklet described Le Printemps in approximately the same terms as the YMCA described the Louvre, "the best renowned Department store in Paris." Michelin & Co. printed a booklet called "Pages of American Glory" containing short ringing histories of American victories in France, fit to inflate the pride of any American who had participated. The booklet finished with pictures of nicely plumped up tires.[40]

The motives of the French may appear venal, the traditional hucksterism of the old world towards tourists, but the YMCA too took an active interest in cultivating uneducated American soldiers as tourists. The YMCA published slim guide books to all parts of France where doughboys might show up. Their booklet of general information about Paris held little that would interest sophisticated travelers. Places of interest included a ferris wheel. A brief parenthesis explained the Place de la Concorde: "(Marie-

Antoinette and many others guillotined)." The parenthetical explanation for the importance of the Louvre un-selfconsciously parodied a sophisticated traveler's worst fears about the unsoph- isticated: "(formerly king's palace, largest in world, now the finest Art Museum in the world – closed except hall of statuary)." The YMCA offered motor trips around Paris, and walks through the Latin Quarter with five to twenty minute lectures given by secretaries. The YMCA intended to teach the moral imperative of tourism. A man should have visited a certain number of sights if he had the opportunity. But teaching men to be tourists taught them to be consumers of culture. The YMCA's efforts, like those of the French, directed Franco/American contact into safe chan- nels, away from conflicts with French civilians and away from conflicts with the army's own hierarchy.

The shifting interpretation of American soldiers as fighting defenders of liberty to consumers took some peculiar forms. The French *Office National du Tourisme* printed its own guide book for this purpose, "The Americans' Guide Book in France." Its author, Baudry de Saunier, dedicated it "To the American Soldiers, who have come to defend *France* – 'The Banner of the World' as Edison says – and with her, *Liberty*." The pamphlet explained that American officers and soldiers "unfortunately cannot spend their leave or convalescence in their own country, but must spend it in France." Nevertheless, with the guide book,

> They could more easily choose not only regions in harmony with their tastes, but would also learn to appreciate the more our country in its extreme diversity... And what is France? Great men have said "Every man has two countries, his own and France!" Intellectually and morally never was a truer word spoken. Physically, it is evident that France, by a wonderful will of destiny, embodies all the most varied aspects of other countries.

Having first identified the American soldier's intentions in France as being entirely France's own – here no fight for democracy, nor President Wilson's fourteen points – the pamphlet identified France spiritually as home to the American. Finally, and more wildly, de Saunier identified France, physically, with the United States. "Other countries have mountains or plains, lakes or forests, sands or prairies; France has all these in turn. She has torrents, cascades, lakes, rivers, streams, water in abundance, extinct volcanes(*sic*), lava and basalt." France surpassed the United States in natural wonders, for, "All these aspects, all these treasures are accessible within a few hours journey, since France in her largest dimension is only 1,000 kilometers." As a lesson in tourism for Americans, the pamphlet stated that to take a trip through France was like taking a trip home, with the distance conveniently diminished.

Having established the logic of an American's desire to tour France in wartime, the pamphlet listed all the famous tourist spots. None of these had anything to do with the plains, forests, or prairies that the French tourist office thought of as the Americans' home. Sands found their way onto the list in the sense of beaches. If an American set out on his leave to find the prairies of home, he would be surprised to find a watering resort at the end of his railway journey. He had some warning. The description of France that so effusively insisted on her lava and basalt ended thus: "In short she is the country of history, of monuments, of curiosities and of gaiety."[41]

The attempt to identify France with the United States showed some strain but it suggested to its readers that what they thought of as home could be represented not only by one place, but by separate attributes of that place that might be anywhere. The French *Office National du Tourisme* could not easily find a logic to train huge populations of unsophisticated Americans to become tourists, but they attempted to tell Americans that visiting parts of France was like visiting parts of America and could be enjoyed in very traditional and *de luxe* European resorts. The mineral springs of France figured prominently in any list of tourist spots. In this particular pamphlet, they were listed with the diseases they could cure. Reading the list, the young American doughboy readers fade to be replaced by plumper, older patrons with their ailments – diabetes, gout, nervous disorders, liver complaints, obesity, and diseases of the kidneys and bladder. Once the American private got a taste of watering places, perhaps he would return in old age, his home defined not by where he happened to live, but by his needs.

Motivated by profit, and in some cases financial survival, rather than the improvement of American soldiers, French hotel keepers yet shared certain aims with American authorities who wished to teach American soldiers to be tourists in order to keep them from mixing too freely with the French and to keep them out of trouble. The method was to give the boys a first class European vacation. There can be little doubt that, in many cases, it was a vacation unlike anything they had ever experienced before in their lives. It must have stood out in most men's memories in as high relief as any experience of the war. Only the memory of combat should have left a more vivid impression.

Though many men participated in this elaborate program, traces of the leave areas appear in their memories in a curiously muted form. To the United States Military History Institute's question on recreation, for example, only one among the twelve men who responded for the Seventy-ninth Division mentioned a leave area. Considering that the Seventy-ninth Division contained in the neighborhood of 20,000 men, and that, statistically speaking, at least 5,000 must have gone to a leave area (about a fourth, or between 400,000 and 600,000 men in the AEF of 2,000,000 enjoyed those leave areas[42]), this one in twelve response needs explaining. The Seventy-ninth Division makes a good example here because it was a unit of white men and it fought well and often, but not so often that it did not have time for leave. It is therefore unlikely that General Headquarters discriminated against it in the matter of leave. Veterans of World War I, when they answered questions about their experience of the war, quite often left out the experience of leave. The members of the Seventy-ninth Division were hardly alone in this omission.

The memory of leave may have faded for veterans for several reasons. Staying in a lavish resort has very little to do with what has come to be thought of as the experience of World War I. The European memory of the war, the successive years in muddy trenches and the annual tragic slaughter in useless offensives has understandably affected the American memory of the war as well. Arguably, this process started very early with the disappointments of the Versailles Treaty and the League of Nations. It had solidified when American novelists of the 1920s and 1930s wrote their disillusioned descriptions of the war. In veteran organizations, men may discuss the experience of combat, which lies at the heart of a man's identity as a veteran, but in such a context a tourist's experience seems secondary. Veterans will not necessarily rehearse a memory of a lavish vacation. The response to the off-duty recreation question, "I liked my ten days at Aix-les-Bains best,"[43] did seem out of place among the archives of the war.

Perhaps such a thought seemed out of place to veterans as they thought about war and filled out the questionnaires.

Woodrow Wilson himself refused to tour the battlefields. Certainly his schedule was full during his trips to Paris after the war, but this refusal has sometimes been interpreted as coldness or a reluctance to face the war's cost in blood. But Wilson's refusal also allowed him to ignore the greater experience of battle held by his British and French counterparts. Wilson the diplomat may have understood the power that Clémenceau as tour guide might have gained on such an outing. Clémenceau had been there while the fighting was going on. By his refusal, he declined to accept a detached tourist's connection to the war. Wilson, the protestant minister's son, understood the difference between symbols of the experience of battle and the reality of battle. He refused to walk on the scene of the theater of a war for whose triumphant finish he felt partly responsible. Other American participants took the tours, but, fifty years later, refused to remember themselves as tourists. Perhaps they came, over that time, to agree with Wilson. Regardless of how complicated by interpretations and representations their lives had become when they answered the questionnaires in the 1970s, they had started the century with clearer ideas of their identity.

The relatives of veterans who prepared papers for donation to research libraries sometimes edited memory when they removed the veterans' letters from their time on leave. In some collections, they explained this editing saying these letters were not of historical interest. On the other hand, veterans and their editor relatives emphasized combat experience. Some veterans edited their letters and diaries to include only a few days of intense fighting out of a year or more spent with the AEF. On the questionnaire distributed by the Military History Institute, to the invitation to make further comments, the veterans most often related some specific battle anecdote.

That the memory of leave faded should not, however, be taken as an indication that the YMCA exaggerated its claims to effective service, or that leave left no impression at the time. One veteran of the Seventy-ninth Division claimed on his questionnaire that his unit had had no time for leave. Along with his questionnaire, however, he included his war diary for the archives at Carlisle Barracks. In the diary, he had carefully recorded a week spent in Chamonix at government expense. The sights, the novelty of a Winter resort, the luxury, the foreign culture, had not been lost on him in 1918.[44] Another soldier who remembered nothing of tourism on his questionnaire, had mentioned his leave in Annecy, a mountain restort near Aix-les-Bains incorporated into the first Leave Area, to his family. With his papers at Carlisle Barracks, his wife included a description of the pilgrimage she had taken with their children to the place he had told them of with emotion, but had officially forgotten.

American magazines accepted tourism as the one way in which cultures could interact. The participation of Americans in a European war, they found, had brought the American magazine writer much closer to the foreign country he observed. Article after article published in America's popular magazines during the war discussed France from a tourist's point of view. Seemingly, American soldiers were not only saving France for democracy or to repay a debt to Lafayette and Rochambeau, they were also saving France for tourists.

The American novelist Winston Churchill described his trip to wartime Europe in *Scribner's Magazine* in terms of tourism and past trips. "The days of luxurious sea travel, of à la carte restaurants, and Louis Quinze bedrooms were gone – at least for a period,"[45] wrote Churchill. But then he found just those emblematic aspects of France surviving the war. He approached the war as a consumer cataloging what he had known:

> The luxury shops appeared to be thriving, the world-renowned restaurants to be doing business as usual; to judge from the prices, a little better than usual; the expensive hotels were full. It is not the real France, of course, yet it seemed none the less surprising that it should still exist.

Like the practiced tourists of Jonathan Culler, Churchill acknowledged a difference between the "real" France and this tourist's France of luxury hotels, but like that tourist he cannot escape the emblematic. His concerns for the survival of the real and the touristic were weighted towards the latter.

> Paris, to most Americans, means that concentrated little district de luxe of which the Place Vendôme is the center, and we had always unconsciously thought of it as in the possession of the Anglo-Saxons. So it seems to-day. The English and Cana-

dians, the Australians, New Zealanders and Americans were much in evidence.

In Churchill's mind, the heart of the tourist's France, that "de luxe" district, had been previously possessed by English speakers in the manner that someone possesses memories. "Unconscious" seems to have meant wistful here. Now, uniformed members of the Anglo-Saxon race had taken quite evident possession of that district. The presence of this army of English speaking men might have struck Churchill as a sign that the Frenchness of the district was becoming adulterated by the numbers of foreigners who had intervened to save it, but on the contrary the presence of these men confirmed the value Americans had always placed on this corner of France. Manifest Anglo-Saxon possession of the tourist's Paris dissolved the distinction between genuine experience and touristic experience of French culture in Churchill's mind. The war had allowed the possession to become genuine. Previously, Paris had existed as a sign of culture in the imagination of tourists who had been there. Possession reified French culture from Churchill's privileged point of view.

Herbert Adams-Gibbons, covering the American Expeditionary Forces for *The Century*, concluded that all Americans shared an innate love for tourism whether they had ever traveled or not. "Americans are born tourists. For most of us there is no better fun, no better recreation, than seeing things," he wrote. "Many of our soldiers may never have traveled before they came to France, but without exception they show the typical American instinct of wanting to see everything and to know all about what they see." The author described soldiers moving from one side of the cultural and class barrier that Dean MacCannell described. They start as actors, but are anxious to become observers. To call this process typically American made a link to ideas about American acculturation and the American idea of a classless society. The distinction between the privileged (the traveled) and the unprivileged (the untraveled) becomes blurred as all Americans learn to think of themselves as cultural consumers at home in a variety of settings, rather than as people acting according to a set of class oppositions.

The blurring of class lines made possible by tourism became clearer when Adams-Gibbons went on to write about soldier accommodations in Aix-les-Bains: "Every man has a chance of drawing Queen Victoria's or J. Pierpont Morgan's or the King of Greece's suite."[46] A desire to see everything, and to know all about what they saw, in the mind of this writer, gave American soldiers the same rewards as the richest men in America, who in turn commanded luxuries comparable to those of the fabulously titled of Europe. Soldiers and nurses did report in letters that they had seen the special chair that was used to lower the corpulent and elderly J. P. Morgan into his bath, but it would be difficult to say how far they could identify their experience of the watering resort with his.

Social blurring did have its limitations in the AEF. Magazines written specifically for soldiers, just like magazines that were intended for a broader public, discussed the experience of the common soldier in touristic terms, but within the AEF military hierarchy required some clear distinctions. In these magazine stories, a common soldier might follow the model of his officer's appreciation of the fine cultural artifacts of Europe, but when his appreciation was not genuine or when he attempted to translate the privileged position of touristic observer into some more material advantage, he would find himself returned to his humble place.

In one such story, "Sammy", the main character ". . . found himself at the square in front of the cathedral. This must be the wonderful church he had heard the officers speak of, so he must see it. He couldn't understand why the officers made such a fuss about a building that should have been torn down and rebuilt anyhow."[47] Sammy did not appreciate the cathedral and, later during his afternoon pass, French customs baffled him. He could not get a meal at a restaurant because he did not know that French restaurants close after lunch and do not open again until late for dinner. Eventually, he returned to his camp with the help of a kind MP, in time for his regulation dinner. He still attempted to impose an unearned superiority gained from his recent leave and so went to the head of the line for "slum." His fellows teased him until he went back to the end of the line. The unsuccessful tourist, the man who had sought material gains from his contact with the ancient or foreign rather than understanding, received humiliation.

He had missed all the signals, French and American. He knew neither that his place in French society was that of the sensitive observer who does not impose his own appetites – he was quite literally hungry in this case – inappropriately on the foreign population, any more than he does on his own people. In both settings he learns his place, and that place is one in a complex society where his own importance has become relative to the whole, rather than corresponding to his desires.

Misapplied tourism appeared as well in *The Stars and Stripes* column "Henry's Pal to Henry" when Henry's pal went to a leave area. In the story "Mademoiselles and a Top," two American soldiers found themselves living in the lap of luxury on leave and tried to take advantage of the situation.

> When we got here a MP steered us over to a place where John D. Morgan and J. Pierpont Rockefeller staid . . . which is all fixed up for a couple of high brows and which is being occupied by only a couple of buck pvts, at present, which is I and Buck . . . I'll bet by just staying here we can cop off any Jane in town when we want to. It is a great advertisement for a couple of buck pvts, who has never had any real chance in the world.

The two soldiers pretended to be officers from wealthy families accustomed to staying in the best hotels and they tried to pick up two nurses. "They were both all togged up in a 1 piece bathing suit and which was kind of low at the top, etc. and I guess that was enough to make anybody want to be a captain or a loot."[48] Their sergeant ran into them and ruined their ploy. Like Sammy, they had tried to use the status of tourism to impose their desires on their surroundings. Like Sammy in the story about an afternoon's pass, they were returned to the place in the scheme of things that the army deemed appropriate. The opportunity to stay in a luxurious hotel remained, but that experience could not be used to gratify some immediate desire. Its value lay elsewhere. Locating that "elsewhere" required a soldier to think of himself as an observer of culture, rather than as a member of a grieving class with material needs and "who has never had any real chance in the world."

A soldier could find appropriate uses for doughboy tourism. These had to do with the expression of his understanding rather than his desires, though presumably he did gain some notice at home when a home town paper printed his letters. Soldiers made use of the exoticism of their experience outside the AEF. A private with an eighth grade education wrote the following letter.

He had recently seen as heavy fighting as any American unit faced, but the experience he chose to share with his community had nothing to do with combat and everything to do with tourism:

> The most important event in my life over here (from a social standpoint) was the leave which I enjoyed during the midwinter . . . The view afforded the traveler from the window is undoubtedly one of the finest in the way of scenic grandeur in the world. To the right is the sea, blue indigo matched only by the bluest sky I have ever seen . . . At Nice as at Monte Carlo one of the finest buildings in the city is the gambling Casino, for the present taken over by the YMCA to house their canteen and provide a dance floor as well as an excellent theatre and writing room. [he goes on to describe the Casino Municipal] The elite gather every afternoon and evening to meet their friends and to observe and display a bewildering variety of styles, the uniforms of the several allied officers producing a color effect that must gladden the hearts of these emotional people. This is France as the American tourist knows it.[49]

The elaborate language may have been his own adaptation of nineteenth-century prose, or have had YMCA secretaries and guide books for models. Some soldiers may have had Mark Twain in mind when they wrote, or reinvented themselves as *Innocents Abroad.* But in either case, it was their understanding of a new situation, and of their place in that situation, not the imposition of their desires on that situation, that made their observations noteworthy.

> I have slept in everything from a hay loft to a hotel where kings have spent their summers and everything that I have seen is about a hundred years behind times. All the houses were built a hundred years or more ago. There is one church here that was built in 1626 and is still being used today.[50]

These men's new familiarity with touristic France made their opinions newsworthy. But they have written naïve letters in terms of the history of the genre. They show none of the desire to get off the beaten track, or find something authentic that no one else has found. They toured in the context of the war. And that was authentic enough.

Unlike Winston Churchill, above, they wrote with no caveats about the wonders of "France as the American tourist knows it" as against some "real France". The first of these authors gave no indication that any more authentic France existed besides the France of the Riviera in wartime, populated by men wearing the polychrome uniforms of the victory he shared. "Socially" the experience has been important because he has moved among these enticing figures. At the same time, he has identified with the French "elite" of the area at least enough to empathize with their emotions in the face of the colorful martial throng. The war has produced its own kind of tourism in which usual distinctions of authenticity have dissolved to be replaced by an exotic standard set by the war itself and American possession. The French elite of the Riviera have become tourists in their own Casino Municipal, and the American observer shared their touristic activity. The touristic sight had become something not French at all, but rather a temporary American possession, a casino rented by the YMCA. The soldier observer has understood this complicated situation for its own sake, and not attempted to influence it.

The second author expressed surprise that a seventeenth-century church, or hundred year old houses, should still be used. Perhaps, he described a more "authentic" kind of French scene than the Riviera. Frenchmen in previous centuries, after all, had constructed that scene for purposes other than the leisure of tourists. But he did not enter into that debate. He made the implicit comparison of the French countryside with the United States, where presumably everything was newer and more convenient. Whether like Twain, he pretended this naïveté, or really judged the backwardness of the French this way, it was his tourist's understanding, not his desires of actions, which he expressed.

The answered questionnaires that the US Army Military History Institute received from veterans of World War I contain the largest standardized body of evidence on the leisure activities of World War I soldiers. It has been difficult to render this information statistically. Still, this evidence, when compared with what soldiers wrote in letters, can begin to answer questions about which soldiers preferred which kinds of leisure time activities and what those activities meant to them. In a sample of two divisions drawn from mixed urban and rural areas, about two thirds of the respondees came from laboring or farming backgrounds and

about one third came from the more educated group made up of
students and men with employment indicating some education,
clerks and salesmen. The students were of college age.

More than half of the soldiers who had left college to join the
army, or who had jobs that indicated some educational background, disparaged leisure time activities while in the AEF or
claimed that no important amount of their time had been spent
in leisure activities. Less than half this group remember baseball,
football, YMCA tours, leaves at the special leave areas and other
organized activities. Very few wrote that they recalled unorganized activities, such as card games, drinking, visiting friends,
or making friends, among the French in nearby villages.

On the other hand, only a fourth of soldiers who had held
laboring jobs disparaged memories of leisure time. More than
half remembered the organized activities, and three times as
many remembered participating in unorganized activities.
Memories of both organized and unorganized recreation were far
more important to men who had been coal-miners and steel
workers or farmers (the two divisions used for this analysis were
drawn from Pennsylvania, Virginia, West Virginia, Maryland,
and the District of Columbia), than for men who had been clerks
and students. Why the less educated group remembered leisure
in its wartime guise, and in greater variety than the more
educated soldiers, is difficult to say. Perhaps for them the novelty
of tourism and culture as something to consume made this part
of the war noteworthy, whereas the more educated had first
encountered these aspects of modern life somewhere else. Americans were all "born tourists," according to Herbert Adams-Gibbons, but only those who discovered this quality in themselves
while in the army thought it worth recording.

Keeping in mind how few veterans responded, their response
to the question, "What forms of off-duty recreation were common?" still divided Americans of draft and enlistment age in
some significant ways. Samples from the Ninety-first and Ninety-
second Divisions told of the following activities: "The usual, some
horseback riding around camp"; "Basketball, football, baseball";
"writing letters, playing cards, visiting friends, and taking in the
sights"; "For some gambling, others women"; "Very little until
war was over, then baseball, football tournaments, debate tournaments"; "Go to towns, fish and hunt in the area."[51] Some of
these activities are things that American men with time on their

hands had always done, and they could be done alone or in groups spontaneously. Activities needing organization fitted the notion, new to many Americans, that leisure time should improve the man, should be, in fact, recreation.

The YMCA approved and organized some of these activities and did not approve or organize others. In the case of some activities, the difference between what the YMCA approved and promoted, and what the men did naturally as an expression of their cultural origins, cannot be made. The men might have played baseball and football spontaneously, for example. The fact that the YMCA approved this activity, to the extent that it supplied the soldiers with a vast quantity of sports equipment, need not point to social engineering. All sports playing, however, as part of a tournament, to determine which was the fittest outfit, or debates intended to sharpen verbal skills for subsequent careers, had a more didactic purpose. By promoting tournaments between divisions, the YMCA could direct the entertainment of many men far more efficiently too. Not many more than eighteen men can be entertained by a pickup game of baseball, but no limit exists on who may be entertained, as both players and spectators of an important match. The YMCA Handbook emphasized matches. And the YMCA history of leave areas presented statistics on numbers of spectators as well as on participants.[52]

"Visiting the neighboring sights" might look like the spontaneous activity of a curious man, but, in the context of the AEF, it almost certainly took place under the auspices of the YMCA. Even writing letters could have a progressive tone, if the contents of those letters were taught by the army or YMCA. These activities could lend themselves to uplift, could help a man to improve himself, and were undertaken with the approval and under the eye, and, in the case of letter-writing, on the stationery of the YMCA or one of the other social welfare organizations.[53]

Those other activities, fishing and hunting, horseback riding, meeting women, gambling, visiting friends, were all things that American men had always done up to that time. They could join a man to some kind of participatory community life where he could satisfy material and spiritual desires and take responsibilities, breaking the tourist's detachment. They could also connect Americans to a pastoral ideal, that for about a third of the soldiers from this sample could remind them of their farm home.[54] The YMCA did not support these activities.

The case that this brief list of leisure time activities was produced by American men at a cultural crossroads can be made by noting how these activities have survived. No one today could say, "the usual, horseback riding." Neither could fishing and hunting be listed in so casual a manner by subsequent generations of more urban Americans. Those activities have become rarer as others, notably spectator sports and sightseeing, have become mass phenomena. Leisure culture among American soldiers in World War I therefore split along visible fissures suggesting social classes or divisions between urban and rural Americans but these splits could easily be crossed if a man accepted the YMCA's touristic training.

Soldiers' relations to French women demonstrated this division in American culture best. American soldiers who married French women came overwhelmingly from the ranks of enlisted men in the AEF. They often came from families with the disadvantage of at least one parent dead. These men attempted to create some kind of community for themselves, to take on responsibility roles even in their leisure surroundings. Officers, more educated Americans and men who could learn to move back and forth over Dean MacCannell's cultural barriers between observers and actors could more often be satisfied with a tourist's and consumer's relation to the place in which they lived.[55]

Men with greater means and greater education could also be tempted to break the touristic mould that defined their relationship to the foreign. Winston Churchill had described Anglo-Saxon possession of a part of Paris through the legitimate commercial means of occupying hotel rooms and café tables. Captain Austin Raymond found a paradise that he described in several letters to his mother, and eventually annexed part of it in a way that crossed the barriers of good tourism.

> My dug-out is very novel – a wine cellar cut from pure white chalk, some thirty feet underground where I live like a mole with no light but candles and lamps . . . I have a large mahogany wardrobe, an equally handsome bedstead with box mattress and sheets, a six foot, beautifully framed mirror, tables, chairs, rugs, cuckoo clock, vases, etc, which my orderly collected from nearby houses. It seems a shame to help

ourselves from the homes of unfortunate people but we may as well do it as the shells will destroy everything eventually. I have also a large silver bowl (about two feet in diameter) and a tall silver pitcher which I have suspicions of having· been taken from the large church across the street.[56]

Raymond's qualms about appropriating French property did not last very long. He eventually sent two vases home to his wife.[57] The poet Alan Seeger committed another example of this kind of high-culture souvenir-taking, and also excused himself by pointing out that the objects would otherwise have been destroyed.

I found finely bound, immaculate sets of Rousseau, Voltaire, Corneille and Racine. The wind and rain that blew in through the immense rents in the walls had not yet harmed them in the least. They were as fresh as the day they left the famous early nineteenth-century presses of which they were the choicest examples.

I took away a few of these volumes, esteeming that the pious duty of rescuing an old book doomed otherwise to certain destruction might absolve me from the gravity of the charge that such an act made me liable to.[58]

Among all the questionnaires from the United States Military History Survey examined for this study, none gave a positive response to the question, "Was there any looting?" Many soldiers remembered theft of various kinds, however, in the AEF. Many diaries and letters referred to baggage stolen from warehouses, stolen souvenirs, and money or watches taken from wounded men in hospitals. Only well educated people actually reported doing looting. Like their less educated counterparts who note more often than they do their time as tourists, the educated note crossing the barriers of culture but in the opposite direction. From enjoying the contemplation of the exotic scenes that they took such evident pleasure in describing – Austin Raymond's fabulous cave, Alan Seeger's library open to the elements – they slip over the cultural barrier and become actors.

The lives of officers ring of "lifestyle." They wrote diary entries that could take the place of the itineraries of the fashionable sometimes reported in magazines today. "Arrived Paris 8:30 A.M. Spent the day shopping. Made a hurried trip through the part of the Louvre that was open," or "Arrived Paris at noon and

went to the horse races at Longchamps." They give the impression of experiences in exquisite localities shared with sophisticated
company. Colonel A. B. Miller of the Marines wrote, "Met my
three interpreter friends and two of their lady chums . . . We
crossed the Loire River, got into a coach and drove to St. Père
de Retz about ten miles away . . . Had the most wonderful dinner
I ever had in all my life. Fortunately the Americans have not yet
discovered this place therefore it is not ruined."[59] This man's
touristic mindset has so far supplanted the special conditions of
the war that his fellow members of the AEF have become the
enemy.

Colonel Miller could easily consume at a high level of cultural
sophistication in France having almost no contact with the
French at all. On November 23, 1917, he described a "musical
evening," at a fellow officer's quarters after which he bought
"Quand Madelon," the ubiquitous song of wartime France.
Thousands of Americans became familiar with this song from
hearing it sung by French soldiers, or by singing it with them.[60]
Miller did not hear French soldiers sing "Quand Madelon," he
heard it at an American officer's party and then bought the sheet
music to send to his wife.[61] Like Captain Raymond's vases, the
sheet music objectified an officer's knowledge of French culture
without his ever having had to participate in it.

Men like these were strangely unattached to French society,
though by education they should have had a greater understanding of French and European high culture than any other
American group. Though their activities were sometimes "typically French", they were the activities of the tourist in France:
eating, viewing, and shopping for luxuries. No matter where they
came from in the United States, they could re-form their own
elite American society in France. Major Samuel W. Flemming,
formerly of Harrisburg, Pennsylvania, and educated at Princeton,
wrote: "No matter where one was in France, if an order came to
go elsewhere, everyone went via Paris, so I did likewise, spending
three days at the Hotel du Louvre which had been turned into
an American Officers Club." Once in Paris, he could easily meet
the old elite of his home town. He described lunches at the Ritz
where he would bump into old Harrisburg and Princeton
friends.[62]

Even the official contact between American officers and the
French left the Americans of rank less involved than common

soldiers. Colonel Miller who, above, visited an unspoilt restaurant described Christmas day, 1917. He started his description with a list of his presents: "Received some very handsome gifts this morning. My lieutenants gave me a gold wrist watch. The 2nd Platoon gave me a beautiful pair of French riding boots and a box of Henry Clay cigars." Next, he conducted a round of official visits to French dignitaries. He returned, Christmas day, to St. Père en Retz with five American friends and ate a twenty-two course meal. "It was wonderful." After that, he participated in the one Christmas event that American enlisted men all over France recalled. "We had a Xmas tree and gave presents to 1,500 French children at the camp." He ended the day at the opera.[63]

Giving presents to French children often appeared in the letters of soldiers as an emotional moment attaching them to France. "Several hundred men lined up and greeted the newcomers literally with open arms. For as far as they went, each man received as a 'Christmas package' one of the boys or girls to carry through the mud to the Red Cross Hut."[64] The scene is touching even as described by a camp newspaper in 1919. And certainly that the men carried these French children through the mud connected each man to a child in a way.

For officers whose education may have prepared them for contact with other cultures, contact meant tourism. Even when less than enthusiastic about what they saw in France, they still thought in touristic terms. "Though the scenery was the same as that which Americans formerly traveled thousands of miles to see, it did not appeal to us in that light, even though it helped to make the trip bearable."[65] Without tourism highbrow, Americans could not understand or relate to France. Where men would describe some idyllic spot as homelike, officers, with great specificity, would plan trips back to the lovely places they saw. "Someday I'll take thee through this country and I'll be thy guide – a fluent French linguist and an old soldier," wrote Lieutenant Joseph Brown. Like others he thought of tourism in connection with combat: "A nice young French Lieutenant directed his battery to fire at a house away across the winding road. I don't know how they do it but all four shells fired were only about fifteen or twenty yards from the mark", he wrote. He went on in the same paragraph: "The Marne Valley is really beautiful, Nin, and we'll have to motor along it – thee and I someday – with Ma and Dad in their cabuche not far away." He combined sightseeing with precision shelling of the Marne valley and the affectionate Quaker "thee," (Brown, though from Philadelphia, was not a Quaker himself).[66]

In dreamy travel plans in the midst of war, officers juxtaposed a private idyl with the mechanized war they shared with the men. For them, the possession of a private escape seemed within reach. "When the time comes, my most precious darling and I are going to have one of those cottages right here in the land which can be a sunny place when it wants to . . . " This captain of engineers had inquired about the price of cottages he could see near his camp and found that he could afford one. In other letters he had considered bringing his wife and child to France.[67] The dreams of regular soldiers would not have been so free to rearrange where people lived. They must have dreamt of how to make themselves at home where they were, with the people around them.

When imagination failed they had to rely on what the YMCA offered or reject tourism entirely and risk disciplinary action. They partook of all the entertainments the YMCA provided at the leave areas. YMCA guides escorted 4,030 soldiers on a tour called "Seeing Old Aix," in groups of 155. YMCA secretaries recorded that 1,758 men played competitive games in the Casino Gardens and that 1,224 soldiers played "Rough House" games in groups of 68 in the Casino itself, presumably on the stage, while 6,890 soldiers watched them do it. The YMCA kept track of its record of service to the serving men.

Altogether, the YMCA reported that 48,298 partook of its activities at Aix-les-Bains. The YMCA counted everyone except ping-pong, chess, checkers and shuffleboard players. This was an impressive number. According to the town's history, however, 113,000 Americans came to Aix, a figure more than twice that size of the Y's activity figure. Therefore 64,702 soldiers either did not go near the YMCA or did so only to participate in the uncounted games. That the most popular service the YMCA performed at Aix was providing bicycles may suggest why this is so. A great many men wanted mobility, perhaps to get away from any kind of organization.

The men who ran the leave areas were very much aware that soldiers were wary of coercion. "They resented very strongly the restrictions upon their individual freedom which the system of leaves involves," said the general report of the system.[68] The men resented orders to take a vacation in a certain place and stay in a certain hotel. But the organizers hoped the men would find sufficient freedom in the area forty miles long and forty miles wide. As one magazine writer put it, "Uncle Sam had paternally arranged for them unknown pleasures. The horses had been brought to the trough. Could they be made to drink?"[69]

Many soldiers did drink from the YMCA's trough. The YMCA offered them a hearty American breakfast at the casino in Aix, familiar eggs, bacon and pancakes that they could not get in their French hotel, and then proposed an activity for the day. "The YMCA bait, sometimes passed up the first day, is invariably swallowed the second." Essentially, the YMCA offered the soldiers something familiar and American in a foreign place and then offered them a tourists' approach – organized tours – to contact with that foreign place. Their energies were channeled into sports and observation.

The touristic model for understanding a foreign culture could spread to become the method for understanding the entire war. Guide books were written for the battlefields where Americans had fought soon after the war. The books combined the new American tourism with the old pastoral and religious American tradition of enjoying landscape. A guide book for the battles around Château-Thierry announced itself as "A friendly guide for American Pilgrims to the shrines between the Marne and the Vesle." Though written by Alexander Woollcott who had reported for *The Stars and Stripes* from the front, its contemplative idyllic tone could perhaps make understandable a mechanical and nightmarish war, but it transformed that war for American memory into something it had not been. "To Château-Thierry American footsteps turn now and always will turn. Trams and busses and motors will grow in number. There will be those who will be wise enough to cover the area on a bicycle and, best of all, there will be the man who will get a knapsack and a stick and set forth to wander idly from stream to stream." The author gently leads his reader back before mechanical transportation, to a more benign past than anything known on those battlefields during the Summer of 1918 when Americans fought there. The YMCA conducted thousands of tours to these battlefields that took in the famous monuments to a French culture that the battles had preserved.[70]

The typical postcard collection that an American soldier or nurse brought home from France in 1919 juxtaposed scenes of wartime destruction with the sights that tourists have always gone to France to see. The photograph collection belonging to Red Cross Nurse Nellie Delisle memorialized a trip she took in the spring of 1919 to the battlefields around Rheims and to the nearly destroyed town and damaged cathedral. The packaged trip, arranged by the YMCA, also took in the concrete structure in a wood near Brécy where Big Bertha, one of the cannons that shelled Paris, was said to have stood. The nurse had a photo of Bertha's empty concrete bowl and a postcard of a child looking small and frail standing next to one of Big Bertha's shells, 1.4 meters high. On the way back to Paris, the tour stopped at Versailles. Nurse Delisle bought a bound collection of tinted photographs of Louis XIV's chateau. At another time, she traveled to Donremy, the birth-place of Joan of Arc. She bought postcards of that place as well. Today, all these pictures are stuffed into a pink French envelope just as she left them.[71] The images of destruction lie in promiscuous contact with the soon-to-be-sainted savior of France, and that canonized virgin with Louis XIV's palace, the greatest monument to French glory, as they do in many other collections of papers of World War I participants.

The nurse's memory of the war consisted of these same destroyed and preserved artifacts. She, and the other Americans who participated in the war, had helped to save France and the French culture represented by the chateau and the home of Joan of Arc. They had saved these monuments from the destruction memorialized in other photographs, and from the engines of destruction memorialized also. Nurse Delisle could absorb the whole story and preserve it as a tourist would, with an album of diverse images mixed with her memories of what she had done for her patients and her country. A way of organizing memories of America's part in World War I that rejected the tourist's vision would have been very difficult indeed.

But not everyone drank at the trough of the YMCA, and those who drank there did not do so all the time. One man who had gone on several YMCA sponsored tours at Vals-les-Bains, and had rented a bicycle as well, noted something strange as he waited to board his train and return to his unit. As he waited, the train carrying the next week's permissionnaires arrived. The

YMCA arranged for a large truck to meet the train and carry off the packs of the men not on it.

> What happened when the train stopped at the stations was some of them accidently missed the train, and some did not want to get on, as they went to Paris and other places. Several days after we were in the town of Vals-les-Bains the boys began to come in to town and a few never got back to their own companies until about time to sail for home. One fellow in Company "C" done that and he got an honorable discharge the same as anyone else. He had the laugh on us for doing all the hard drilling and sleeping in barns. The MP's could not imagine how so many men got away from the train.[72]

Some Americans still preferred to lite out for the territory on their own.

4 "Mad'moiselle from Armentières, Parlez-vous?" Sexual Attitudes of Americans in World War I

> From gay Paree he heard guns roar,
> And all he learned was je t'adore
>
> "Mademoiselle from Armentières"

The territory, free from the improving restrictions of the army, to which many men wished to "lite out" was the company of French women. There was a practical side to the way in which army authorities treated men's relations with women. First of all, they were concerned with the inefficiencies caused by veneral disease. In three general orders from General Pershing in his first six months in France, and in numerous publications and publications and lectures, American men learned the army's policy on relations with women. Soldiers were expected to remain continent. The army would offer improving recreation to keep them away from women. The army would provide prophylaxis, and, under some circumstances, would enforce its application as well. Soldiers could be court-martialed and punished for contracting venereal infections. Unit commanders would be held responsible for high levels of veneral disease among their men. Pershing personally inspected the reports of venereal disease every day. As a result of these efforts, and medical treatment among civilians near concentrations of American men, the venereal rate among American soldiers in September of 1918 was less than one case in a thousand soldiers.[1] The other armies sustained far higher rates of disease per thousand soldiers: the Canadian and Australian armies 150; the German army 110.2; the French 83.19; and the British 30.[2] Though the September 1918 figure was probably unusually low for the AEF because of the heavy combat involvement of American troops at that time, the comparison with the other armies is still striking. By a combination of

means, the American army had avoided a major drain on man-
power.

The Americans managed to come to a solution that solved the
problem of veneral disease in keeping with their ideological goal
of improving Americans while they served. Much of this "improvement" took the form of simple restraint, but the sex
education soldiers received from pamphlets and lectures as part
of the program taught them to think, probably for the first time,
in a detached and scientific way, about a part of life that the
society they grew up in had shrouded in taboos.[3]

It comes as no surprise that the United States Army in
combination with a progressive government should have restrained soldiers contact with women for a combination of
practical and idealistic reasons through a combination of practical and idealistic means. But that does not mean these authorities
had reached an agreement on what the standard of behavior
towards women should be, or that it would conform to the social
realities of the foreign place where it would be applied. In a much
recounted and revealing incident, French Premier Georges
Clémenceau wrote to General Pershing offering licensed and
medically inspected houses of prostitution for American soldiers.
While considering the situation, Pershing sent a copy of the letter
to Raymond Fosdick, head of the CTCA, with instructions to
show it to Secretary Baker. Baker read the French suggestion
with dismay, saying, "For God's sake, Raymond, don't show this
to the President or he'll stop the war."[4] In the story, three
progressive moralists, Fosdick, Baker and Wilson are linked
against the Frenchman, stereotypically indulgent, but pragmatic,
in sexual matters. Pershing, the military man, interested in the
efficiency of his men, did consider the option, but eventually
chose other methods.

Rejecting Clémenceau's solution to the problem of contact
with women marked a misunderstanding of the strains the
American presence put on the French, aggravated by the enforced division of labor between uplifting American women and
the physically available French. Both the advocates of improved
morality and of army efficiency tended to ignore the French
women and the society where their regulations and propaganda
efforts took effect. Clémenceau's licensed brothels, unless better
managed than those of other armies, and in conjunction with
prophylaxis, would probably not have reduced the venereal rate

so effectively as combined dissuasion and prophylaxis. It would have done nothing to convince families of soldiers that their sons would come home morally improved. But licensed prostitutes would have contained the problem of contact to a definite part of French society by extending the touristic model for contact between cultures into the sexual realm.

The army and the Wilson administration eventually chose a program that was both more efficient and bore less moral stigma than licensed houses of prostitution. But the army and the progressive Wilson administration were not in total agreement on the standard of behavior towards women they wished to achieve. The army's inclusion of marriage in the restraints on contact with women marked a difference. To maintain its efficiency and keep its men clear of conflicting responsibilities, the army would willingly have eliminated marriage, temporarily, in the lives of the men in its charge. The progressive administration, believing that the war could be conducted in such a way as to further social goals, was unwilling to accept the army's suggestion to detach a period of a man's life from social norms and responsibilities.

In the absence of clear enforceable restrictions, men for whom education or social background made the improving standards of the United States Army's propaganda plausible were naturally still attracted to French women and found themselves establishing their own limits on the touristic detached contact with the society of a foreign place. Those soldiers who were inclined to escape the military authority and standards of behavior that extended over them even during periods of leave, found their own difficult paths into French society. Some men for whom culture meant participation in ritual and community started their own family, overcoming barriers of language and culture.

The war itself, with its violence and uncertainties, probably made young men's need for women's companionship and comfort more urgent. Some American soldiers kept a popular series of French postcards called "Le Poilu Permissionnaire" as a souvenir. The series portrayed a French soldier returning home to the embraces of a woman. He traveled from the front to her bed in just two images. Once with his woman, he ran the gammut of love: "amour ardent," "amour fol" (he chases her wearing a nightshirt and a helmet), "amour calme" (they are in bed together), "amour tempéré" (they eat together), "amour d'antan" (they promenade together), "fini l'amour" (he returns to the front by way of the railroad station). The series connected the idea of sexual excitement and bliss, and also calm domesticity in the company of a woman, with the idea of being steadfast in the face of the enemy. War has prepared this soldier for love, and even provided some of the erotic props for love – that helmet. Conversely, the sexual and emotional satisfaction and warmth that he feels when he has spent time in his home has made him calm and ready to face the enemy fatalistically once more.[5]

The makers of souvenir postcards and the soldiers who bought them were not alone in making the connection between sexuality and combat. Women observers made this connection too. A soldier's projected masculinity could seem to have increased as a result of his fighting. A writer for *The American Red Cross Magazine* wrote of such a perception in an article describing men coming to a canteen just after battle. She called the article "Just Real, Real Men!"

> I can't tell why it was, but the sadness of it all, the far-away homes of those boys, their goodness in doing just what they thought we would like, and their quietness, nearly broke our hearts! And they are so big! They tower over everyone, and have great broad shoulders, and big voices – just real, real men![6]

Combat in World War I, that so often has been called emasculating, actually enhanced the virility of these men in the eyes of this woman author. But she did not experience this strong masculinity as only sexual, she noted the men's need for home as well.[7]

The British military historian Richard Holmes has found the analogy between a soldier's first experience of combat and his first experience of sex throughout the history of war. And he has examined the connection between combat and increased sexual activity, pointing out that it includes not just a desire for physical gratification, but also "for affection . . . for positive evidence that, despite the upheavals of military life, one still remains a valuable and valued person."[8] He wrote that World War I was no exception. "It wasn't that you were in love with anyone in particular," he quoted a British soldier as writing, "it was simply that you took a quite especial delight in female society, and without really planning to, you yet did all in your power to attract them."[9] Those deeper voices and shoulders held so broadly may have resulted from such a semi-conscious effort on the part of the returning soldiers described as "just real men" to attract women, while their sadness, quietness and obedience all point towards a deep need for affection.

Messages about sex and emotion could be extremely complicated for a man who tried to live up to the ideal of continence while in France. He might express wonder and disapproval at venal sexual relations he saw around him, at the same time as asserting his own masculinity through self-control.

> ... In the same compartment there was this rake of an American officer who was on his way to the U.S. he said because he'd had pneumonia but I guess there was something else. And with him 2 regular Parisian chickens, reddened cheeks and hair and everything, and he was having some time. He told me "not to be slow," but I had a big advantage on him as he couldn't speak a word of French and so I talked to one of them and I guess I'd better tell you Baby that I *did* like her perfume ... I changed cars to get out of it – that's the first experience like that I've had and I thought I'd better tell you all about it as I tell you about everything and it wasn't [*sic*] nice party for me to be in – me thinking about my 2 Pets [his wife and his daughter] *all* the time.[10]

This officer expressed both manly interest in the women, and his powers to resist bolstered by thoughts of his home. He called the officer with the women a "rake," as if, for him, the only precedent for womanizing came from literature, not from any experience at all. And the letter is also testimony of his need for the affection of his own women, who are so far away. Telling his wife about such an incident might look cruel; he unsettled her needlessly. But he needed her response. She understood. They wrote to each other at least twice a week, and sometimes several times during a single day.

Another soldier who accepted the message of the YMCA and who had spent two weeks fighting just at the end of the war insisted in letter after letter to his mother that he did not look for women, but that they looked for him. He wrote that when women called him beautiful, they actually just admired his glasses! "One is sure to fall unless he [*sic*] had trained himself thoroughly in the art of self-control," wrote this veteran of the Meuse-Argonne offensive:

The American soldier is having his hardest fight right now and thousands will not go home with their comrades. They will "fall" wounded at the battle of Paris or Marseille or Bordeaux or any place where attractive women are. They "fall" fighting alone, in a one-sided contest. And believe me, it is no easy fight with a real and constant temptation presenting herself in a most alluring form at almost every turn.[11]

The YMCA played an important part in teaching soldiers to survive this battle. This soldier recounted an incident where he thought of the words of a YMCA lecture to save himself, and he let his mother know that he always stayed at the Y when in a strange town.

One day, surrounded by women on a park bench, he nearly succumbed when one of them flashed sunlight off her hand mirror into his eyes.

I am falling, falling, my senses reel. I must break the spell or I will be a moral coward. The effort is great but I at length swing my mind to thoughts of home and I have won.[12]

This soldier insisted that all the attraction was on the side of the women. He could not understand how such healthy fine looking women could behave in so apparently depraved a way. He did not think the war had enhanced his masculinity, but that it had somehow rendered French women boy-crazy. He overheard a French woman and an American who had just met, having this conversation in a train:

'It is a pretty day.'
'O! . . . yes.' He answered, 'You speak English.'
'No! Jus a little.' The train then stopped.
The girl spilled the beans, 'I loff you!' She said.
'Same here.' He answered.
'Just one keess,' she volunteered holding up one finger.[13]

At about the same time, a friend of his received a proposition while on his way into a church. Of these events, he wrote, "We are all astonished. Is it one of the effects of the war or is it natural?" He found his answer, and decided that he understood French women better, when he was told that for every four single young women in France, there was only one marriageable man after the war. The metaphor he chose to use in his explanation echoed the central example of Darwin's *On the Origin of Species*, bird reproduction. "It is nature. They are competing with one another like a bird with brilliant plumage, like a butterfly. They become veritable magnets in obtaining a mate."[14]

The French women he met on trains as he traveled about after the war, following the United States Army's program of tourism, had a different opinion. "But we are not looking for beaucoup mademoiselles." He and his friends told them. "Ah! Yes, but you are. All Americans are looking for women," the girls who shared their compartment had replied. This young man learned slowly the idea that war increases a man's attractiveness, even his own.[15] He thought of little else besides women while he waited to go home after the war. One can still feel the mutual sexual tension in him and his interlocutors while reading his letters some seventy years later. Everything he said about those women could probably have been said about him. He, too, sported a gaudy kind of plumage, that of a veteran. He, too, sought out the opposite sex. And nothing exists in his descriptions that sounds mercenary, either on his part or on the part of the women. "I loff you," said the French woman. "Me too," said the American. They meant it. And this rather innocent exchange can inform an interpretation of the bawdier lines of "Mademoiselle from Armentières, Parlez-vous?"

Eventually, the tone of his letters became calmer, his wonder at these women lessened. He had attempted to hold himself to an ideal of self-control, to hold French women at a certain distance, to observe them as a curiosity of nature. Perhaps understanding their nature eventually led him to understand his own. In any case, in his later letters, he insists less on the restraining influence of the Y.

Less restrained contact between American soldiers and French women has left plenty of traces. Evidence exists to suggest that American soldiers had few difficulties making the acquaintance of French women. The *Physionomie de Paris* reported with unflagging interest the daily conquests of Americans in Paris in the bars and restaurants of the more expensive quarters. In the songs submitted to the police for censoring before public performance, the indefatigable sexual appetite of Americans, and their constant success with women, were stock subjects of humor, sometimes spiced with a certain jealousy.[16]

Certainly, the comparatively ample pay of American soldiers played a large part in their amorous successes. Americans could afford prostitutes much more easily than the other allied soldiers, and they could offer sufficient money to women who were not prostitutes to persuade them to consider some sort of relationship that might approach prostitution. The Adjutant General distributed memoranda warning that "The Provost Marshal and plain clothes men of the Intelligence Police have been ordered to report all ranks and militarized civilians who are seen in cafés and other public places with prostitutes and women of questionable character," and warning that an officer could be court-martialed for consorting with a prostitute.[17] Brothels were officially off limits to American soldiers. But soldiers seem to have found a way to get what they wished for, sometimes by simple boldness. One soldier described overcoming the language barrier:

> Wooley vouze chusaa veck me, supposedly French for will you sleep with me. An old timer who has served in the Phillipines introduce jig jig which they claimed meant to same thing. The French prostitutes soon took it up and it became the question of the time.[18]

Complaints submitted by the French civil authorities to the Liaison officer at Nantes – by no means an isolated case – indicated the rest of the method for picking up a woman when brothels were restricted and the subtleties of the culture were unfamiliar:

> It has been brought to my attention that depravity is constantly increasing in the zones of Nantes and St. Nazaire.
>
> The consensus of opinion of these different reports seems to be that one of the principal reasons for this state of things is that American soldiers are not allowed to frequent licensed houses of prostitution.
>
> The barring of American soldiers from these houses seems to make them bolder in accosting and picking up women on the streets, and also causes them to make most tempting offers of money, and this in these times of stress and difficulties that we are going through, causes many women to succumb, who otherwise would not.
>
> It even happens that American soldiers are getting so bold as to make their propositions in the streets to women who

are not of easy virtue and so commit most regrettable mistakes.[19]

The French regional commander seemed most disturbed by the spread of "depravity" from classes of women of "easy virtue," where such things were tolerated, to other classes of women. The boldness and money of Americans toppled the resistance of some French women and caused this disquieting behavior. It was complaints like these that had led to Clémenceau's offer of licensed houses of prostitution. And such complaints increased after the Armistice.

The French historian of prostitution, Alain Corbin, has pointed out that World War I increased "sexual misery" to such an extent that it set the regulation of prostitution back by fifty years. This regulation had become a generally voluntary matter, aimed not so much at restricting sexual contacts as at restricting the spread of disease. During the war, separation of couples, the large number of French widows who found themselves forced to support families alone, and the large concentrations of men away from both the restraining force and emotional ties of family and society, lead to a vast increase of prostitution and sexually transmitted diseases.[20]

It is hard to gauge what these relationships meant to the men and women involved by measuring "sexual misery" and reading police reports. But there are few records of the feelings of the participants. The song the American Expeditionary Force sang most often, and for which Americans invented most verses, was named for a French woman, "Mad'moiselle from Armentières." In the words, they recorded some clues. She held a secret: would she speak or not? Perhaps the question at the end of the oftenrepeated first line interrogated the singer's companions, perhaps himself. Parlez-vous? Could he communicate with this mad'moiselle? How would she judge him?

Many verses undermined the dignity of the army and even the singer:

> The Yanks are havin' a hell of a time
> Wadin' around in the mud and the slime,
> Twelve long rainy months or more,
> I spent hunting for that war.

But they always end with the nonsense phrase, "Hinky dinky, parlez vous." Hinky Dinky, so close to "hanky panky," asked will Mademoiselle sleep with the American singers. Could he communicate sexually? Sex, expressed by the nonsense phrase, "Hinky dinky," transcended language and cultural barriers. The song takes a subversive stance towards the usual measure of an army's effectiveness, its efficiency in war, and concentrates instead on the sexual aftermath enjoyed by individuals.[21]

Military men in authority knew quite well that the song described the sexual relations of American soldiers to the French, but some interpreted its meaning only as hostility towards the French and as an insult to French men. French men deserved the insult according to one colonel, who referred to the song in his memoirs. He wrote of it as part of his description of the stereotypical French peasant. "He [the peasant] seemed completely unconcerned at the scandalous implications of some choice and bawdy verses of 'Hinky Dinky Parlez Voo,' mostly sung in his direction by a few 'vocalists,' hastily gathered for the purpose."[22] The colonel overlooked the mockery of the American Expeditionary Forces and the individual singer's self-mockery expressed in the verses above, and he also overlooked the triumphal aspect of the song for Americans. Soldiers had made some connection in a foreign place, carried out a personal foreign mission and learned something in a foreign country beyond the obligations of battle.

> From gay Paree he heard guns roar,
> And all he learned was je t'adore

or

> My Yankee sweetheart looks askance
> At all the mail I get from France

are verses that hardly insulted French men, but they did contain something of which a colonel might not approve. The first of these two verses placed personal and sentimental life in opposition to the military duties of a soldier. The second verse undermined the notion of the domestic sphere in the United States that, according to the propagandists, should have motivated the soldier to do his military duty. The stand-in for the "Yankee sweetheart" in France could be an unavailable American nurse or YMCA worker. The soldier had preserved an emotional life beyond uplift while in the AEF. Under the verses of this most boisterous humorous song may be found the need for affection Richard Holmes wrote of and the "Just Real Men" of the *Red Cross Magazine* writer.

"Mademoiselle from Armentières" did contain plenty of insulting verses, insulting to either French men or women.

> Mademoiselle from Armentières
> Hadn't been kissed [other verbs could be sung here]
> in a thousand years.

> With her I flirted I confess,
> But she got revenge when she said yes.

> The doughboy he had beaucoup jack,
> 'Till mademoiselle got on his track.

> My Froggie girl was true to me,
> She was true to me, she was true to you,
> She was true to the whole damn army too.

These, probably the kind of verses the colonel remembered, could warn American soldiers against relations with French women. These verses tend to reinforce the importance of the army and its violent mission by depreciating the sexual distractions a soldier might find around him in a foreign place. The last verse suggested that relations with foreign women had somehow become part of the standard of army experience like training. But the song elaborated by American soldiers comprised far more varied and subtle reflections of the soldiers' feelings for Mademoiselle.

The musicologist, Lieutenant John J. Niles, called this the "song of songs whenever white army men get together."[23] But he objected to it and to many other songs of white American soldiers because he did not care for the crude way it portrayed Americans' relationship to French women. Of another song, popular with American soldiers, he wrote, "This is perhaps the most pathetic piece of drool to come out of the war. The French is atrocious and the sentiments are almost enough to cause a nice big gauge war between two very long standing allies. But here it is, just as it was sung countless times."

> Quand la guerre est finie
>   les Américains partis

> Laissez les pauvres Françaises
>   un souvenir Bébé.
> (When the war is over
>   the Americans leave
> Leaving poor French women
>   a souvenir baby.)[24]

Niles tended to see the verses in terms of what they might mean to the French men, and perhaps he disapproved of the satisfaction and attested proof of virility it may have meant to the singer. Two other verses of this particularly objectionable song appeared in Niles's book, *Songs My Mother Never Taught Me*, with an illustration by A. A. Wallgren, the cartoonist of *The Stars and Stripes*. Sexual bravado was the song's principle message. But there is another message in the song. The singing soldiers, through intimate contact with French women, have broken through the limits of a tourist's experience of a foreign place. They have turned the tables on the YMCA, and left a souvenir, rather than bought a souvenir to take home. Certainly the song can carry a cruel message to the French, but the French were unlikely to hear it. It also carried a message of triumphant individualism in the face of standardizing authority.

Niles had kept a musical journal of the war and, in 1927, he published *Singing Soldiers*, a volume of the songs of black American soldiers with the following explanation for his omission of the songs white people associated with the war:

> The imagination of white boys did not, as a rule, express itself in song. They went to Broadway for their music, contenting themselves with the ready-made rhymes and tunes of the professional song-writers who for reasons best avoided now did not give up their royalty checks for the chance to secure the safety of democracy at thirty-three dollars per month.[25]

Two years after *Singing Soldiers*, in 1929, perhaps succumbing to commercial pressures, and requests of white veterans who did not find familiar songs in a book where they expected them, he published *Songs My Mother Never Taught Me*. This second volume contained about fifty songs sung by white soldiers, starting with the bawdy "Mad'moiselle from Armentières," and including standard military fare like "Marine's Hymns," and the caisson song of the Field Artillery. Niles's heart was not in such a project and he attacked some of the songs. But clearly the book did not bear out his assertion that white Americans did not express their imagination in song. They either expressed themselves with the songs produced for a mass culture or they expressed escape from that culture in a triumphal cocky tone of which he did not approve. But a song like "Bon soir, ma chérie," can either be interpreted as a crude insult to French cupidity, or as a more general frustration at the commercial quality of sexual relations.

> Bon soir, ma chérie, comment allez-vous?
> Bon soir, ma chérie, je vous aime beaucoup.
> Avez-vous un fiancé, ça ne fair rien –
> Voulez-vous couchez avec moi ce soir
> Oui, combien?
> (Good evening, my dear, how are you?
> Good evening, my dear, I love you very much.
> Have you a boyfriend? That makes no difference –
> Do you want to sleep with me tonight?
> Yes, how much?)[26]

Military authorities considered relations between French women and American soldiers unfortunate if unavoidable, and impossible, except on the crudest level. When left to military authorities, organized meetings between men and women could be intense, but limited. On some occasions, soldiers could receive an elaborately orchestrated welcome by women seemingly designed to reinforce mutual desire. Lt. Clifton Cates described such a meeting between men just back from the front and women, in a letter to his mother and sister, July 13, 1918. His regiment had been ordered out of the fighting at Belleau Wood to participate as actual blooded veterans in the July Fourth parade in Paris. He and his marines were of considerable symbolic importance on parade.

> We literally ran out of that wood and we all heaved a sigh of relief when we got beyond range of their guns – the first time since May 31st. We met other details from the other companies at a designated place then proceeded to Gay Paree . . . We rolled into Paris the afternoon of the 3rd.
>
> The morning of the 4th we got up early and cleaned up and tried to look halfway decent, but we still looked like a bunch of bums.

[During the parade on the Champs Elysées] you cannot imagine the cheer that would go up as the French people would recognize the marine flag. One continuous shout . . . They literally covered us with roses – would carry each bouquet a piece and then drop it – then another girl would load me down with more flowers . . . Even every little kid [word unreadable] would yell, "Vive la Marine." I am glad that I joined the marines.

Then three hundred men and four officers and myself went out to the largest ammunition factory in the world for lunch. We rode out and first went thru the factory. It was a wonderful big factory and employed 10,000 girls – a very good class of girls and not the kind of person usually finds [*sic*] in factories. They gave us marines another grand welcome as we filed thru. We then marched into an enormous dining room. At each table there was an American ribbon on one chair so a soldier would sit at each table. We were above in the club rooms [he eats and drinks with some French generals and colonels and pretty girls] where we could look down on that angry mob – over 10,000 and mostly girls. It was wonderful to look at that mob in one dining room. Champagne opened at a signal like a German barrage, 2,000 corks popping 40 feet into the air at the same time. After lunch [and toasts] they sat the chairs up on the tables and danced for two hours – the girls literally fought over the men.[27]

This mammoth party was followed by an overnight leave until 6 AM, when Cates and his men found themselves once more on their way back to the front via a rest camp. Their trip to Paris, where they were both spectacle on parade and tourists of a kind, was a twenty-four hour pause during the business of the army.

For many French women, the war seemed to offer new opportunities. They took jobs in manufacturing and services formerly reserved for men and at higher wages than women had enjoyed before. But no lasting changes in the role of women in French society resulted from these changes in work status because relations between the sexes became more polarized. The spread of prostitution among women who would normally have had other means of supporting themselves and the aggressive sexual attitude among new veterans were aspects of this retrograde stereotyping of sex roles. Françoise Thébaud, the French historian of women during the First World War, concluded that "war that exalts masculine values and radically separates men and women does not seem to me to favor an evolution of the role of the sexes."[28] She found that, when men returned from war, they wished to return to a life as ideally domesticated and dominated by themselves as their lives had been hyper-masculine at the front and dominated by forces beyond their control. The party at the munitions factory described by the American lieutenant, though probably enjoyed by the participants, can be seen as a grotesque illustration to Thébaud's analysis. The war had placed those women in a new position as money earners. But the war had placed the men in a position of sexual power more likely to promote frustration than any kind of understanding between the two sexes.

American women connected to the war effort in France found themselves in a very different position from French women. They enjoyed the same financial privileges as American soldiers and the same social privileges as officers. Being comparatively few in number, they could choose when and with whom they socialized. When they socialized with enlisted men, against the regulations, they found themselves in the powerful position of "treating" these men by the very fact of taking a risk for them. These women could set the limits on social behavior, on a date or at a dance, something that in working-class American urban society had become the privilege of the one who paid for amusements. One nurse wrote that, after the ban on dancing with enlisted men was lifted, she no longer had any interest in them. Perhaps her interest faded when her attentions were no longer a valuable gift. Men found that, with American women, the war had turned the tables on them even while, with French women, they enjoyed a dominance more extreme than they would have found in many American cities.[29]

Nurses were a teasing symbol for soldiers. They could not associate with enlisted men, and yet the nurses were presented as the kind of healthy girl every American boy should want. They represented a desirable ideal and yet enlisted men were subordinated to them. The angel nurse was a standard feature of songs from Broadway sung by American soldiers. From the lyrics to the graphics of the sheet music, they presented the nurse as a powerful savior, who yet was a key to satisfying domesticity. "My Angel of the Flaming Cross" told of fears chased away by an angel. The decoration of the sheet music featured storks nesting on chimney tops: after fear will come calm domesticity, the constellation of symbols said. "The Girl with the Little Red Cross (on her sleeve)," presented the nurse as a Gibson Girl ideal.

> Her hair is golden,
> Her eyes are blue,
> Her lips are roses,
> Her heart is true.

The graphics that went with this song showed a powerful, idealized woman, but one that thoroughly subordinated men. The capable woman supported the soldier in his death agonies. She maintained her vigor. He was wan and bloodless. "My Red Cross Girlie the Wound is Somewhere in My Heart," presented the nurse as an empowered Madonna. There are two men in the graphics – one draped over barbed wire and the other draped, still showing signs of his wound, in an arm chair. The message is fairly clear. The men might desire nurses, but a wound provided the only way to get close to one. And once close to a nurse, in a hospital, the enlisted man still lived under the army's authority now embodied in the nurse.[30] "This is the life!" wrote one soldier from his hospital bed.

> The nurses are great and it is equally great to see an honest to goodness American girl, who can speak your own "lingo." The guy who wrote that song, "I Don't Want to get Well," certainly did express my sentiments, concerning the present time.[31]

Not getting well would mean he could stay near the nurse, not that she could become available to him. He got well soon enough and found himself on his way back to his unit.

The best women were far away. The United States Army preferred Lady Liberty to all other females. Officers brought their men up on deck as their transports left New York for one final look at the Statue of Liberty. The soldiers dutifully wrote home that they had thought of her soberly and of "all she represents," and then gone below again. After Lady Liberty, the US Army preferred "Mother," as a symbol to fight for – safely distant and vaguely disciplinarian. Thoughts of home could motivate a soldier to fight, or, as in the examples just above, could keep a man out of entanglements with French women.

These two women, "Mother" and "Liberty," found themselves side by side and even confused in *The Stars and Stripes* on May 10, 1918, in anticipation of Mother's Day. "The Gal We're All Fighting For," announced the headline across the top of page one. The Statue of Liberty appeared over a watery horizon in a dramatic pencil drawing. Soldiers in the drawing can see the statue from France and gather from that vision the inspiration they need. She can give them strength, but also she can see them and perhaps register their shortcomings on the tablet she carries. Next to the drawing, under the headline, "Home Folks Waiting for Great Shipload of 'Mothers' Letters,'" the editors of *The Stars and Stripes* had placed an article about how every soldier should send a letter home on Mother's Day, May 12. Who did the paper mean by the "Gal We're All Fighting For," and whose watchful eye rose majestically over the horizon, "Mother" or "Lady Liberty?"[32]

The week before, a drawing of "Mother" herself appeared at top center of page one in the place of "Liberty." She rushed from her back porch, decorated with a service flag, to receive her Mother's Day letter from the postman. Her right hand stretched out for the letter, her left clutched, not Liberty's tablet, but her ample breast. Her soldier son owed her this letter because:

> You know what Mother's letters mean to you. You know how much she puts into them, how much you can read between the lines of her longing for you, of her prayers for your safety and uprightness and well-being.
>
> But you've no idea what your letters mean to Mother. You've no idea how many times she reads them.

Nobody could escape from the instructions to put the best face on the war, and thus participate in auto-propaganda. "Write home. Pack the page with love and good cheer. Fill it to the brim with reassurance, for you know how mothers worry." If a man had no mother, he must borrow or designate one:

> If you have suffered the greatest loss that can come to a man, if you have no mother to write to, then send your greeting to the one who is nearest and dearest to you in all the world and who has done the most to take her place. Write, if you will, to your bunkie's mother, telling her how he is fairly bursting with health, telling her what a lot all the men in his squad think of

him, warming her heart with the news of his prowess he himself was too shy to write.[33]

Even if a soldier decided that a girlfriend had done the most for him, the paper asked the soldier to think of her, on that day, as a mother surrogate. And if he desired the preferential treatment Mother's Day letters received, he had to address the envelope as "Mother's Letter."

General Pershing made the whole operation official on May 10, 1918.

> I wish that every soldier of the American Expeditionary Force would write a letter home on Mother's Day. This is a little thing for each one to do, but these letters will carry back our courage and our affection to the patriotic women whose love and prayers inspire us on to victory.[34]

Mother's Day remained an important event in 1919, commemorated with a YMCA pamphlet for the Army of Occupation entitled "Mother's Day on the Rhine." It featured a poem called "The Dearest Mother."[35]

Many soldiers sent the letters that the army, the YMCA, the chaplains, and *The Stars and Stripes* told them they owed their mothers. When the army asked soldiers to give their mothers reassurance about their health and "uprightness" the army turned individual soldiers into propaganda agents. Obedient soldiers presented the idea that army life increased health and morality. Some soldiers had taken to this propagandistic practice long before Mother's Day, 1918. "Please for my sake don't worry about me as I am well and happy, besides leading a good straight clean life,"[36] wrote one soldier to his parents from training camp, using the vocabulary of a YMCA secretary. Another put into verse the ideas of General Pershing's message about Mother's Day communication:

> For what the world holds good and true
> Was taught by her and not another
> And the dearest thing in all the world
> Is she whom we call mother.[37]

The military worked for the proliferation of this sentimental language of mother love. Army propagandists understood that love of a mother or home, far across the ocean, may easily become equated with love of homeland. Love of a woman who is nearby, especially a foreigner, does not so easily enhance patriotism. "Mother" got the positive public relations. The reputation of French women suffered.

Marriages between Americans and French women created a problem for the army: the new wives became dependent on the army, would need transport to accompany their husbands back to the United States after the war, and fostered a loyalty in their men for themselves, not to the organization and goals of the army. A man's mother, a female safely far from the theater of war who had little means of controling her son, could become an icon, served by love, enhancing a man's resolve to perform his military duty. Admiration or love for a Red Cross nurse, in her way a distant figure for enlisted men, could also stimulate a man to become a better soldier. But a French woman as wife, not as strumpet or allegorical figure of Alsace-Lorraine, existed outside the realm of female symbols the United States Army could manipulate.

A French wife could come too close to the front where she might have a deleterious effect on toughened soldiers. A French general explained his army's preference for prostitutes over wives near combat thus: "Easy women and prostitutes are a necessary distraction, whereas wives, who represent the home, soften the heart."[38] Though, officially, the American army did not believe American soldiers needed the distraction of prostitutes, they certainly did not desire the softening effects of wives who came too near their men. Rules prevented women volunteers to the Red Cross, the YMCA and other organizations, whose husbands were in France, from serving overseas.

The army and the American popular press did the best they could to push the French woman into the role of harlot. Magazines, developing a new version of an old stereotype of the French woman, wise and cynical in the ways of love, thrilled readers with articles about the possibilities of Americans debauched by French women but remained silent on the subject of American men and French women marrying.[39] The army regarded French women with sufficient hostility to attempt to abrogate the personal right of a man to marry whomever he pleased. The Judge Advocate wrote to General Pershing on June 18, 1918, saying that he would write to Washington seeking permission to issue an

order against marriages. No such permission, however, was forthcoming from President Wilson's government.[40]
When it could not prohibit marriages, the army took no position at all on this question. This non-action itself became an obstruction. On September 16, 1918, the military attaché at the US Embassy in Paris requested a statement from General Pershing's headquarters or from the War Department on marriages, as he received daily inquiries. The Adjutant General at General Headquarters replied that "such inquiries were irregular and unauthorized and should be disregarded."[41] This non-policy insured that relations between American soldiers and French women would remain as irregular as possible.

By keeping these relations irregular, the army reduced any claims French women might make upon it. Lieutenant Colonel Albert B. Kellogg, who compiled documents around the marriage question for the Army War College in 1942, cited the case of a Sergeant H. who had had relations with a woman, S., who wrote to General Headquarters requesting aid. The records maintained a discretion beyond concealing the names of the parties, but presumably S. was pregnant. After investigation, H.'s regimental commander wrote that, "If approved by higher authority, Sgt. H. will be given the option of marrying this woman or standing trial." Higher authority did not approve. The Divisional commander wrote, "There is no evidence showing unwillingness on the part of the woman and it is not thought that under the circumstances related that the demands of justice or discipline require that the request of Mme. S. be granted or the man be brought to trial."[42] Clearly, the interests of the army lay in keeping its men and itself free from obligations to French women. "Willingness" (to have sexual relations) on the part of the woman was sufficient reason to ignore her request, regardless of what H. may have promised. At lower levels of authority, regularizing the situation through marriage seemed a possibility. At the higher divisional level, the soldier and the army needed and received protection from obligation and got it at the expense of the reputation of the woman.

The army regarded any of its men as a good catch. A soldier in the AEF often possessed as much as $10,000 in war risk insurance. From his pay, which was far greater than that of a French soldier, an allotment could be deducted for his wife. The commanding general of the Thirty-sixth Division wrote on March

7, 1918, to the Adjutant General that 350 marriages had taken place in his division between August 1917 and March 1918.

> He believed that in many cases the women involved were designing persons of questionable character who contracted marriages for the purpose of obtaining allotments and ultimately perhaps the insurance.[43]

The shift in loyalties from mothers to French wives disturbed the army in ways that could be counted in dollars and cents, in addition to the more intangible loss of an American mother as a stimulus for bravery and patriotism. In April, 1918, the Bureau of War Risk Insurance received an average of 750 requests a day for a change of beneficiary from mother to wife. The army saw in this the possibility of abuse.[44]

The army could not prohibit marriages, and its non-policy towards marriages could not stop a couple with any determination. Hence, some authorities worked at discouraging marriages through other informal means. On November 25, 1918, the Director of War Plans Division, General Staff, wrote to the Secretary of War on the subject.

> If the Army with its great numbers of chaplains and its numerous auxilliary agencies devoted to the purpose of aiding the men and keeping them straight, cannot by the use of those agencies prevent the problem suggested from becoming a serious one, commanding officers at camps where it is a serious problem, can help by making such restrictions on leaves as will keep the men within bounds.[45]

The army had two methods of keeping men from marrying French women. Officers routinely refused to give their men permission to marry, and through camp newspapers and chaplains, the army mounted a propaganda campaign against marriage. One officer stated his reasons for refusing permission to marry in a letter to his Commander in Chief as follows:

> When Private W. asked permission to marry I refused, as I did in other cases, on the ground that this was no time to be undertaking new responsibilities and obligations; that we were over here to fight when the time came; and to spend the rest of the time getting ready for it and not to marry and raise

families. If Private W. is allowed to marry this girl it will lead
to a number of other cases just exactly like this. I have been
through the whole thing twice before in Cuba and the Philippines.[46]

This colonel very nearly followed the model of General Headquarters to such requests, except that General Headquarters
would inform a soldier that he did not need permission from the
army to marry: "Permission refused," read their usual letter in
these cases, "if given, it would not affect the competency of the
soldier to marry under French law."[47]

The soldiers' newspaper, the *Oo La La Times* of St. Nazaire,
written largely by Army Chaplain and Episcopal Priest, Henry
Russell Talbot, propounded a version of how it was hoped
soldiers would treat France and French women that changed as
the army and the chaplain became aware of the problem of
soldiers marrying. The paper started on October 30th, 1917, with
a very positive version of both the quality of the men in the camp
and the prospects of mixing with the French and receiving some
benefit from French culture.

> The enlisted personnel – the men – have wide experience and
> travel, some left highly lucrative positions, a considerable
> proportion are college men and a great many are mechanics,
> therefore it is easy to see that one is continually rubbing
> shoulders with men worth while, men able to keep life from
> becoming humdrum or sordid, even if he were not always
> getting new views of a beautiful country and studying French
> as well as War.[48]

The newspaper presented the war as an educational experience.
The writers intended the newspaper in part as a propaganda
organ to reassure parents at home about their clean living sons,
but mostly they conceived it as a way of presenting the soldier's
life to the soldier in a manner beneficial to the US Army.
Personal jibes, intended to change soldier behavior, appeared in
the very first issue. These often struck at the lack of education of
the men mentioned and could be interpreted as persuasion for
attendance at the classes in French that were given at the Camp
in St. Nazaire.

Sergt. Hart is to be seen quite often pondering over a French letter. Too bad Lee, you have to let someone else read them.[49]

As the personal items became more biting, the paper became an improving scourge to the men who read it. Discouraging and embarrassing men in their relations with local women held first priority in the paper's list of behavior modifications.

> Private Scharlau, the "lady killer" from Chicago, has succeeded in making another hit, this time he has captured the affections of the "Pride of the Fishing Smack," the two *sou* queen."
>
> Private Robinson has lost faith in the Fair Sex. Private Speck Green can probably explain this.[50]

The *Oo La La Times* did not just throw its ice-water on relationships that looked mercenary on the part of the French woman, but on any sign of affection or even generosity shown by an American man for a French woman.

> Recently when we asked Austin why he walked to work, he said all the autos were tired. The other day, however, when we saw him on his way he was pushing a heavily laden wheel barrow down Rue Ville Marten for a Mademoiselle. It is true he has a very tender heart but we have some doubt as to his sympathy for the tired autos.[51]

Apparently, a man could not help a French woman with a large burden without exciting the prurient speculation of the paper.

> Mess Sergt. Wheeler is of late making a great many trips into the country supposedly buying green vegetables. But there are some who have doubts. Those who know her say that she is not as green as she looks.[52]

Too much attention paid to a woman drew the attention of the *Oo La La Times*. The implication of the newspaper's message was that French women could not be faithful. If a soldier showed signs of making a commitment to a woman, it behooved the paper to demonstrate that she was not worth it, just as it behooved military authorities to protect soldiers from personal entanglements if she appealed to them.

These news items appeared unsigned in the paper, but other articles, some over the Chaplain Henry Russell Talbot's signature, point to his improving spirit.

> To all those fellows who had a mademoiselle out promenading on Thursday evening, and just couldn't break the "date," I want to say that you missed something that was an equal to our entertainment on Wednesday evening. [on Wednesday evening the Chaplain had recited poems of Robert Service]. The majority of us, I am sure, had never heard of the Loire River, where it was so well explained by our guest, the Chaplain.[53]

By teaching the soldiers to be tourists, the chaplain hoped to keep them away from more direct contact with the French.

But substituting education for a chance to promenade with the Mademoiselles proved a tricky business. After all, knowledge of French culture and the French language could lead to intimacy between soldiers and French women. The first edition of the paper presented learning French and encountering French culture as advantages to be taken by American soldiers in France. The sixth number, on April 10, 1918, presented learning French in a more equivocal light in an article entitled, "Our Own Little French Lesson."

First, the article discussed French in a humorous vein and reduced the language to the foundation word, "Combien," and then three categories: "Mademoiselle, Manger, Souvenir." The language was further reduced to food because "the subject of Mademoiselle is very delicate, and besides there is the censor." The article eventually taught soldiers to order an omelet, bread and butter at a restaurant and delivered a warning:

> We warn you against trying to say anything to the lady (the waitress) beyond what you have learned. She'll answer you, but what the . . . ? She look [sic] silly, you look ridiculous, both turn around, you begin to walk to the door, *dix sous* look like a fortune compared to your feelings in money. You par [sic] by mutual agreement . . . We can't make the warning to [sic] strong.

The *Oo La La Times* never set any records for proofreading, but the errors and ellipses in this "warning" render its reading difficult to the point that one reads the errors. The writer first reduced all communication between French and Americans to commerce, and then warned the soldiers away from any commercial transactions, save the purchase of food. But the brief scenario about the purchase of a meal inevitably returned to the subject of relations between men and French women, at which point the author's writing skills failed him.

The subject of Mademoiselle, read sex, was too delicate for a direct approach, and souvenirs might include, after all, a "souvenir bébé." The little scenario of the restaurant was intended to prove that the language barrier raised an insurmountable barrier between the French and the Americans. The writer did his best to keep that barrier intact. But the article did something else as well by rhetorically establishing that the only relationship an American soldier could have with a French woman rested upon the word, "combien," how much. The author insisted that the relationships the language barrier prevented were of a low order.

Even when the relationship of an enlisted man manifestly involved more than a commercial transaction, the newspaper could triumph venomously at its failure. For example, when the marriage of Private Joseph Mondyka did not take place:

> The girl got next to him and told him to beat it. He is up against it. He fell off the water-wagon. He is now confined to the barracks for thirty days. We also understand that the Captain gave you a bawling out at inspection last Sunday. We thought you were a previous service man Joe – what does the Captain think?[54]

The chaplain editor followed the spirit of orders never made explicit in regard to the men's relations with French women. Nobody ordered men not to marry French women. After the Armistice, however, when military urgency no longer justified denials of permission to marry, the campaign against marriages did not let up. Confining a man to barracks for thirty days and giving him a public dressing down were certainly effective ways of keeping him from renewing his court.

Standards were different for officers. When Captain Edward Taliaferro married "Mlle. Maguerite Tournier, the charming daughter of the [French] Commandant and Madame Tournier," the *Oo La La Times* described a "Brilliant Franco-American wedding."

> The two smiling sisters of the bride, assisted by two officers of the regiment very effectively made the customary collection for the poor of the war.
> A daughter of France and a son of America united in marriage symbolized for us the union of the two nations in friendship and affection. We hope that other eligible young officers, and we have them, quite a few, will be as fortunate as our Captain Taliaferro. We think they will.[55]

For officers, the paper could suspend the exigencies of the war, and look forward to a whole rash of marriages. The captain and his bride, in spite of the war, honeymooned on the French Riviera. And later, Major Bullard, of the same military organization, did marry Hélène Tournier, the sister of the new Mrs. Taliaferro, and that couple were given the same fanfare. Colonel Kellogg found no evidence of restrictions or barriers erected by the army to the nuptials of officers. The *Oo La La Times* regarded even the abbreviated nuptials of Major Bullard as a model, though he left his marriage bed for the front. "A Honeymoon in the trenches may not be according to the usual form, but to our acclaim of congratulations we add a note of envy for we would like to get up there ourselves."[56] The paper saw no contradiction between marriage and war for officers. And by writing of a "honeymoon" in the trenches it had made the connection between sex and fighting that has been made by others.

Very few American officers married French women. The rash started by Captain Taliaferro spread to major Bullard. The Tournier girls whom these officers married, daughters of a superior French officer, were certainly an exception. When American officers married, they tended to marry American women, and those American women tended to be nurses. Nurses too carried the rank of officer, and until well into 1919 were not permitted to associate with enlisted men. The wedding involving the highest ranking Americans found in French marriage registers for this study involved a Lieutenant Colonel and the YMCA Director at Brest.[57]

Officers could approach nurses and stay near them much more easily than enlisted men could. Special arrangements could be made for officer social life. At the American Expeditionary Force University, the educational institution that the US Army improvised near Beaune after the Armistice, officers, nurses, YMCA and Red Cross personnel made a social group. Busses, reserved specially for officers and nurses, took them from camp to town. The bus schedule fit their social schedule. The last bus stopped at Beaune's movie theater, and on Wednesday and Saturday nights, busses retrieved officers from their bi-weekly dances at the Hôtel de la Poste.[58] After the war, nurses attached to the Army of Occupation in Germany, danced so often at the parties of officers that the surgeon in charge of the hospital at Coblenz had to order them to desist.[59]

Marriage registers in city halls across France tell of many other successful courtships, but they don't involve American officers or nurses. In the usual pattern set in French marriage registers, a working-class girl with one or both parents dead, more frequently the father than the mother, married a working-class man, currently an enlisted man in the AEF also with one or both parents dead, more frequently the mother than the father.[60]

From what the marriage registers recorded – the occupations of the couple, their parents and the names and occupations of four witnesses – these women married into a situation for which they had no model, and committed themselves to a partner of a foreign culture, and to traveling to a foreign country, of which they knew little, often not even the language. But the situation they left behind them through these marriages, a very precarious situation indeed, hardly involved fewer risks. In the different parts of France examined, the death rate of their fathers varied from a third to a half. The death rate of mothers varied from one in twenty to one in three. Fewer than one in twenty of the brides who married Americans in the towns examined had both parents living. They had few apparent prospects. Yves Henri Nouaillat, in his study on American soldiers at Nantes and St. Nazaire, divided the women who married Americans into two groups according to profession. Those who listed their professions as maid, waitress, typist, laundress, etc., he said, could have been women that Americans met in the course of normal commercial life, while the women who did not work signaled an American's integration into a French family. He maintained that the mar-

riages took place on every social level.[61] The data collected for
this study from Beaune, Brest, Dijon, and Aix-les-Bains showed,
however, that many of the women who had no work also had no
father, and some of them had no parents at all. There was hardly
a "family" for the American man to attach himself to. Far from
representing every social class, the brides tended to come from
families of manual laborers. Very few listed parents with
property, and those who did came from families of café owners
or hoteliers, indicating the path by which an American could
introduce himself. Nothing indicated that these women were
"designing persons," as the Colonel of the Thirty-sixth Division
above suspected. On the other hand, marriage to an American
soldier may have appeared to be a solution to a very insecure
situation.

Of those few marriages that did involve American officers,
nearly a fourth were to French working-class women. In all but
one of these cases, either the man's mother had died or he was
an orphan. The couple that combined people from the most
unequal social backgrounds involved an American doctor, with
the rank of lieutenant, the son of a lawyer, and an orphan who
listed her occupation as *ouvrière*, (worker). In this case, the
lieutenant's mother had died, making him fit the pattern set by
orphaned regular soldiers. The cases of officer marriages are too
few to allow more than speculation, but the patterns set seem to
indicate that the death of parents had a profound effect on how
a man perceived himself. A possible conclusion to be drawn from
the remarkable numbers of motherless Americans who married
French women, is that the lack of a mother, the symbol so
frequently employed by the army to encourage loyalty to home
and country, freed men to marry outside their own culture.

Few marriages of enlisted men with American women occurred
in France, less than 1 per cent of the marriages examined. In
these cases, both the man's parents still lived and he came from
a middle-class background. Though rules prohibited American
women, Red Cross nurses and YMCA workers from consorting
too closely with enlisted men, enlisted men still managed. Ethel
D. Warner, a nurse with the Red Cross, actually preferred the
company of enlisted men to officers. She filled her journal with
descriptions of clandestine parties held by nurses for groups of
enlisted men, of impromptu dances between trains in railroad

stations, and of enterprising enlisted men who climbed into her train compartment to share a journey with a nurse.[62]

Multiple standards operated in the army. Officers, if not encouraged to marry, could still do so and become a model held up not so much to be emulated as to symbolize Franco/American harmony. Enlisted men could marry but did so against the wishes of their commanders. American women, connected to the army either as nurses or volunteers with one of the agencies concerned with the soldiers' welfare, could not consider marriage without threatening their officer status and facing the risk of being sent home. General Headquarters of the AEF made itself quite clear on this point in the case of nurses. "It is the opinion of this office that in the event of such a marriage, the discharge of the nurse would be ordered and she would be sent at once to the United States," the Adjutant General wrote in response to a nurse's inquiry, August 29, 1918.[63] The Adjutant General either relaxed this rule just before and after the Armistice, or the threat of being sent back to the United States, and away from a new husband, no longer mattered so much when in all likelihood the new husband would soon return to the United States as well. In the marriage registers of Brest, for example, one American nurse married on October 22, just before the Nov. 11, 1918, Armistice. After that date and through August 1919, eight American nurses married. The nurses invariably married American officers.

Not all soldiers in the AEF could hope to woo, let alone win, an American nurse while in France, but many followed the pattern set by those cards entitled "Le Poilu Permissionnaire," from war to domesticity. To the question on the United States Army Military History Institute questionnaire asking what they had done following discharge, many wrote, "got married and looked for a job." In many war diaries and journals, enlistment and marriage bracket the war experience. Often the only part of their lives for which these men left a written record was a packet of saved war letters or the war journal. Like a romantic novel, their story ends with marriage, but not until they are back in the United States.

For one large group of Americans the war included few romantic elements – neither successful combat nor marriage. A preference for the "original song productions" rather than the songs of Broadway, had lead John Niles away from the singing of white men to a study of the songs of African-American soldiers. He made the following comments in the introduction to his volume of their songs:

> By reading the lyrics of the songs on the pages that follow, one will see that the love of woman is very seldom referred to . . . After all going to war is a very masculine occupation and it is natural that the sights, the sounds, the odors, the tasks, the endless days of mud *should* make up the "fiendishly illogical hodgepodge" from which the soldier and the sailor concocted their songs.
>
> Women had to do with the madness that was war. Many of them had their first opportunity to prove a previously unexpressed nobility. Many of them were brave beyond the usual understanding of the term, but somehow they seldom got into the original song creations that became a part of our army and navy's kit and baggage.[64]

In the songs of African-Americans that Niles recorded, mothers appeared, but no mademoiselles, no nurses, and no women war workers. His statement that "The sights, the sounds, the odors, the tasks, the endless days of mud" provided the material for songs held true. In this, as in so many aspects of the war, the experience of black-American soldiers opposed the white American soldiers' experience. They found themselves operating within a system of contrary standards. In *Singing Soldiers*, exclusively devoted to the songs of black soldiers, not one song takes as its subject the love of women in any form. They take their subjects from the work and lives of black soldiers: digging ditches and graves, carrying loads, cleaning clothes, from exhaustion, death, scratching insect bites, and longing for home.

One song talked about "mother," but she had a very different role to play than the patriot mother contemplated by *The Stars and Stripes*, General Pershing, and at least some white soldiers. This mother knew war meant nothing but hardship and possible death for her son, not the achievement of health, clean living, and enhanced manhood.

> My mama told me not to come over here –
> But I did, I did, I did.
> My mama said they surely would shoot me dead –

An' they did, they did, they did . . .
I tried to keep my secret from every shot and shell –
But "long come one that made me tell . . .
My mama said not to come over here,
But I did, I did, I did.

In other verses, his father tells him not to go to France, and finally his pastor tells him not to go. The black man's home, represented in this song by mother, father and pastor, far from supporting him in his patriotic duty, opposed it.[65]

Mademoiselle from Armentières had no place in the lives of black soldiers, and they sang different words, "Lordy turn your face on me," to a tune that approximated the white soldiers' song. Black soldiers asked God for protection, not Mademoiselle for approval.[66] As an African-American YMCA worker explained, white America had exported its prejudices to France.

> American prejudices had not only been carried across the seas, but had become a part of such an intricate propaganda, that the relationship between the colored soldier and the French soldier is more or less a story colored by a continued and subtle effort to inject this same prejudice into the heart of the hitherto unprejudiced Frenchman . . . In talking with the soldiers, and ultimately with the French people, we were told that the story of roughness of colored men was being told to the civilians in order that all possible association between them might be avoided. They had been systematically informed that their dark skinned allies were not only unworthy of any courtesies from their homes, but that they were so brutal and vicious as to be absolutely dangerous.[67]

It would be difficult to make systematic distinctions between the race prejudices that the French held before the war and prejudice formed by American influences. If this YMCA worker told the truth, however, it would have been very difficult for a black soldier to approach any French woman.

American authorities made the effort to influence French prejudice. Rule number three of the guidelines for relations between the French and the Americans, compiled by the French Military Mission stationed with the American army, stated that "Americans become greatly incensed at any public expression of intimacy between white women and black men,"[68] and therefore all precautions should be taken to prevent this occurrence. These informal rules seem to have had some effect and in some places, taken in conjunction with already existing French prejudice, may have taken on the quality of hard and fast regulations.

In the town register of Chambéry, where black soldiers took their leaves, not a single American married a French woman during the war years. In neighboring Aix-les-Bains, however, where white soldiers spent their permissions, marriages to Americans reached as high as half of all marriages during the month of June 1919. And even in Dijon, a provincial capital like Chambéry, but having no specially large American organization attached to it, the marriage rate to Americans varied between one in twenty and one in ten during the first six month of 1919.[69] This absence of all Franco/American marriages suggests that in Chambéry stricter restrictions against marriages were enforced than in other places where there were no Afro-American soldiers. Such a practice could have prevented inter-racial unions without making a rule addressing the question.

American authorities seem to have kept even black American women away from black soldiers, reserving their services as YMCA and welfare workers for white soldiers. The entire staff of the first YMCA for black soldiers established in France was soon sent home, presumably for their very success in raising the spirit of black soldiers. Certainly, the memoir of Addie W. Hunton and Kathryn M. Johnson, two black YMCA workers who found positions serving black units, recounted one struggle with race prejudice after another.[70]

White soldiers too had obstacles to overcome in their relations to women, but those obstacles fell away in the face of determination. Men at the leave area of Aix-les-Bains, for example, managed in the brief ten day's time they were in the city to court and marry a French girl. The French authorities of Aix made special dispensations to allow American soldiers to marry without producing the usual documentation confirming their single status. And, while on leave, these men escaped the eye of their officers who almost certainly would have found means to stop the marriages. Their path to matrimony was eased while on leave, but in other ways, those weddings still represented an enormous step. Even if the girl were willing to leave her insecure position as a working girl perhaps with no father providing her home, the soldier had to convince her that he could support her. A joke in *Yank Talk*, a review of American Expeditionary Force humor, made light of this difficulty in a manner aimed at keeping Americans away from French women: "When the girl of your choice asks you if it is really true that you have beaucoup automobiles back in the States, it is usually the best policy to say: 'Je ne comprends pas.' "[71] But the sarcastic words of a French newspaper in December, 1918, just before the avalanche of Franco-American marriages started, indicated that the French understood quite well the tendency of Americans to exaggerate when they talked about their riches: "It is said that all the charming girls of St. Nazaire who have married American soldiers are certain to accompany their husband to the United States and find their home luxuriously appointed on New York's Fifth Avenue."[72] Even having convinced the French woman that she should marry him, the American soldier had to contemplate the cultural difficulties. "Wouldn't it be funny to be married and then have to teach your wife to speak your language?" wrote one officer home to his own wife after visiting a Franco-American couple.[73]

The soldiers who married went from battle or camp to a strange French town and found themselves on the margin of life there. Feeling a need to participate in the social life around them and wishing to express their new sense of maturity and enhanced masculinity that battle had given them, they married someone they found in that town, someone also somewhat on the margin of society. Missing parents and a precarious existence were not the only connection between an American soldier and a French woman. A baker from Boston, Massachussetts, married the daughter of bakers in Dijon; a grocer from Cleveland, Ohio, married the daughter of a Dijon grocer.

These weddings needed witnesses. For a moment, a little party formed in the city hall and a union was solemnized. Between a half and two thirds of the marriages took place with a mix of French and Americans present. Usually, the American soldier would bring a friend, mechanics tended to be supported by other mechanics, cooks by cooks, Military Police by their friends in that service. The French woman would have some family member, an aunt, an uncle, sign the marriage register. In very few cases were weddings dominated by Americans, and those were cases of American officers marrying American nurses. In more than a

third of the marriages, the American found himself alone, surrounded by the family of his bride, or a few family members and
a clerk from the town hall, or a waiter recruited for the purpose
from a nearby café. Often the same clerks and waiters appear as
witnesses at several weddings. These American men threw themselves into a foreign situation. They can only have done it
because of a profound belief that marriage represented an
important and inevitable step in their personal evolution. They
must have believed that their life's progression, a progression that
included the experience of World War I battle, had lead, inexorably, to the point where, as mature men, they should take wives
and form families.

For American soldiers, training in the American army had
presented a model for standard behavior and manliness characterized by restraint and detachment and comparison with others
in a very large group.[74] Of course, men have always been able to
compare themselves with others, but participation in the AEF
vastly increased the possible scale of this comparison. Combat in
the war might have shattered such careful constructions of
identity, but soldiers both reported that they faced fear and death
alone, and that everyone else felt the same thing. In combat, they
experienced both their central individuality and a deep reaction
shared with other soldiers. In traveling around France, they
might have experienced a sense of themselves and their cultural
identity alone against a foreign background, but their steps and
reactions were carefully guided. They could move on and off the
guided path, and some did, without necessarily rejecting the
restrained touristic identity imposed by the YMCA. A soldier's
relationship to women provided another test of that new standard
of behavior where manliness and strength were measured by
self-restraint and detachment. Almost no soldier could combine in
his life both the uplifting womanly American ideal of the ubiquitous posters and songs, with the promise of personal contact.

There were exceptions. For some officers, the war took on a
rose-colored glow and became the background for a personal
romance. Lieutenant John D. Clark, who had fought in the
artillery with the Second Division and was with the Division
during its principle engagements, remembered the war not for
the fighting and the life and death struggles, but as the time he
courted Nurse Emma Marie Zangler, whom he called "belle of
the AEF". She preserved menus and invitations supporting this

claim. The letter that accompanied his and Nurse Zangler's journals and photograph albums to the US Army Military History Institute at Carlisle Barracks told of his part in victory, but it had little to do with making the world safe for democracy.

> The illustrated invitations near the end of it [Nurse Zangler's album] indicate that she was the belle of General Headquarters. The Major Price referred to was on General Pershings staff and reputedly was the youngest colonel in the AEF (age 26). By a strange coincidence, in August, 1919, the respective ships on which we were returning to the United States arrived on the same day – mine in Hoboken, his in Brooklyn. Each of us had sent a radiogram asking her to meet him at the dock. She met me, we were married in 1920 and had a wonderful life together until her death in 1962.[75]

This Second Lieutenant's great war victory fits the pattern of a hero's tale. He faced the danger, received the most desirable woman as his reward and lived happily ever after. Nurse Zangler hinted at the outcome of their story in the earliest pages of her characteristically undated diary of the voyage to France. "Large concert tonight [attended?] by all – enlisted men, officers and nurses. Sang songs and had a wonderful time. Talked to Jack Clark – dandy boy – against rules of course – but all rules can't be kept."[76] Clark started the war as an ambulance driver and then changed to the artillery. There he became an officer, and could consort with nurses openly. His and Nurse Zangler's albums often contained photographs of the same scenes, picnics, and dances at the Grand Hôtel, Vittel. All the evidence supports Clark's assertion that she was the "belle" or even the princess of the AEF, and behaved accordingly. In her photographs, she is always perfectly dressed and coiffed; in her diary she noted, sometimes with exasperation, sometimes with resignation, the omission of tablecloths at dinner; and frequently managed to have breakfast in bed! Snatching her from a colonel was no mean victory. Clark's good fortune must have been as rare as Nurse Zangler was herself.

For most enlisted men, American women carried the baggage of the restrained uplifting relationship between men and women crusading for a cause. French women bore the burden of the more personal and physical relationships. American women were present, if scarce, in France as nurses, YMCA employees, Salvation Army Lassies, and members of other welfare organizations. In the roles assigned to them they cared for wounded men, gave them encouraging talks, served quantities of food and drink in canteens and in YMCA huts and at leave areas, they provided entertainment, organizational services and a warm atmosphere. They also served as models for propaganda on posters and booklets. Idealized women, either keeping home across the Atlantic, or doing war work, sometimes Liberty herself, encouraged and provided motivation for American men to do their duty.

5 "A Grave Diggin' Feelin' in my Heart:" American War Dead of World War I

> I've got a grave diggin' feelin' in my heart –
> I've got a grave diggin' feelin' in my heart –
> Everybody died in de A.E.F.,
> Only one burial squad wuz left' –
> I've got a grave-diggin' feelin' in my heart.[1]

For the first time, in 1921, the body of an unidentified soldier was buried at Arlington National Cemetery amid great pomp and designated as the "Unknown Soldier." Many American soldiers went missing in World War I. Many collections of letters from soldier sons trail off with unsatisfying replies from Red Cross officials, company commanders, YMCA workers, and liaison officers. The officials answer with brave optimism, with sympathy or formality, the pleas of parents for information about a son from whom no letter had come in over a month, or whom the War Department had announced wounded by telegram and then seemed to forget.

With the burial of the unknown soldier, an end could be put to the anxieties and inquiries of parents. Not only might *the* unknown soldier's coffin contain the unlocated remains of their own son, but the remains in that coffin represented as well an apotheosis of uncertainty and a finite translation into patriotic gesture of a very infinite problem – the meaning of individuals killed in great masses in a war whose dominant strategy was attrition. The question, "What did he die for?" and the grand but uncertain answers, for democracy, for freedom, to save us from German awfulness, answers which, by 1921, held less and less relation to any reality or even any popular feeling, could all resolve themselves in this gorgeous national pageant where an uncertainty became enshrined in an inscribed marble tomb.

The other belligerent countries, too, developed new ways to memorialize death in the service of the nation on an unprecedented scale. The ceremony at Arlington reflected similar burials of unnamed soldiers at the *Arc de Triomphe* in Paris and Westminster Abbey in London. The details of each specific ceremony, and of the complementary burying of the other war dead, named and unnamed, along with the memorialization of those for whom no body had been discovered, all addressed needs and aspirations of the different nations involved.[2]

The ceremonies of the United States follow similar patterns as those of other countries, but with added dimensions having to do with the heterogeneous population of the country, the nationalist aims of American progressives in government, the relatively late entry of the United States into the war, and the small number of American war dead when compared either to the American dead of the Civil War, or to the French, British or German dead in World War I.

All these memorializations after World War I contemplated the connection that normally exists between names and bodies, but that the destructive power of the war had destabilized. The British case, examined by historian Thomas Lacqueur, demonstrated the variety of possible monuments to names and bodies. The unknown warrior at Westminster was a body without a name. The British also built the Cenotaph in London, a tomb bearing neither a name nor containing a body. In France, they built Menin Gate, the walls of Tyne Cot and other monuments in their sector of the western front, for the inscription of the thousands upon thousands of names of the dead. They also dug 1,075,293 graves in France, which ideally marked the resting place of body and name together. But with the grave markers, as with the other monuments, names and bodies slip away from each other. Unidentified bodies occupy 180,861 graves, and 336,912 stones mark the spot where a named man was thought to have disappeared. Lacqueur's analysis of these memorials emphasized their "hypernominalism" that could represent, by either names carved in stone or rows of stone markers, the immense sacrifice of the British in World War I, without entering into the controversial question of memorializing the cause for which the sacrifice was made.

Together, the names and headstones are like shadows of the dead, standing in one-to-one correspondence with the fallen, representing them to the living in their ungraspable quatitative specificity. They are like the army of the living, both democratic and individual in their singularity, mere numbers in their aggregate. But their precise meaning was neither defined nor definable. Each of the living was free to remember as her or she chose.[3]

Lacqueur's analysis could apply to the American case as well. The war aims pale beside the numbers; before either the void of the Unknown Soldier or the silent testimony of the approximately 30,000 American World War I dead in France.

The numbers of American dead, however, between 70,000 and 100,000, cannot compare to either the British figures for World War I, nor to the over 600,000 dead of the Civil War when the US had a population a third of its 1918 size. Why then did World War I and not the Civil War spark the innovations of "hyper-nominalism" and the Unknown Soldier?[4]

In fact, at Gettysburg and other Civil War battlefields, individual graves and monuments with names marked a movement towards naming all the fallen, but the memorialization of names never overwhelmed representations of "The Cause" either for Union or for States' rights. In World War I France, however, no American fought for anything so clear as the Union. Thus, for Americans it seems logical to make the insubstantiality of the causes for which the Allies, except for France, fought in World War I bear more of the responsibility for the way the Federal government memorialized the effort.

Beyond the lack of clear war aims, the special technological and strategic conditions that not only separated so many men's bodies from their names, but also tended to undermine the tenuous connection between war aims and war costs seem important in motivating memorial innovations. Elaine Scarry has written that war has a two part structure, one the dominant activity *inside* war, or injury, and the other, the contest that determines the winner *outside* or after the war. The poverty of World War I strategy produced a deterioration of both these interior and exterior parts of war.[5]

Bodies, the measure of injury, vanished in the mud and shelling, while military aims and objectives, the contest, lost all direction, in the trench stalemate, except for the production of enemy bodies. In other words, when strategy became reduced to the strategy of attrition, injury and contest collapsed into one. The innovation of the elaborate memorializations afterwards make sense as the creation of paths back to some comprehensible national identity after a war in which strategic and national purpose was all but lost. Contemplating all the possible combinations of bodies and names on the western front induces a sense of sorrow, but also of national identity that includes all the heroic and tragic possibilities in the available evidence of suffering.

When John Dos Passos asked rhetorically of the contents of the tomb at Arlington, "How can you tell a guy's a hundred percent when all you've got's a gunnysack full of bones, bronze buttons stamped with the screaming eagle and a pair of roll puttees?" he expressed more than dismay at the fact of the body rendered incomplete and nameless. He also called into question the government's attempts to reconstitute that body and, with it, to reconstitute an idealized American nation: "Make sure he ain't a dinge, boys. Make sure he ain't guinea or a kike,"[6] Dos Passos continued. He pointed fun at the fears of white nativist Americans, who though willing to have their patriotic emotions moved by such a national symbol as the Unknown Soldier, might yet balk if they thought too clearly about what went into the make-up of that national body.

The African-American singers of the Grave Digger's song at the head of this chapter made the further connection between reconstituting the body politic and attrition. The song imagines the strategy of attrition followed to its extreme, and absurd, limit: a war in which all soldiers have been killed except one burial squad. The song is the sardonic comment of people who have no power over the make-up of the nation's body politic, in fact their people have been excluded from it by Jim Crow laws and voting restrictions, and yet they understand perfectly how that body politic may be reconstituted using the bodies left by war. In this unspeakably melancholy song, where the singers lament the fallen soldiers and their own fate as grave diggers, yet there is hope as the singers recognize the importance of those who dispose of the dead after a war of attrition.

The Graves Registration Service answered John Dos Passos's question, making sure the Unknown Soldier was "a hundred percent" by guaranteeing that his identity could never be found out. The broader question of how memorialization eventually overcame the difficulties posed by a war of attrition required almost the memorial variety that the British employed after World War I.

In choosing the Unknown Soldier, in transporting him to the United States and burying him at Arlington, Army authorities part invented and part copied a magnificent celebration of the loss of individual identity that came with death in World War I, replacing it with a national identity. The Graves Registration Service chose four bodies from four different battle site graves. They chose bodies for which no documentation existed to indicate the date of death, and on which, upon exhumation, no identification could be found. They brought these bodies to the Hôtel de Ville at Châlons-sur-Marne, a town at the center of what had been the American sector. There, in a ceremony witnessed by French and American officers and with a military band in attendance, blindfolded Sergeant Edward Younger chose the unknown soldier by placing a bouquet of white roses on one of the four coffins after having circled them three times. As the *History of the American Graves Registration Service, Q.M.C.* stated, "The circumstances and details connected with the selection and forwarding of the "Unknown Soldier" with the magnificent cortege and farewell furnished by the French government is a splendid chapter."[7]

Because essentially a void, he could absorb the disparate patriotic projections of a whole country with no racial or ethnic barriers to interpretation. Because tragic and painful in his end, he could raise a whole population's pain to the level of tragedy. The soldier in the tomb could take on any identity. The tomb itself was built of stone funerary architecture classically arranged to be understandable to anyone.

Thousands viewed the casket of the Unknown Soldier as he lay in State in the Capitol, hundreds of thousands watched him taken to Arlington, and their delegations, including veterans, immigrant groups and black-American groups all payed him homage and claimed him as one of their own.[8] The symbol of the Tomb of the Unknowns has continued to attract over four million visitors each year, second only to the sensational Air and Space Museum, as a Washington D.C. tourist attraction.

The Tomb of the Unknown Soldier, now called the Tomb of the Unknowns, has retained its position as the most important American monument to war dead, even today when loss of identity is no longer such an important part of death on battlefields. Historians have estimated that one in three soldiers who died in the American Civil War went unnamed. No one of them

has been singled out to represent the loss of the country. At
Arlington, 2,111 of these, from both North and South, lie in a
mass grave under a common monument. During World War I,
about 10,000 American soldiers were buried without identification, a ratio of unknown to known of between one to seven and
one to ten, depending on the figure for war-dead used.
Astonishingly, by the time of Vietnam, only one recovered body
remained entirely "unknown." Under pressure to make a controversial war fit the pattern set by World War I, in 1984,
Secretary of Defense Casper Weinberger chose that body, really
only six bones and three per cent of a body, for the tomb. He
had all documentation attached to it shredded to keep it unknown. The ratio of unknown soldiers to known has dropped
then from about one in three to zero, in a hundred years. The
practice of designating one unknown soldier to represent all the
nation's dead from a war had in fact started when record-keeping
and accountability of the cost of war had begun to catch up with
the destructive power of war.[9]

Such a symbol might not contain America for the literary or
intellectual. The literary critic Walter Benn Michaels has described American culture just after World War I as slipping into
a contemplative realm where old white protestant prejudices
could remain safe despite the presence in America of a new
generation born in America, but of immigrant and often Catholic
and Jewish parents. Michaels concentrated on the transformation
of racism into an American aesthetic in the literature he examined. "Making itself available for aesthetic contemplation turns
out to be America's way of making more Americans,"[10] he wrote,
explaining the appeal of Hemingway's and Fitzgerald's books. If
the American writers who went to France suffered disillusion as
a result of the war, they were partly disillusioned by a military
and governmental establishment that could create cultural symbols for America too democratic and too standardized for their
point of view. America's great authors of the 1920s set out for
France to write about America in which old values could be
preserved, just as the last of the doughboys along with the
Unknown Soldier boarded ships for home bearing the values of
mass society.

Of the expatriot writers, only John Dos Passos directed his
fiction directly against the reactionary force of the symbols of
American confidence generated by the war. The vast specificity

of his trilogy, *U.S.A.*, has the effect of unmaking symbols and icons, from Thomas Edison to corn flakes. He attacked the symbol of the "Unknown Soldier" by inserting into his description of the blurry pompous sentimental burial ceremony at Arlington first the possible details of the unknown's American origins and then the necessary details of how he became unknown. He listed a series of backgrounds all over the American social and geographical map – " . . . across the railroad tracks, out near the country club, in a shack cabin tenement apartment house exclusive residential suburb . . .". He then continued: "The shell had his number on it. The blood ran into the ground. The service record dropped out of the filing cabinet when the quartermaster sergeant got blotto . . . The blood ran into the ground, the brains oozed out of the cracked skull and were licked up by the trenchrats, the belly swelled and raised a generation of bluebottle flies . . .".[11] The author attempted to bring his readers to face death as the brutal effect of war on human bodies at the moment in his narrative when the official world attempted to turn death into a symbol sufficiently vague to teach Americans to be American.

Dos Passos went to the trouble to resist the symbology of the Unknown Soldier for the same reason that the War Department embraced it. Death in World War I had a role that it had not held in previous wars because the armies engaged on the western front followed a strategy of attrition with which they were never quite at ease. The American Expeditionary Forces contributed the telling numbers to this strategy. That was their great purpose. The northern armies fought the American Civil War with a similar strategy, after General U. S. Grant took over their direction. But the American memory of the Civil War has often emphasized the South's resourceful maneuvering against that strategy. In the latter stages of the war, parents and wives of Civil War dead accepted their losses as personal tragedy rather than as sacrifice to the nation.[12] No one ever completed the connection between personal loss and national victory in that war, so complicated by the fact that part of the nation triumphed while the other went down in defeat. The 2,111 unknown dead at Arlington remained a jumble of bodies under a single marker, never raised to the position of national symbol. Lincoln himself, in his famous address at Gettysburg, had to ignore half the dead on the field when he stated that "we can not dedicate – we can

not consecrate – we can not hallow – this ground. The brave men
who struggled here have consecrated it far above our poor power
to add or detract." Those dead in Lincoln's words should
re-dedicate his listeners to the struggle for northern victory. The
rhetoric of Woodrow Wilson would have taken the liberty of
turning them all into a symbol for the united nation.

Attrition, in its crudest form, meant the destruction of one side
while the other still had sufficient energy and organization to
invade, or in the words of the "Grave Diggers' Song," sufficient
energy to bury the dead. In practice, perceptions of imminent
destruction and disorganization played an important role. In the
end, the perception of the inevitability of the destruction of the
German army along with the political collapse of the country led
the German military commanders to sue for an Armistice. Many
factors went into this calculation, but that Germany found herself
out-numbered was chief among them.

German generals only found their armies out-numbered once
they had to count Americans in the same way that they counted
their own troops. The French, too, had not known how to count
Americans. And their anxieties, as well as the Germans' hopes for
the incompetence of American arms, appeared in popular songs
as well as in official reports.

> The Americans are here, William [here Kaiser William II]
> The Americans are here.
> They have given France
> Their dollars and their valor.
>
> American soldiers!
> What a delusion that is!
> All those business tyros
> Weren't born to the military.[13]

According to the song, no one, neither the French nor the
Germans, questioned American business ability. The French
were able to begin to translate this American trait into military
prowess while voicing their skepticism through the Kaiser. Business ability, efficiency and economy did not count in this war
where bodies were required.

Only when American units had participated in the halt of the
last German offensives at Belleau Wood and Château-Thierry in

July, 1918, did the Germans learn how to count Americans. Of the consequence of those battles, the German Field Marshal von Hindenburg wrote:

> We had been compelled to draw upon a large part of the reserves which we intended to use for the attack in Flanders. This meant the end of our hopes of dealing our long-planned decisive blow at the English army.
>
> In these circumstances the steady arrival of American reënforcements must be particularly valuable for the enemy. Even if these reënforcements were not yet quite up to the level of modern requirements in a purely military sense, mere numerical superiority had a far greater effect at this stage when our units had suffered so heavily.[14]

Von Hindenburg gave the impression that only the wearing down of numbers counted and that Germany had drawn on her last reserves. General John J. Pershing quoted this passage in *My Experiences of the War* and offered no critical comment to indicate that anything beyond the numbers of men, not their ability, not their leaders, had mattered. In fact, in his summing up of the events of July and early August, 1918, the Second Battle of the Marne, the most successful period of American belligerence, General Pershing emphasized numbers in his own words as well.

> While our forces had played important roles in halting earlier German offensives, there were available here for the first time sufficient American divisions to join with those of the Allies in striking a decisive blow. The power of American arms brought to bear in the Marne salient made it possible to crush the last enemy offensive and commit him entirely to the defensive . . . Nearly 300,000 American soldiers were engaged in these operations, sustaining more than 50,000 casualties.[15]

General Pershing concluded his war memoir by reiterating the importance of numbers to the American contribution to the Allied victory.

> It need hardly be restated that our entry into the war gave the Allies the preponderance of force vitally necessary to outweigh the tremendous increase in the strength of the Germans on the Western Front, due to the collapse of Russia and the consequent release of German divisions employed against her . . .

There was a total of approximately 300,000 American troops engaged in [the] Second Battle of the Marne . . . In the middle of September, an army of 550,000 Americans reduced the St. Mihiel salient. The latter part of September, our great battle of the Meuse-Argonne was begun, lasting through forty-seven days of intense fighting and ending brilliantly for our First and Second Armies on November 11th, after more than 1,200,000 American soldiers had participated.[16]

Few other historians of the Meuse-Argonne Offensive would have described it as "brilliant." But only with that one word, reminiscent of either heroism or inspired leadership, did General Pershing dilute the grim message that numbers alone counted. He did not elaborate his message. He caused his reader to imagine what a war, where men counted only as cannon fodder, looked like and felt like. Pershing gave the barest facts of this horror, and then only when recounting the logistical difficulties of the battle: "A total of 173,000 men were evacuated to the rear and more than 100,000 replacements were received."[17] These casualties and the men who took their places became bodies to move over already strained communications systems. The suffering wounded men "evacuated," perhaps with missing limbs, were hardly more passive than the replacements who "were received." Any action or initiative of these armies of men as individuals did not count in Pershing's account of the war either. The Germans knew and understood the numbers. That did matter. The Germans realized that the imbalance was too great, the destruction of the German army was inevitable. They realized this as early as October 3, 1918, when their commanders insisted that their government treat with the Allies for peace.

That the German army was not destroyed has allowed Germans to this day to insist that the Allies never defeated the German army in the field at the end of World War I and that, instead, revolutionary political forces gave the German army a "stab in the back." In fact, by the time of the Armistice on November 11, the allied armies had taken back much territory that the Germans had held for years, and, in some places, were advancing as much as five miles a day, with only ruined roads and rain holding them to that. The Allies did not "defeat the German army in the field," only if that meant entrapment or destruction. The German defeat resulted more from exhaustion, the exhaustion of a whole country involved in a total war. The Allies won, after all, a war of attrition.[18]

Karl von Clausewitz's famous definition of a general's aims – the destruction or entrapment of the enemy army – could not be followed in World War I by maneuver or surprise, by the skill of commanders or the bravery and spirit of the men. If one side took to the offensive, it had first to prepare the way with a massive artillery assault of the other side's machine gun emplacements, communications, barbed wire and trenches. With this cannonade completed, the attackers would climb out of their trenches and make their way across no man's land burdened with several days' supplies, to take possession of their enemy's now partially destroyed position. They continued their advance through the enemy system of trenches, hoping to emerge at the back of the enemy's lines. Large numbers of fresh troops could then come through this gap. These fresh troops would then attack the flanks and rear of the enemy whose defenses faced forward. In theory, the enemy could thus be destroyed, but this never happened. The longed-for gap never materialized. It became necessary to defeat the whole country.

The military technology, that both sides shared, kept the gap a phantom for several reasons. The very immensity of the artillery bombardment before any offensive with a hope of decisiveness precluded surprise. The enemy almost always had time to prepare. And, if the fantastic preliminary shelling did not get the message across (it lasted a week before the Somme in 1916 and needed, 1,500,000 rounds of ammunition[19]), then the massing of troops and supplies behind a particular area visible to reconnaissance planes would do the trick. As one army brought up men anticipating that they would make a gap and then flow through it, the other army could put men in position to fill the gap. Even if the attack took them by surprise, the defenders could move their men in trains and trucks to contain the gap much more swiftly than the attackers could move their men on foot carrying several days' supplies through the morass their successful bombardment had made of several miles of trenches. Without the bombardment, the advancing men could be cut down by machine gun and rifle fire from the enemy trenches. With the bombardment, they lost the possibility of surprise and soon found themselves wallowing in the destruction their own high explosives had created.

In practice, the bombardment did not always have the desired effect, making the offensive position harder still. At the Somme, for example, the greater part of the 1,500,000 rounds of various kinds of ammunition caused surface explosions and did not destroy the deep shelters where the German machine-gunners had taken refuge. From the moment most of the British soldiers climbed out of their trenches to start across the devastation towards the German lines, they were the target of German machine-gunners. Many historians and eye-witnesses have described the pointless carnage that resulted. Men were mown down in their ranks.

Both the allied and the German armies essentially repeated this scenario on the western front throughout the war. The commanders knew the advantages of a defensive position. As early as the Russo-Japanese war of 1904–5, European and American observers, including John J. Pershing, had witnessed very similar war conditions. As early as 1897 (1903 in the United States), the French military theorist Ivan S. Bloch had published *The Future of War*, in which he concluded that,

> At first there will be increased slaughter – increased slaughter on so terrible a scale as to render it impossible to get troops to push the battle to a decisive issue. They will try to, thinking they are fighting under the old conditions, and they will learn such a lesson that they will abandon the attempt forever . . . War has become impossible, except at the price of suicide.[20]

Bloch hardly stood alone in his analysis of mechanized war with industrial might behind it. Plenty of evidence existed to support him from the American Civil War onward. And even if he had created his thesis with no supporting evidence, the First World War quickly provided all the evidence anyone could want. The British fought their terrible and well-known offensive on the Somme in the Summer of 1916, but the battles fought before and after that demonstrated exactly the same thing. Attack would not succeed. Bloch had erred in his analysis where he insisted that men would learn not to advance into mechanized fire, or not to order their fellow soldiers to advance into such fire. Officers continued to give such orders and the men obeyed. In the Fall of 1918, more than two years after the Somme, essentially the same tactics were employed, with little more success and very similar casualties, by the American army in the Meuse-Argonne offensive.

Offensives might not succeed in taking ground, but they remained the last defense against the admission that war had become a matter of attrition pure and simple. Generals might talk about a *strategy of attrition*, but the fact that every year of the war saw massive offensives mounted demonstrated that commanders never became easy with this idea.

The commanders could not accept the notion of attrition probably because of the passivity that concept implied. Once a general had admitted that he could only succeed by defense, by shelling the enemy's trenches while his own were shelled as well, he had given up any belief that his military expertise mattered to the outcome of the whole war. Just as importantly, he had admitted that none of his men mattered, except as targets to draw, and eventually exhaust, the enemy's fire. All their individual heroism and their careful training, the national genius of which each soldier represented a cell, would count for very little. The outcome of a war that should have determined the dominant nationality of Europe, with all the Darwinist overtones implied, would have proven nothing beyond the fact that one group of powers had a greater population of young men to throw away than the other.

The *strategy of attrition* grew as a kind of shadow of reality behind other more aggressive ideas. At the same time that Bloch published his thesis pointing out that increased fire power coupled with defensive concealment precluded offense, Ferdinand Foch, later the supreme commander of the Allied armies, published *Principles of War* in which he noted that "Any improvement of firearms is ultimately bound to add strength to the offensive." He claimed to have made a mathematical proof of this by simply noting that an attack of two thousand men could lose twice as many bullets as a stationary force of one thousand men. Both *movement* and *numbers* counted here; but Foch neglected to note the effect that defensive cover, for example trenches, would have. One of Foch's disciples took his theme further and insisted, at the courses he gave to future French strategists, that any offensive plan was better than any defensive plan and that criticism of the offensive theory was evidence of moral weakness and could disqualify a man for high command. Eventually, he developed the French doctrine of the *offensive à outrance*.[21] The moral imperative to offense eventually warped the data of other factors, such as economics, politics or military technology, that might have offered arguments for defensive strategies. As Jack Snyder, the historian of offensive ideology in the era of World War I, concluded:

> At the most general level, the period between 1870 and 1914 was conducive to offensive strategies. The Franco-Prussian War, although it demonstrated the devastating effect of defensive firepower, seemed superficially to show that modern wars could be short, offensive, and beneficial. At the same time, social Darwinist thinking made tests of military strength seem inevitable and "natural," and prevailing economic ideas suggested that these wars had necessarily to be short, decisive, and hence offensive.[22]

When American commanders arrived on the western front, they too believed in offense and in action. American officers were disgusted by the lack of activity in the "quiet sectors," where allied commanders first sent them to become accustomed to trench warfare. Quiet sectors existed, as historian Tony Ashworth has explained, as an outgrowth of an informal "live and let live system" in which infantry men on both sides recognized that offensive activity resulted in dangerous retaliation and that personal survival was best served by a strict inaction in the trenches. Commanders wished to keep the killing machine in action in order to destroy enough men and material of both sides to reach a conclusion. From posts in the rear, they could always destroy such "live and let live" systems by ordering artillery attacks. Men and junior officers in the trenches of such sectors, sometimes recognizing their own high officers as a greater threat than the soldiers opposite them, preferred to maintain such systems. Americans, fresh to the war, insisted on night attacks and control of no-man's land. After all, these American troops had to prove themselves. Typically, their first assignment was to such a sector, whereas their European counterparts found themselves rotated to such sectors after service on an active front or in an offensive.[23]

The German generals could never rely on a strategy of attrition or of defense. The younger Helmuth von Moltke, in charge of German war planning from 1905 to the beginning of the war, shared a predilection for the offensive with his military contemporaries, but also had inherited a legacy of successful brief wars fought by the Prussian army against Austria and then France under his uncle, Helmuth von Moltke the elder. In the war with Austria and then the Franco-Prussian war, the difficult political problems of the unification of Germany had been resolved by military aggression. This legacy of successful military aggression solidified into dogma under Alfred von Schlieffen, chief of the German General Staff from 1891 until 1905, who perfected his famous plan for a two front war in response to the treaties that joined France and Russia after 1891.[24] The von Schlieffen plan, including the encirclement of French armies by a flanking manoeuver through Belgium, and then a quick transfer of armies to the Russian front, was essentially a gigantic shell game, to make German soldiers worth more than the Russians and French who would out-number them.

Alfred von Schlieffen set his considerable organizational ability to prevent Germany's becoming involved in an extended war of attrition for he appreciated the delicacy and interdependency of industrial economies, and considered that such a war would mean ruin. "A nation's existence depends upon the uninterrupted continuation of trade and industry, and a quick decision is necessary to start the wheels of industry turning again. A strategy of attrition is impossible when the maintenance of armies of millions requires the expenditure of billions."[25] In the actual event, von Schlieffen's plan, as modified by Helmuth von Moltke the younger, did not overcome the mechanics of machine-gun and trench. Both sides became bogged down in the famous stalemate from which both sides periodically attempted to extricate themselves through costly efforts to regain the offensive.

The war set a pattern of attrition very early of between three thousand and four thousand dead a day. And it kept it up for four years through the months' long battles that gained no territory, until the Germans had run out of everything at the same time as the Allies were re-supplied with men and material from America. The war had become a machine producing death. Once America entered the war, the Allies just had to keep the machine going and it would have the desired effect on Germany. If anyone's individual skills mattered, it was organizational skills of manufacturing and transportation.[26]

Death under these circumstances became the single product of war, the single measure of success. Offensives produced more death more quickly than the defensive waiting under shell fire. By advancing, an army might lose vast numbers of its men, more than it captured or destroyed of the enemy. But it would speed the whole process up. And, in a perverse way, losing his own men could enhance a general's reputation. Military units stand along a scale of bravery and valor determined in part by their losses in the battles in which they have fought. At the end of descriptions of battles in divisional or regimental histories, the casualties are mentioned with understandable, though perverse, pride – to maintain order as a unit while sustaining heavy losses and to pass the endurance test of combat deserves praise, though the people who hold the strongest right to that pride are dead. Logically, their replacements and other people around them, if not their survivors, will require a new test.

The rhetorical direction of memorials, however, attempted to spread their accomplishment around, even to their relatives and geographical origins. The program to the First Annual Belleau Wood Day Memorial Service, sponsored by the US Marine Corps Club of St. Louis, June 11, 1922, and dedicated to the Mothers, Fathers, Wives, Brothers and Sisters of the dead, took just such a trajectory.

> Why this memorial service? Out of the eleven hundred and some odd men from St. Louis and the district 109 are missing today. They have reported for duty with their Maker in Heaven. That is over ten percent of the men who served, a much greater percentage of mortality than was sustained by any other organization. Most of these men were killed or wounded at Belleau Wood...They who have paid the supreme sacrifice, they who were privileged, if you please, to succeed in that in which I know many of you would have been only too glad to offer yourself....[27]

The program to the service answered its question, "why hold this memorial service?" by saying in effect that these men did not die in vain. They died to prove that their survivors and families, most of whom have never seen battle, would die in battle if given the chance. The figures given in the program yielded a casualty rate somewhat under ten percent. The author's slight exaggeration of the figure emphasizes the importance of high casualty rates to such an event.

Immediately after the war, divisions with long active service and heavy casualties printed special bulletins recounting their activity, their casualties and claiming the honor of having been first in both. Newspapers picked up this information and an article in *The New York Times* imagined a competition between divisions to settle this question.[28]

Amateur historians of their own units pointed with pride to the casualty lists. One member of the Fourth Division wrote "I can't help but feel just a bit proud of the old fourth. There are many tiny white crosses in France today, thousands of them, which read – 'Fourth Division.' "[29] Ralph Williams of the Second Division dedicated his autobiographical fiction, *Luck of a Buck*, to his division which he calls "second to none." First among the accomplishments in which the Second Division led, he listed proudly, "More men killed or wounded than any other Division in the AEF."[30] Non-military institutions took some pride in their war dead as well. Yale University published a special "New Year Greeting" on November 18, 1918, in which secretary Anson Phelps Stokes listed the university's many contributions to the war. "May the men of Yale continue to uphold the high tradition of their university in the spirit of the one hundred and fifty graduates and former students who are known to have made the supreme sacrifice in the cause of Freedom."

With time, veterans could accept a death price with an utterly military explanation that they would not have accepted during the battle. Murvyn Burke, who had been a private at the time of the war, offered an explanation of the battle of Cantigny that his own officers would have applauded. The attack, he stated, actually "was for psychological reasons – or in Military talk, morale." French and English morale was low at the beginning of 1918, Burke explained. The Germans wished to prove that they would not have to count American soldiers as the equals of Germans in their attritional calculations. The battle was a test, and the quantity of the men lost and of the suffering withstood proved the point to the Germans. "Our losses could not be justified by the importance of the position itself, but they were many times justified by the other great and far-reaching considerations. None of these things were known to the man with the rifle in the foxhole – he was just doing his duty."[31]

In World War I, the dead themselves became a necessity for national war aims. A degree of sacrifice to the nation and the nation's power became an aim of war. Arnold Toynbee has written of the "oblation of military human sacrifice to the religion of nationalism."[32] Nationalism finds its justification in wartime – the greater the number of men sacrificed, the greater must be the deity nation. The usually humanely motivated military historian, Liddell Hart, looked more for nationalistic justification than for a quick finish that would have saved lives, when he considered the battles at the end of World War I.

> It was well that the Armistice had tarried long enough to allow the offensive of November 1st to take place [the second part of the Meuse-Argonne offensive]. For it provided a counter-poise to the bitter memories of the first phase – more truly the first battle of the Meuse-Argonne, and a proof that when purged and refined by experience the American Army could produce leadership and staff work worthy of the gallant sacrifice of their fighting troops – the American nation in arms.[33]

The reputation of American arms and the prestige of the American nation represented by her arms, counted more to Hart than the men, British, German, French as well as American, who lost their lives needlessly in the last week of the war. For Hart, the suffering of individuals in this case came after the prestige of nations. But justification of the individual powers and genius of commanders seems to have come first of all, for only through the efficiency of these commanders coupled with the "gallant sacrifice of their men," could the nation find expression and could the sacrifice find meaning in economical victory.

Liddell Hart entitled the first edition of his history of World War I, published in 1931, *The Real War*. The introductory explanation of that title reappeared in subsequent editions. In that introduction, he identified the conflict over the meaning of the war between the suffering of individuals, the advance and retreat of grand strategies, and the rise and fall of nations.

> Some may say that the war depicted here is not "the real war" that this is to be discovered in the torn bodies and minds of individuals. It is far from my purpose to ignore or deny this aspect of the truth. But for anyone who seeks, as I seek here, to view the war as an episode in human history, it is a secondary aspect. Because the war affected individual lives so greatly, because these individuals were numbered in millions, because the roots of their fate lay so deep in the past, it is all

the more necessary to see the war in perspective, and to disentangle its main threads from the accidents of human misery.[34]

Liddell Hart pushed human suffering to the periphery of history, even as he evoked that suffering, because he assumed more efficient strategies would in fact reduce that suffering. He chose the words "torn bodies and minds" deliberately to show the importance of a strategy that would minimize them.

Elaine Scarry has described at length this tendency of military thought to escape from the fact of injury as the product of war. Liddell Hart moved consciously from the language of injury to the language of strategy as contest for a humane purpose, but other historians make that move drawn to the language of contest as the only means of making sense of battle.[35] For example, military authorities speak in sanitary terms or in terms appropriate to the athletic field or other contests. "We mopped up some machine-gun nests during the afternoon," a report might state or, "The sides were even for the afternoon's match," or "from check the situation quickly deteriorated to check-mate," or "the army delivered a knock-out blow." With a small act of imagination, sanitary expressions, such as "mopping up" – extremely common military talk to this day – can become graphically *the* metaphor for the bloody affair it has so often represented. The language of contests, however, perhaps because it expresses that aspect of war related to determining a winner, resists interpretation back down to the level of individuals receiving injury. The "knock-out blow" maintains its connotation from the boxing ring, violent certainly, but also decisive and contained, when applied to war. But the words "knock-out blow" in the military context convey only the metaphorical sense of a whole army defeated. It does not convey anything specific, not one soldier's bruised face, and certainly not the individual injuries sustained within a defeated army.

Scarry suggested a purpose in this rhetorical evasion of the fact of injury in war texts. These metaphors make the translation, otherwise missing, from the fact of injury in war to determining a winner of the contest, the other aspect of the structure of war. Notoriously, war itself eludes, and World War I particularly eluded, a decisive end. Even after a "knock out blow," which neither side but rather time finally delivered in World War I, the field of contest moved to the conference table. And after the conference table, of course, history has taken over the endless task of interpreting and evaluating the importance and outcome of the war. The meaning of the war dead and their actual torn and suffering bodies have been important bargaining chips and talismans in these negotiations all along, though almost impossible to face steadily as the only product of the war. The multiple memorials after World War I, some to names, some to bodies, solved this problem in one way. Historians solved it in their narratives that move back and forth between the fact of injury and the fact of contest, and soldiers, as they could, in their own writing, or as they assisted families reconstituting the history of particular bodies, and names, did the same thing. As Elaine Scarry wrote, sense could be made through different evasions of injury as the product of war:

> It is not that any one person moves through the four [different forms of evasion] but that a population as a whole, in their separate murmurings, keep articulating back and forth across their entirety the full series as though to keep the words in the air, to keep them from landing where they can be seen and assessed.[36]

Was the war worth the suffering, a historian might ask. Liddell Hart would reply that such a question cannot be answered, that the questions of wars must be considered in the broadest historical terms far from the suffering of individuals. And why must war be considered like that? Because, wrote Liddell Hart, it involves the suffering of so many individuals, historians must learn the larger forces behind their suffering. As Elaine Scarry wrote, human suffering and the product of war fade in and out of the discourse, evading focused attention: "War entails a structure of physical and perceptual events: it requires both the reciprocal inflection of massive injury and the eventual disowning of the injury so that its attributes can be transferred elsewhere, as they cannot if they are permitted to cling to the original site of the wound, the human body."[37] In other words, just as Liddell Hart found, in order for meaning to emerge from war, the pain suffered by individual bodies must be translated into history. As Murvyn Burke might have said, soldiers with a rifle in a fox-hole were possessed of one sort of information about war: injury, fear and discomfort. The commanders knew something else, the nature of the contest. Years later, these disparate versions of the battle enhanced one another. Suffering set a high price on the outcome of the contest, and the outcome validated the suffering when the soldier could discuss the events of battle in the terms only available to officers at the time of battle.

While making meaning out of their battle experiences, soldiers moved the issue of death in and out of focus in much the same way as military historians. They did not forget the carnage of war, nor were they particularly reticent about recording it. Rather, talk of wounds or suffering required strategic placement in letters and journals to maximize the meaning of those who had suffered or died.

> I have not dwelt on the horror of it all, but war does something to a person. To see blood and carnage everywhere as men, horses, and mules are blown to bits developed in us a certain savagery and hate that pushed us on toward a terrible enemy with a willingness to see him destroyed.[38]

Thus, one soldier for a moment seemed to hang onto injury as the central aspect of war. He gave few details about the blood and carnage, the destroyed men, horses and mules, yet this list of living things gives the impression that he saw their destruction at close range. He may have known affection for some of these persons and animals. When he translated his experience immediately to revenge against a "terrible enemy" and a desire to destroy him, this terrible but vague enemy did not bleed, nor did he lose his limbs in the face of the author's fire in the narrative, he simply vanished into a sea of hatred.

This soldier wished to protect his family from unpleasant truths. But he also wished to reveal the extent to which war had changed him. Extended passages in the memoir discussed his evasions and approaches to revelations about the horror of war:

> Before I reached home, I decided that I must clear my mind of all the terrible experiences of the past two years, as much as possible. It would not be right to make my family and friends sad and uncomfortable by inflicting upon them the horrors in which they had no part.[39]

He wished to protect his family, but he also wished to be recognized as someone who had seen tremendous suffering and become a man because of it. "I was different and not the carefree boy who went to war. Now I was a man older than my years for

I had seen so many wounded dead and dying," he wrote. He married and his new wife helped him to forget the war by forcing him to remember it. In fact, he wrote the memoir to satisfy her curiosity about a part of his life. "Soon I began to collect the bits and pieces of the two years of war and hide them away in a hidden corner of my mind." He both collected and hid his experience. Suffering surfaced and sank to make its meaning for him.

Some official language of death tended to disguise suffering from relatives, but the relatives seem to have required news of the lost body, as well as assurances as to the cause for which it was lost. During periods of combat, keeping up with the correspondence of death must have severely taxed officers. People naturally made mistakes. Sometimes, authorities employed strategies to enhance the significance of a soldier's death after having first given the impression that no one had quite kept track of his presence, alive or dead. Private John Blaser sent a final letter to his brother back on the family farm in the West on May 28, 1918. "Over here . . . landed here . . . pretty," are the only words legible in the communication. On August 24, the War Department sent their standard telegram informing the next of kin that John Blaser had been wounded. On October 5, the Red Cross sent a letter to Blaser's brother, presumably in answer to an inquiry, stating that they had no information about the wounded private. On January 4, 1919, again presumably in answer to an inquiry, Captain Jared I. Wood wrote to Blaser's brother saying, "Your brother, Pvt. John Blaser, was killed in the head fighting at Sergy on the Ourq River. His body was buried near where he fell. He was killed outright by hostile fire." At about the same time, the Red Cross sent another letter "confirming" that Blaser had died of wounds on September 16, but that no record could be found of the hospital where he died. An undated newspaper clipping preserved by his family reproduced a second letter from Captain Wood.

> Sir: Pvt. John Blaser was killed at Sergy, France in the hottest fight I have been in. He was very good and was a great help to me in making this company the best in the Regiment. It was men like him who won the war. He was killed in action and not carried to a Base Hospital. We buried him near where he fell, but his body was later moved to the American Cemetery by the Graves Registration Bureau.

Of course, a considerable difference exists between dying of wounds perhaps in a hospital some time after a battle and dying at once from an injury to the head. No one can have been certain as to Blaser's fate. The Red Cross admitted as much. Captain Wood, had he actually known what had happened, would surely have corrected the erroneous telegram of August 24, 1918, long before January 4, 1919. But in the absence of information, Captain Wood reduced Blaser's suffering as much as possible. Thus, he invented a quickly fatal wound to the head. Because of confusing information, Blaser's brother must have written again asking for details and receiving the second letter from Captain Wood in which details, the River Ourq and the head wound have disappeared, their place taken by "hot" fighting and a patriotic interpretation of Blaser's service – "He was very good and a great help to me . . . It was men like him who won the war."

Captain Wood's letters cannot have convinced the Blaser family and yet in some sense his words gave the family and Blaser's home town what they wanted, a doughboy hero. Private Blaser had written to his brother before he embarked for France indicating that he hated the army, that he was something of a discipline problem, and that he had no friends. Blaser's own words would tend to undermine what his captain subsequently said about him. Yet, the family gave the local newspaper the letter in which not only John Blaser's odd yet not unpleasant character – his best moments in the military, he wrote, were spent far from discipline and authority, guarding a sceptic tank – but also his body disappeared to an unnamed graveyard. Of course, preserving the whole collection of messages from the War Department, the Red Cross, and Captain Wood, complete with all the contradictions in those letters, indicates that the family reserved some judgment.[40] The meaning of John Blaser's death became one of those uncertainties that the Unknown Soldier could finally put to rest.

John Blaser made part of a chaos of wounds and bodies left after the continuous battles through the Summer and Autumn of 1918 that received rhetorical anesthesia well into 1919. Howard Munder wrote his last letter home on August 31, 1918. His father Charles received it on September 21. In the week following that letter, the family received news that their son was wounded. Charles Munder then wrote to the War Department and received a telegram stating "wounded in action, degree undetermined."

The War Department had previously misdirected the telegram. On October 18, the father wrote to his son's company commander, James F. Cooper, and received no answer. On November 8, he received a reply to an inquiry to the Red Cross saying that no information was available but that "If your boy is in a hospital, he is getting the best care that our skillful doctors and wonderful nurses can give and a great percent of the wounds that do not prove fatal at first inevitably get well." Perhaps the Munders were heartened by the Red Cross's optimism because by this time they had received news from "a lad in our son's company that Howard was shot in the stomach and still alive at the end of a week."

Soon Charles Munder started making carbon copies of the letters he sent to the War Department and to other organizations seeking information. He and his family tried every avenue they could think of. Howard Munder's file at Carlisle Barracks contains hundreds of these sad letters. On November 14, 1918, Charles again heard from the Red Cross: "We hear nothing but praise of the splendid work being done for the boys in the hospitals in France." Sometimes the news seemed promising. In February 1919, a neighbor received a letter from her boyfriend who was serving in France. He wrote, "I inquired about Howard Munder, Co. G. of 109th Infantry and they told me at Division Headquarters, in fact, showed me the record they had. He was wounded September 6th and was evacuated to a hospital somewhere in England. They had no record of him dying, they told me perhaps he is on his way home by now. I could have found out what hospital he was evacuated to but would have had to go to the Division Sergeant." This young man came closest to revealing the information Howard Munder's parents so desperately wished for, but like the army itself, he had other things on his mind than the doughboy who disappeared. The rest of his letter was taken up with his own business.

Finally, on September 27, 1919, P.C. Harris, Adjutant General, wrote a final letter to Charles Munder. "In view of the length of time which has elapsed since he was last heard of, it is accepted at the War Department that he was killed in action, September 6, 1918 and a notation to that effect has been placed on the official records." Munder's stomach wound – notoriously painful – and his survival for at least a week after, his possible evacuation to a hospital in England and the year of anxiety for his mother and father were eliminated in the words "killed in action." The adjutant continued his letter to say where to apply for the war risk insurance and pay due to Bugler Howard Munder. On October 6, 1919, a YMCA secretary sent Mrs Munder Howard's diary found in the mud near Fismes (Aisne), France. Howard had written his last entry on September 5, 1918, "Went to company under heavy fire. Machine gun 77's."[41] The printers of this diary had put spaces in the front for the owner to inscribe certain personal information: "shoe size 7c; hat 7; collar 14; drawer 38." At the very last then, Mrs Munder, to whom the diary was sent, received news of her son's body. He was small and plump, not a martial or heroic figure. Shoe and hat sizes could not make up for the missing body, the evidence of suffering.

No monument to the war could have suited such people as the Munders better than the "Unknown Soldier." The meaning of their son's suffering, the manner in which he disappeared and then reappeared only as his suffering, as a stomach wound, or as the fact of his hospitalization, could be layed to rest in that casket at Arlington with the unidentified contents. Yet, the fact of their retaining, for so many years all those letters searching after Howard, and sending them all eventually to the US Army's archives, shows that they were never satisfied. They wished Howard's life and death to have meant something. Howard himself had worried. He was small and had bad eyes. He could not shoot a rifle. He was no kind of soldier and knew it. He only hoped he would be a better businessman for the experience. Early in his army career, he had written that he hoped for a discharge because of his inability to shoot a gun. "I look forward to when I am discharged, which I hope is real soon."[42] Yet, the army did not give him up, and only with difficulty could sense be made of his sacrifice.

No one seemed able to make Howard Munder into a warrior. His tiny feet, 7c, did not command much respect or even notice. Unit clerks did their best to keep up with inquiries and personnel, but the task must have been demoralizing at times.

Every day, we receive letters from mothers and relatives seeking information about some of the boys who have been killed or wounded. Some of the most pitiful and pathetic letters! We always give them our careful and particular attention. In some cases, we have no record at all – such letters are, indeed, the hardest to write.[43]

They were hard to write because the parents desired some assurance that their son's death had meant something. This meaning shared the requirements of Elaine Scarry's "structure of war" that is to say it required movement from the injury sustained by an individual, complete with details, to the contest in which the larger structures of armies and nations were engaged. Having established that the son, or husband or brother had not been a vaguely defined casualty, or cannon fodder, that someone had recognized the dead soldier for himself, that he had died among friends, and of specific wounds, the official could move on to the heroic blandishments so apparent in Captain Wood's second letter about John Blaser. When no one could supply the details of death, as in the case of Howard Munder, the official found himself unable to say anything about the cause in which the young man died. Munder became a name without a body, without verifiable injuries, and worth only the amount of his insurance policy. The "Unknown Soldier", of course, as a body with definite injuries but without a name, could be buried with all the honors due a soldier who died in a cause.

Red Cross workers, officers and buddies, all helped supply the necessary details of an individual's death. For some, a network of condolence organized to bring the death into focus with the war. Lieutenant Charles Robinson's immediate commander, Captain Joseph B. Bersky, wrote to Robinson's parents and arranged for a witness to Robinson's death to write as well with details. Bersky supplied assurance that Robinson had stayed away from women, suggesting he had kept his body fit for sacrifice: "I feel that you should know one thing. Doubtless you have heard of the temptations to which a man is exposed over here. I want you to know that your son lived in the midst of these temptations unsullied, that his life was clean." Lieutenant W. O. Kleinstuber supplied, and, in a sense, shared the details of Robinson's death at the behest of Bersky:

> I have just received a letter from Captain Bersky in which he asked me to write you concerning your son's Charles death.
>
> On about October 24th Charles and I were assigned to the same Battalion of the 318th Infantry.

From that time on we were pals, shared our blankets every night and everything. I was also struck in the head by the same shell that hit Charles.

We were operated on by a very competent surgeon. But poor Charles had a badly fractured skull and his brain was lacerated and infected.

He was given a very impressive military funeral which I attended, befitting his rank as an officer and Hero of the U.S. Army.

Although his loss cannot be replaced to you, yet you have a good reason to be mighty proud to have had a son who was brave enough to sacrifice all for love of his country.

Hoping this gives you the information you desire . . .

Captain Bersky set the stage, insisting that Robertson's body had remained pure and worthy of the meaning that would come to rest on it. Lieutenant Kleinstuber then fulfilled the requirements of the structure of war. The lieutenant provided details of the death, validating his witness by his intimacy with the deceased, and he provided the patriotic context, "for love of his country."[44] Witnesses in a position to provide authentic details seem rarely to have withheld them to spare the feelings of parents. From the closing of the lieutenant, in fact, it seems that the parents in this case requested details of their son's death.

Colin V. Dyment, the Red Cross worker in charge of records for the Ninety-first Division, created a document, perhaps unique for the AEF, in its rigorous attention to accuracy, that arranged the suffering of the entire division into a single narrative. He recorded all the major wounds and the deaths of the men of the Ninety-first Division, including interviews and testimony from witnesses, accolades from officers, last words where possible, and educated speculation drawn from circumstantial evidence when no witness was available. He planned to send several pages of this "account of Death" to the emergency address of every man killed in the division along with a chronological account of the movements of the division. "With the help of a good map of France," the next of kin could place the death of their loved one into both its geographical setting and its emotional setting amid a host of other suffering.

Whoever lived at the emergency address would pick up the story of damage to the human tissue of the Ninety-first Division at full flood. At first, it would make no sense. After about a page, names of officers and places, of messengers and commanders would repeat. Death would start to form a pattern. Colin Dyment suppressed little for delicacy's sake. Halfway through the copied section, the name of their son or husband or brother would appear with some details around it, the names of companions perhaps familiar from letters. There would follow about five more similar events, and then the narrative would end as abruptly as it started. A letter accompanied the selection from the "account of Death" that spoke to the issues of the war for which this man had died. For members of the Ninety-first Division, the two sides of the structure of war, injury and contest, were represented at their death in a manner complete yet discrete, one part from the other.[45]

How soldiers thought of the death they saw around them differed somewhat from how they thought they ought to re-present death to people far from the battlefields. When coming upon someone unknown, dead in a field, some soldiers emphasized how close that body still seemed to life.

> Something that was a man once, lies up in the field and another here, wearing the kaki [sic] uniform. Boys who yester-day were alive and crossing the fields as we are. But nearly always the kaki uniform lad seemed just to have gone to sleep. I remember one, a mere boy, with yellow-gold hair who looked up into the sky, blue as his eyes must have been.[46]

The idealization stood out in this case, but Loren Duren, who wrote this passage in his memoir, saw plenty of bodies. Soon, as if relinquishing one narrative style for another as his experience of the dead mounted up, his tone changed. He described burying the dead.

> I shall very briefly describe it. Memories like that aren't pleasant. Indeed some things I cannot write for it can do no one any good. We were divided into groups, each with his work to do. Some brought the bodies in from the fields where they had fallen, while others were digging those trench graves. Then we covered their bodies, made wooden crosses; those silent, rude, markers standing so naked against the sky for those who had made the supreme sacrifice. I helped cover the bodies and we laid them in the trenches twenty-four in a row

and we buried two hundred and twenty-two there on a little rise of ground by the side of a shell torn road, just outside of all that was left of torn little Chezy village.

If one could forget those horrible torn remains of our boys. For a week or more they had been in the fields in the rain and mud, some grotesquely mishapen by gas, left sitting up and still grasping their canteens for a last drop of water as the clouds of gas overtook them. While others were ripped open by shrapnel or machine-gun bullets. Six or seven of our own boys were buried there, two who had been chums, a bugler and a runner. They were always together, so we buried them there, side by side. Many of the lads had letters or pictures in their pockets which were sent back to their people. Little keepsakes and trinkets, we buried with them. Oh, if one could only forget those awful silent heaps. The smell which arose from those decaying bodies was almost overpowering and many of us were compelled to wear gasmasks while bringing them in. A few bodies actually burst when the first shovelful of earth was thrown on them and in other awful wounds were piles of maggots, heaving and crawling. God it was awful.

I am glad that people here cannot know these awful things, for knowing, one could never never forget. One had to keep always in mind that last week, last month, one had hiked, slept, ate with these boys. They had made the sacrifice; we were doing the one and only decent thing left to us. When the graves were leveled off and a neat white fence had been built around the cemetery, there was a short service of prayer and a salute of guns and we left them there on a little rise of ground, by the side of a shell-torn road.[47]

Loren Duren started his narrative of death with an idealization of it, a youth whose eyes only yesterday were blue as the sky into which he stared. And he finished with an idealization as well. He not only ended his description with "a neat white fence," he copied out the lines of "Flanders Fields" by John McKae. But, between these conventional brackets, he found himself drawn to record details that he is glad the general population does not know. With his fellow soldiers, he dug mass graves and put into them people he had known. In the presence of the "torn" bodies, and in the shadow of a "torn" village, they said some prayers. The service included a military salute through which the military reason for the destruction of these men was symbolically re-presented as well.

In the minds of soldiers, no impenetrable barrier seems to have existed between the grim details of death and the rhetoric of the high purposes for those deaths. There seems to have been no resentment at the fact of a war of attrition. In fact, as time passed for veterans and they could understand better their position in the war, they seemed to have accepted the strategy of attrition as reasonable.

The pacifist Quakers, who organized an ambulance service, printed a propaganda booklet that members of their service, The American Field Service, purchased as a souvenir. They entitled this book of photographs *The Absolute Truth,* and certainly they intended it as a pacifist tract. The book contains only black and white photographs mostly taken by the US Signal Corps. Its only text is the brief captions to the pictures. The majority of the photographs portray dead men showing varying degrees of their final agony. "Alone:" a German lay awkward, yet purposeful across a welt of ground near a field of weeds, his equipment around him, his face missing. "Where they fell:" Germans, identifiable by boots and mess kits, stiff in rigor mortis, one with a huge hole in his neck and a clenched fist, another wore an expression of horror. "No Man's Land:" swollen bodies in a field having the look of bodies in a Brady photograph of a American Civil War battlefield. "Our Boys:" the dead arranged like a munition belt of bodies, with one handsome dead profile show-ing. "Almost Buried:" a young man, his blond hair still ruffled by the wind, with still intelligent eyes and a sensitive mouth looks into the distance held sitting up by the weight of a collapsed trench that crushed the lower half of his body. "Aviator's sacrifice:" a charred legless aviator lying near the wreckage of a plane. The photographs, always graphic, and their captions sometimes heavy with irony, included about twenty pages. The booklet conveyed a strong message: war has no glory in it for individuals. The dead may sometimes even be handsome still of face, those are destroyed just as much as the dead with faces missing. War even destroyed aviators. These specific men, some still recognizable, were the product of the destruction of this war.

The booklet contained a few photographs, however, of living men. Stretcher bearers carried the wounded. Medics offered aid. The man who kept the booklet indicated wherever his picture or one of his companions appeared as stretcher bearers. Though this was a propaganda booklet, the very fact that it memorialized important, if grim, moments for some men, made it a memorial to a heroic period in their lives. So strong was the structure of war that, depending on the context, a Quaker pacifist tract could actually be interpreted as an advertisement for the heroic possibilities of war. "This is me," wrote Neal Beroth of his image among stretcher bearers, this was his moment in the war. He kept the booklet along with a collection of the special commendations and the official citations of the Second Division, to which his ambulance unit was attached. Alone, the booklet of photographs might have had a pacifist effect. In the context of a man's war memorabilia, it could take on quite another meaning.[48]

Americans not involved in the actual fighting represented death differently. In her journal, Nurse Ethel D. Warner emphasized the difference between the experience of war for the men who fought it, and for her, a nurse who only saw the wounded result. "The war had become a reality by this time. It certainly wasn't because the boys discussed it much," she wrote. She described funerals at a hospital graveyard with a different tone from that used by men who had been in battle.

> There were two artificial wreaths for the use of the graves for the whole cemetery. They were snatched from the last graves to be laid upon the fresh dirt of the newly made ones. If there happened to be three or more deceased victims in one day it was a toss-up as to who would get the wreaths.[49]

She counted the bodies, but she replaced patriotic sentiment with cold irony.

She recorded with muted pride the comparatively small contribution she and her American colleagues made to the hospital graveyard, only 438 dead out of 37,774 patients, less than 2 per cent. The pride of this medical worker lay in how small the number could be kept.

This nurse described wounds with clinical detail both in general and specific cases, but again with no sentimental statement interpreting those wounds. She left out the discourse of the high-flown cause. Expressions like "supreme sacrifice" and "love of country," which appeared in other texts like essential parts of speech, found no place in her memoir. "The shrapnel wounds were usually long and deep and it was not unusual to see a patient with wounds from his head to his feet." She described, unflinchingly, the appearance and effects of Dakin drip, an antiseptic wash administered deep and continuously into the lacerated intimate portions of men.

In the letters they wrote to parents, nurses spoke of the body before them, but not of the war. Charlotte Gailor, writing two weeks after the death of Clarence Hackett, wrote a letter that minimized the pain he suffered, and that portrayed Hackett as thinking fondly of home and with gratitude for his parents. Writing just after that period of the war when American soldiers enjoyed their greatest military successes, July 1918, the period in which Hackett received his mortal wound, she left that role out of her brief letter.

> I went to see him about 8:30 the evening before [he died] but he was asleep and I didn't disturb him. He did not realize he was going to die and in fact was hardly conscious the last two days when he was so sick. He had been put in a room by himself and died very quietly in the morning at 7:30 while the night nurse was with him.
>
> The men in the ward with him say he was a brave lad, and they used to talk about how nice it would be when the war was over and they would be home. Clarence said he was going to try to repay his folks for all they had done for him.[50]

Her letter may recount nothing less than the truth, though she reported the conversations among the soldiers as hearsay and some of the phrases, "brave lad" for example, might have been comforting formulas. If she did write this letter arranging plausible details to lend comfort, her idea of what would comfort differed greatly from the ideas of officers and men who saw fighting.

Chaplains, men who presided over the funeral services of soldiers and who must have presided at the bedside of many a wounded man's death, took the opposite course from nurses: they .emphasized the meaning of the death without the suffering of the body. In the words of one Chaplain, the body of the dead man starts in the middle distance, the length of a football field away from any witness, and recedes into a reassuring ether:

> No one was near him when he died yet he was but 3 hundred feet from his company. He had no suffering, and his body was

not mutilated, something for which we may be most thankful. He was loyal and brave, and gave himself to make this world a better place to live in. He was 'faithful unto death,' and now, his is the 'crown of life.'[51]

In this case, the necessary wound left no mark, and though no one stood near enough to tell, Lieutenant Logie did not suffer. The man's body became lost in the rhetoric of high causes. Distance from the particular body, along with an official position in the hierarchy of death, caused the chaplain to represent death as this extreme imbalance between the language of suffering and the language of high purposes of the suffering.

Chaplains saw it as their duty to transform men's bodies into the essence of American purpose and patriotism during burial services. World War I caused a torturing of language in many official realms as old forms were fitted to modern destruction.

An imperishable page in America's history has been written; how glorious and significant, only future ages can reveal. But it was not without cost. All over France, in bloodstained, crater-pocked battle fields, in Base Sections and Hospital Centers, groups of rough, white crosses mark the places where sleep those who made the supreme sacrifice.

We have met here today to dedicate this cemetery. But it needs no dedication within our power to make. It has received its consecration from the deathless spirit which burned as a torch in the bosoms of the men and women who lie here.[52]

Thus, a Chaplain dedicated an American cemetery near a hospital in Savoie. He never came closer to the death of the men and women he buried, who died of wounds and flu, than to mention bloodstained fields quite a distance from his hospital. And instead of Lincoln's simple statement that the men who struggled at Gettysburg must cause his listeners to rededicate themselves to the preservation of the Union and government by, of and for the people, the World War I chaplain evoked a "deathless spirit which burned as a torch in the bosoms" of the dead. His rhetoric had dropped the fact of dead flesh while at the graveside, and he had brought forth an evanescent essence of American nationalism for his listeners.

Death and the occasion of burial offered a unique propaganda opportunity. In the presence of wounded bodies, the rhetoric of the significance of the contest could take flight. The first American soldiers to die in combat in World War I were Corporal James Gresham and privates Thomas Enright and Merle Hay. "Give till it hurts," readers of war bond posters depicting these three men were told. "They gave till they died." But just as the war lingered on to the conference table at Versailles, to become a cause for World War II, Gresham, Enright and Hay continued to give long after they died. The plan called for their service into eternity. As a French general, acting as propagandist for Franco-American relations put it at their graveside,

> These graves, the first dug in our national soil and just several steps from the enemy, are like the hand-print of our allies, hitched securely to the common weal and affirming the will of the people and the army of the United States to fight with us to the end, to sacrifice whatever is needed, to fight to a definitive victory, for the most noble of causes, the liberty of peoples. That is why we would ask that the mortal remains of these young men stay here, that they be left to us forever.[53]

The message was clear. Once American blood had soaked into the earth of France, America would find herself more firmly committed to the French cause. General Bordeaux, in his speech at the graveside of these three men, spoke of the monument that would stand over them and the future passer-by who would read the inscription and wonder at the commitment of one distant republic for another.

General Pershing remembered the deaths of Gresham, Enright and Hay on November 2, 1917, and agreed with the sentiments expressed by the French general who spoke at their funeral.

> A group was caught in a box barrage and although the men made a courageous resistance against the large raiding party three were killed, five wounded, and twelve captured. These were the first casualties that had occurred in our army to units serving in the trenches. The French took charge of the funeral ceremony and turned out a formal guard in addition to our own. The services were conducted by the Fench General Bordeaux, who came with his full staff and delivered a beautiful oration over the graves ... This joint homage to our dead, there under the fire of the guns, seemed to symbolize the common sacrifices our two peoples were to make in the same

great cause. It seemed as though their death had sealed a new pact of understanding and comradeship between the two armies.[54]

General Pershing explained how these three soldiers lost their lives. The Germans had mounted an elaborate if limited offensive – a box barrage to cut the men off from their fellows, a large raiding force – in the quiet Vosges section of the line in order to capture some American soldiers for intelligence reasons, and in order to test the metal of Americans. The action cost American lives, but in doing so, gave live proof to the Germans that Americans would soon take up their positions. The message of General Bordeaux gave the interpretation to the Germans of the message already delivered by the captured Americans and the dead. At this moment, the quality of their fighting meant little, the fact of their presence meant everything. The French made sure that the message got across correctly.

In agreeing with the French on this matter in November of 1917, Pershing already found himself out of step with some public opinion in the United States. Citizens of the home towns of at least two of these soldiers felt that any monument to them should enhance their place of origin, not some spot in distant France. Movements for memorialization occurred immediately. By November 6, 1917, Pittsburgh had named a street after Thomas Enright.[55] Along with a memorial service for James Gresham, the people of Evansville, Indiana, started a movement to bring his body home and erect a monument to him in a public park.[56] By November 28, the War Department had refused a request from Pittsburgh for the body of Enright and established a policy of not sending any bodies home until after the war, ostensibly to save on French rail traffic.[57]

Interest in the fate of American war dead increased after the Armistice. Areas of concern spread and included not only the final resting place of soldiers but also accountability and the reverence the bodies received in a foreign place. Did every grave contain the man whose name it bore? What became of a soldier's personal effects? As a lecturer at the Quartermaster Corps Motor Transport School put it in 1922,

The history of the American Graves Registration Service in Europe abounds in facts which clearly indicate the intense

interest the entire nation takes in the burial of its military dead.
This interest increases with the cessation of hostilities, and be
it Armistice or treaty of peace, to the Graves Registration
Service it is a clarion warning that its operations will then be
carefully scrutinized.[58]

The Graves Registration service had the "sacred obligation,
made by the War Department to the people of the United States,
that the graves of American Dead should be perpetually honored
and cared for."[59] Yet the Service did not have a good reputation,
and no unit wanted the job of gathering and caring for the dead.

Soldiers could view the task of picking up the the dead of their
own unit with a sense of duty and humanity, as expressed by
Loren Duren above. Some expressed a kind of relief when they
found themselves returned to a sector where their unit had lost
men and they could pay their final respects and decorate the
graves. But for the whole army, the task encompassed much more
than the digging of some trenches and laying in the bodies. The
digging and burying went on for years. The record-keeping
became a herculean task even for the American army that had
lost relatively few men.

Black soldiers did the actual searching for American dead on
the battlefields, they did the gathering up and the burying and
re-burying, at least during the earlier periods of the GRS
activities. Later, the GRS hired French labor. The history of the
GRS did not mention the fact that black soldiers did the burying,
and that black non-commissioned officers must have verified the
identity of the graves' contents. Black women YMCA workers
Addie Hunton and Kathryn Johnson, while dignifying this role of
black soldiers, may have given a reason for this omission in the
history.

> Strange that the value of such a task did not gather full
> significance in the minds of all American soldiers. Strange that
> when other hands refused it, swarthy hands received it! Yet,
> perhaps, not so strange, for Providence hath its own way, and
> in these American cemeteries in France we have strong and
> indisputable evidence of the wonderful devotion and loyalty
> and the matchless patience and endurance of the colored
> soldier. The placing of this task – the most sacred of the whole
> war – in his hands may have been providentially planned. It

may have been just another means, as against the force of arms, to hasten here at home the recognition and enforcement of those fundamental principles that for four long years had held the world in deadly struggle.[60]

The work connected to taking care of American soldier dead was too sacred to be left to black soldiers. As much meaning attached to the disposition of the dead as attached to combat in this war of attrition. The histories therefore left out the fact that African-American soldiers took care of these tasks. African-Americans could be kept away from combat, but burying the dead, back-breaking, smelly work with the possibility of disease, fell to their lot. The role black soldiers played in labor battalions, unloading ships and building roads, found its way into reports. Caring for the dead did not.

The Graves Registration Service was organized under Major Charles C. Pierce as early as May of 1917. Pierce had had the same job in the Philippines and had accounted for every man according to the history of his service. The war in Europe, however, confronted him with larger problems. His service was "hampered by insufficient personnel and its ideas as well as its apparent duties could not be effectively carried out from the beginning." They got behind, "and could not maintain that close contact with the advancing lines essential to the proper and accurate recording of burials as well as the prompt concentration in battlefield cemeteries."[61]

The Graves Registration Service continually expanded until it contained 150 officers and 7,000 men. This small army located and dug up the mass graves like the one described by Loren Duren. Duren recorded disgust, certainly, at the smells and sights, but still the men in his unit had found the time for a certain humanity in the procedure carried out, after all, for former companions. They had placed those friends, that bugler and the messenger together. For the GRS men coming later, these were "charnal house" conditions. They placed the bodies in boxes and re-buried them in local graveyards or established a new cemetery. A non-commissioned officer determined the identity of the body and recorded it.

After the Armistice, the GRS rechecked the battlefields and graves and removed some to new sights. In one 640 square kilometer area, they registered 12,000 bodies that they had missed during the war. By February 1919, they had combed 20,480 square kilometers looking for dead Americans. They ran into some extraordinary difficulties. A direct hit from a German shell had buried fourteen men seventy-five feet underground. Rivers and canals had flooded parts of battlefields and cemeteries. Their problems had only begun. In September 1919, the war department decided, for the first time in American history, to repatriate the dead.[62]

The War Department had succumbed to very strong public opinion. The "Bring Home the Soldier Dead League" lined up several arguments: that American parents, unlike their British counterparts (the British brought no bodies home), were too far away to visit; that the presence of American bodies would have just the effect General Bordeaux had spoken of and would involve the United States in future wars abroad; that the French morticians and coffin makers wanted the bodies to stay; and that the soldiers would wish to return home.

The "Field of Honor Association," counting General Pershing among its members and backed by Colonel Theodore Roosevelt, Jr., who had recently started the American Legion, lined up approximately the same arguments turned around. General Pershing spoke for the dead:

> Could these soldiers speak for themselves, they would wish to be left undisturbed, where with their commanders they had fought their last fight. The graves of our soldiers constitute, if they are allowed to remain, a perpetual reminder to our allies of the liberty and ideals upon which the greatness of America rests.

The "Field of Honor Association" suspected a plot by American morticians and defended the French by citing touching stories of village women dividing up the task of caring for the graves of Americans among them.[63]

Congress decided to do all things for all people. It appropriated $8,451,000 or about $250 a body, to bring home the dead whose families requested it. Later, Congress would spend $650 to send each war mother or widow who so desired to France, to view her son's or husband's grave. The task of sorting out which bodies stayed in France and which went to the United States fell to the GRS. So far, the policy of concentrating burial grounds had resulted in 505 American cemeteries. In the Summers of 1920–2, in what their history referred to as their "final drive," the GRS dug up all the bodies once more to tag some for the US and some for the five permanent American cemeteries in France that the Fine Arts Commission in Washington had had designed. In the Summer of 1921, at the height of its activity, the GRS repatriated 31,945 bodies to the United States and sent 400 to nearest kin in Europe, mostly to Italy. There were 7,523 bodies that had to await shipment and were re-buried or stored temporarily near their port of embarkation. The French worried about disease and the fact that so much rail traffic was devoted to shipping bodies. But, in the long run, some of this re-arranging may have proved efficient. The British established cemeteries wherever forty or more soldiers had fallen, which resulted in something on the order of 3,000 burial grounds and correspondingly high maintenance costs.

Eventually, 45,588 dead Americans found their way back to the US and 764 to their country of birth in Europe. Public opinion insisted that no American stay in German soil. Thus, the GRS brought over 2,400 flu victims in the Army of Occupation back to cemeteries in France or to America, regardless of the wishes of their families.[64]

A cloud of suspicion hung over the Graves Registration Service. The War Department received letters every day complaining of "indifference, negligence, and in some cases theft of articles many of intrinsic as well as sentimental value" of the dead. Investigations showed that, in the case of theft, the GRS men probably arrived too late on the scene to perpetrate the crime. As a controled experiment, the War Department investigated deaths aboard returning troop carriers. On one ship where 54 men had died between France and the United States, in only 21 cases did the bodies land with any personal effects at all. On another ship, only 9 out of 27 bodies arrived with effects. What personal items there were never had any value. Sometimes a nickel watch had been substituted for a gold watch.[65]

Independent agencies offered testimony to disprove the charges of negligence. A commission from the Grand Duchy of Luxembourg found that adoption of the sanitary methods of the Graves Registration Service for exhumation and putting bodies into coffins would greatly improve the sanitary laws of their own country. Typically, an independent investigator from Massachussetts wrote enthusiastically about how her anxieties about the GRS had been laid to rest,

> I have never been so profoundly touched as I was with the tact and courtesy of the officer in charge and with the reverence and order with which the work was done.
>
> I soon realized that not only for myself but for mothers and other sisters I had a mission in seeing every step of the procedure that I may return to America and speak with authority for what the Graves Registration Service stands for.
>
> Only those who have lost their dear ones can appreciate that feeling of uncertainty regarding the disposition of our dead when we have the all too prevalent impression that was mine before I came.
>
> I cannot say more than had I known beforehand what I know now I would not have come on such a long journey and I most certainly feel that if others shared my knowledge a very much less percentage of bodies would be going home.[66]

This investigator seems principally to have worried about the reverence with which bodies were treated by the GRS and by the French. That must have been the uncertainty she spoke of that had motivated people to cause Congress to bring the bodies back to the United States. She did not address the other uncertainty: just who reposed in which grave.

The official history of the GRS only addressed the problem of identification procedurally. It described how a non-commissioned officer had to place the mark of the GRS on the approved grave. It further described lengthy documentation, forms sent in multiple copies to different offices. But it never attempted to explain what happened when the soldier's identification discs had come unattached and the body and papers become too decomposed for easy identification. Nor did it offer any estimate of how often that happened or how often a family requested a body's return, when the GRS did not have one to offer. They included no statistic on the accuracy of naming after four years of digging up and re-burial.

Systems were elaborate, but broke down. Henry Bartol, the liaison officer stationed in Lyon, took charge of burying Private William Hill, the first American soldier to die at the hospital in that town on June 7, 1918. He reported his actions very carefully. He followed a French plan for burial, having the body placed in

Carré M. 5, *Première Fosse* (Square M. 5, First Trench). Subsequently, he received very detailed instructions from his superior, the equally conscientious Captain Forbes:

> Grave number one should be placed at North East corner of lot and should be dug at a distance of eight centimeters from border of allee number five and one meter ninety centimeters from line dividing American lot and French lot on the side bounded by allee number twenty-six. Blue Prints and instructions will follow by mail. Officer from Graves Registration hopes to visit Lyon in about a week.[67]

"*Première Fosse*" and "grave number one" did not occupy the same spot. With the best will in the world, Bartol had caused difficulties for the GRS. He left no record of having dug up William Hill in order to re-bury him along official lines. The GRS men who came later may have done so.

Speculations on just how often the name attached actually fit the body came from more informal sources than the official history. Mervyn Burke returned to the United States with members of the Army of Occupation in 1921, and told the following rather cynical story in his memoir:

> Shortly after leaving port learned that a good portion of the cargo consisted of about 1,500 bodies being removed from French Battlefields where they had been buried, and taken back to their homes in the U.S. The Organized Morticians had put on a big campaign to bring them home to their loved ones and had gotten Congress to appropriate $250 for the burial and also an appropriate headstone for the grave. Any extras, of course, were to be paid for by the family and we should not be surprised to learn that those extras showed up in nearly every instance.
>
> I found that several of the G.R.S. people were on board and from them learned that only about one in ten of the caskets could be sure of containing the remains it purported to. The others had a sufficient number of the proper bones to make a complete skeleton, and that was that. They felt, even more strongly than we did, that the pressure to 'bring them home' amounted to little more than a racket.[68]

Mervyn Burke went on to compare this racket to other prohibition era rackets. Perhaps he or his informant exaggerated. By the

time he wrote the memoir, he had become a man of the twenties
with the corrupt government of Harding to disparage. He was no
longer a doughboy under the moral suasion of Woodrow Wilson
and General Pershing. But a 10, or 20 or 30 per cent accuracy
record of the GRS men would not have satisfied anybody worried
about the identity of the soldier in the coffin.

Some people probably put their fears about the identity of the
man in the coffin to rest because they needed bodies to support
their particular cause, but the strength of meaning provided by
possession of a body, any body, was such, that it settled questions
of identity and doubts about purpose by its own presence. A body
is already the sign of what was a man or woman. Having made
the one act of interpretation, it is perhaps easier to make the
second, that if it is the wrong body, then it can be the sign of the
right body, or a sign of all other bodies. Receiving bodies home,
families assured themselves that their son or husband would be
cared for symbolically, while perhaps some other family cared for
the right body. Every soldier body that came home was in a sense
an unknown soldier carrying a symbolic weight of the man buried
at Arlington, but with his purpose defined by his family, and his
meaning laid to rest in the context of a family plot in a local
churchyard, rather than a national military cemetery. That
meaning could be entirely personal and affectionate. A family
might feel their dead simply belonged at home. Or they might
bring their dead home to support an idea of American isolation.
They might leave their dead in Europe to advertise a new notion
of America as a world power, or they liked the idea of Americans
in a great cause maintaining their place for ever. Or they might
feel, as Theodore Roosevelt did when he learned of his son
Quentin's death, that a soldier's body belonged on the field
where he fell.[69] In any case, these bodies were potent symbols put
to rest in family grave yards.

Those left to the state could be used for causes, which however
worthy, they might not have agreed with. Addie W. Hunton and
Kathryn M. Johnson used their attachment to the dead for their
cause, the uplift of their people.

Looking out from our little kitchen window of the "Y" barrack,
we saw what seemed to us a wonderful sight. Two long lines
of soldiers were before us – one moving slowly over the hill
and the other coming up the main road – each man bearing

on his shoulder a single white cross that would rest above the grave of a fellow-hero. Quickly our mind traveled back over the centuries to Him who had borne the cross towards Golgotha, and we saw in these dark-skinned sons of America bearing those white crosses, something of the same humility and something of the same sorrow that characterized the master, but we also beheld in them the Christ Spirit grown large, beautiful and eternal with the ages.[70]

These two African-American YMCA workers were watching preparations for an inspection of the graveyard at Romagne by General Pershing. They might have seen Christ in the grace of the black soldiers who carried those white crosses. They were setting the stage, using the strongest symbols available, for the continuation of their struggle with a culture that gave them a subordinate role.

The dead have held an extraordinary place in American culture. Americans, far more than Europeans, have tended to equate culture and civilization with the manner in which the dead have been treated. Philippe Ariès has pointed this out, discussing the park-like settings for graves, and the elaborate ritual around the funeral home in the United States. "The city of the dead is the obverse of the society of the living, or rather than the obverse, it is its image, its intemporal image. For the dead have gone through the moment of change, and their monuments are the visible sign of the permanence of their city." In the nineteenth century, the United States was so characterized by change that such signs of permanence took on special importance.[71] Stanley French has discussed the invention of the park-graveyard as proof that America had culture and history during the nineteenth century, when rapid urban growth and industrialization were wiping out material evidence of both. The park-graveyards of the nineteenth century became premier tourist attractions, places to take foreign visitors.[72]

The American graveyards in France, while emphatic reminders of the participation of the United States in the war, also carry a perfected democratic version of the American park-graveyard abroad and became a touristic destination for Americans and Europeans too. In many ways, those graveyards re-enact the American Expeditionary Forces' role. Like American units at Belleau Wood and Soissons, they were well placed. They occupy uniformly dramatic settings at the top of hills, visible from a long way off in the flat countryside where Americans fought their important battles. Annette Becker, historian of World War I memorials, has given them first place in grandeur and as tourist attractions in the eastern French landscape that had very few attractions before.[73] They eclipse the graveyards of other nations by their arrangements. The builders used quantities of white marble for crosses or stars of David over every body, and in the classical monuments and romanesque chapels that dominate each site. The perfectly geometrical landscaping produces a democratic effect where each grave appears at the center of star shaped perspectives of green paths stretching in every direction. Grass and trees – American species adapted to the French climate – are kept in perfect condition. The American dead have been concentrated just as they were in the war. Pershing struggled hard, throughout American involvement in the war, to create a unified and independent American army operating in its own sector. The French and British always considered that the best use of American divisions was as replacements in their own sectors but by the Saint-Mihiel offensive in September 1918, Pershing had at last succeeded. He commanded the dead just as he did the living, not allowing his units to be spread among foreign commands. They make an impressive and permanent American presence today, just as the AEF made an American presence on the battlefield in the war of attrition. They mark an outpost of American culture that American tourists can visit abroad, and an American stage upon which American dignitaries can act in a foreign place.

Of course far fewer American dead from World War I lie buried in France than the dead of other countries involved. The numbers vary depending on how and when the counting was done and partly because the cemeteries represent an open-ended American presence in Europe. Bodies of men who died from wounds were not always included in early figures. Soldiers and nurses from the Army of Occupation and other units stationed in Europe in the 1920s and 1930s were added. Bodies were repatriated. Bodies were added from World War II, increasing the scale and significance of the cemeteries. American men and women serving with NATO forces have been buried in cemeteries built for World War I. Figures between 70,000 and 100,000 American World War I dead are common. Of these, the Graves Registration Service stated with unblushing precision that it shipped 45,588 to the United States and 764 to European places of birth. Thus, as few as 25, or as many as 54 thousand Americans dead from World War One were left to be memorialized in those cemeteries.[74] The dead in the British, French and German cemeteries number in the millions. At the American cemeteries, until World War II, architects consciously used landscaping and materials and concentration to mask the small numbers of American dead who might be invisible among the dead of other countries in any other arrangement.[75]

General Pershing continued to serve among these armies of the dead. Between the wars, he traveled among the American grave-yards, overseeing the construction in stone of the permanent counters from the war in which each side waited for the other to run out of men and material. He had concentrated his troops once more into a progressive vision of American values: democracy, faith, and the power that comes with unity and efficiency where every man knows his place. He dedicated his memoirs to the Unknown Soldier in 1931. But, as with other progressive attempts to organize Americans in World War I, many escaped the cemeteries. Like the men refusing to become good tourists, a good proportion of the dead, with the help of their families, lit out for the territory, in this case home.

Guardians of those same graveyards, as late as 1986, recalled General Pershing's visits and his contemplative promenades on horseback – he would send his charger, Blackjack, ahead of him by train. Horse and rider would move together among the rows of white crosses, but sometimes they strayed from the regimenta-tion of sorrow and into the nearby woods.

6 "The best place to live on Earth:" Lessons for the Doughboys' Return

But give me towns to westward, where
life moves not so slow,
With fewer castles, maybe, – more future
and less past

"Deauboie," "Farewell to Coblenz"

To help dampen complaints about delays in returning to the United States, *The Stars and Stripes* published, soon after the Armistice, a cartoon epitomizing the paper's ability to bend soldiers' thoughts in a direction desired by army authorities, while appearing to ignore that hierarchy and appealing to the good sense and better nature of soldiers themselves. Alexander Woollcott described this particular cartoon in a *Saturday Evening Post* story of 1928, "It was a chill corner of a battlefield, bare as the face of the moon. The drawing showed two stretchers covered with a muddy blanket. It was a sight too many of us had seen not to have known from the very contour and folds of those blankets that there were dead men underneath – dead men waiting for the burial squad to saunter past and stick them somewhere underground. But it was the title of his cartoon that transformed it into as telling a tale as ever I saw – effective in its little movement of time as sometimes a hand may be when it is lifted to still a tumult. The drawing was called 'The First to Go Home.' "[1]

On one level, the import of C. Le Roy Baldridge's cartoon could be understood like the reminder to children who won't eat, that other people in the world go hungry: do not complain, you are much better off than others. But as a drawing, coming from a fellow soldier, and not from any apparent authority, it commanded greater respect. It gained power from the unresolvable meaning of bodies themselves: it was a drawing of unknown bodies, that could be signs of specific dead or signs of all the war dead, which at the same time are signs of the living, and signs of

188

the causes for which men have died and the living have struggled. That the dead should be called "The First to Go Home" pretended that the question of what American dead represented had been resolved. They had gone home to God who knew their worth and the worth of their sacrifice, and the news of their death would eventually reach their homes in the United States, where loved ones would undertake the sentimental resolution of their life's meaning and the meaning of their loss. Though in fact little was certain about the identity of the dead just after the Armistice, and it would take years to determine their final resting place and move them to it, the AEF's newspaper made a certainty of death and left the surviving soldiers with the task of finding certainties in life worthy of that sacrifice.

Unable to return home to the United States for the first six months after the Armistice, most soldiers saw their lives and their purpose as uncertain. Discipline and morale suffered as a consequence. The army quickly helped American soldiers make uplifting interpretations of the part they had taken in the war. The tourism of the American Expeditionary Forces ranks as such an effort started almost a year before the Armistice. The education program of the AEF culminating in the founding of the American Expeditionary Forces University at Beaune, in the Côte d'Or section of France, represented the most conscious expression of the notion that the war should have produced Americans better equipped for the future.[2]

This extraordinary educational program cannot be understood separately from the context of the war as conducted by Americans: the fighting, the leave area system, the memorialization of the dead. That context made the claims of the educational program believable and desirable, though like the leave area system, and like the cartoon of "The First to Go Home," the education program also served the very practical purpose of quieting complaints until the real task of the army – after the Armistice its return home and demobilization – could be accomplished.

The organization of the American army's educational system and the curriculum at the American Expeditionary Forces University at Beaune formalized and taught a version of American progress. The army's post-Armistice educational aims, elaborated by General Pershing's staff in February, 1919, were aimed at needs of soldiers in their future role as civilians pushing the United States forward. The orders creating the AEF University made this quite clear: "This citizen army must return to the United States prepared to take an active and intelligent part in the future progress of our country."[3]

The army established secondary schools at army posts and, for army divisions, high schools and technical schools came into being. These schools offered everything from horseshoeing to automobile repair, telegraphy to telephone wiring, all to cover the possible needs and the educational desires of members of a society moving into the twentieth century. Division commanders had ordered surveys of their units to determine educational needs. Orders permitted 15 per cent of any AEF unit to go to school, relieved of all but one hour of military duty per day. At the beginning of American involvement in the war, Secretary Baker had made the analogy between college students and soldiers when considering army recreation, now the army accomplished the transition from soldier, through student, back to new American citizen.

Arrangements were also made to send American soldiers to the universities of France and Britain for the Spring term of 1919. And since those "university opportunities" were of graduate character and were "therefore available only to selected men of high educational qualifications," an AEF educational center was established to provide college and technical training beyond that offered at division educational centers.[4] This educational center became the American Expeditionary Forces University at Beaune, an institution intended to reproduce in France the atmosphere and training of an American university for 40,000 men, to contain an agricultural college, a technical school, and to provide elementary training.

Colonel Ira L. Reeves, the military "president" of the University – he resisted whenever he could the more military title of commander – explained the purpose of the university:

> We are here to serve the Army primarily, and it is the wish of the Commander-in-Chief, as I interpret it, that every effort be made to return the soldier to his home a better qualified man in every way to meet the obligations which will confront him in civil life, that he left when he enrolled as a soldier to fight his country's battles.[5]

For Reeves, a soldier had "enrolled" in the army the way he might enroll in a class. In either case, he had every right to emerge edified by his experience. The war should have made the world safe for democracy, while it trained individuals for the future.

According to the army's University Council, the AEF University held a position at the cutting edge of American education. They had the power and the freedom to found a university without history, along completely rational lines, suited to the needs of students and America.

> The absence of hampering traditions and the presence of unusual problems all suggest an opportunity of organizing here such an educational system as many of us should like to see in the United States – that is, a system so unified from the elementary to the graduate schools that every man can find in college, in the post school or in division school classes, the particular instruction that he needs. The entire system will be represented at Beaune.[6]

In the middle of the United States Army, a progressive, rationalized, democratic educational institution grew. Any soldier with a high school diploma could go. The University would fulfill the progressive principles of efficiency and uplift by providing a coherent program from elementary through graduate school to the broadest possible range of American citizens.

As they improvised a university, administrators at Beaune were understandably self-conscious, even defensive, about the innovative role their university would play. They wanted to include all kinds of Americans and meet all their educational needs, and they wanted their institution to compare well with institutions in the United States. In their final report on the AEF University at Beaune, they made careful comparisons with other American institutions. They explained the differences saying that theirs was the university leading the way towards more democratic education, offering what the students desired. For example, far more students at Beaune chose business courses than did students in the United States. The explanation for this was simple.

> The students at the American E. F. University in Beaune were ordered in from among all high-school graduates in the American Expeditionary Forces, with the understanding that

they would be given instruction in such subjects as they
individually desired ... The registration given here may be a
fairly clear indication of the proportion of men graduating
from high-schools who desire higher education in some form
of business, but are persuaded they can afford neither the time
nor the expense.[7]

The report implied that if universities in the United States
followed the same kind of pragmatic approach to students,
offering them what they wanted and what they could use, similar
concentrations of business students would be found there. The
engineering school at Beaune was under-subscribed, when compared to its counterparts in the United States, because of "The
eager desire for a better knowledge of how to do real things well."
Apparently, fighting, or at least involvement in war, had taught
young Americans to get results. Men who had become pragmatic
in the army, considered engineering, with its insistence on
mathematics and physics, too abstract. Their university, rather
than upholding abstract standards, reflected a new, pragmatic
standard.[8]

The tension between democracy in education and the maintenance of standards in education ran through all discourse about
the institution's goals. The final report of the University addressed the "absence of our accustomed American machinery for
entrance examinations," by saying that, "The work of education
in the Army has obviously a teaching rather than an examining
function." In the view of the administrators, it was "more
important that we should help any member of the AEF who
desires to improve himself than that we should issue certificates."
Thus, the university opened the doors to higher education to
anyone who wished for it in the army, which is to say to a very
much broader cross-section of the population of the United States
than had gained that privilege at home.

African-Americans seem to have been excepted from this open
admissions policy. The university documents do not include any
stated policy on race. Letters to and from Colonel Reeves
indicate that he would have favored an integrated institution, but
he reluctantly accepted the status quo of the segregated AEF.
Reeves himself wrote to a fellow university administrator, regret-
ting the necessity of segregating the farm school at Beaune. He
must have assumed that the preponderance of black soldiers

would require agricultural training and that they would have to be kept separate from white student-soldiers. The existence of several letters from African-American soldiers requesting information about the AEF University showed that no one made it clear to soldiers whether or not the university would uphold the army's policy of segregation. These letters also show that if any African-American soldiers attended classes at the university itself, they must have been a tiny minority.[9]

Excepting African-American enrollment, the men who directed the University accepted the lack of restrictions on admissions, and relaxed testing, for practical reasons, and because the students, rather than being unformed American youth, had already submitted to their nation's standard in service. Their task was to turn that newly formed national standard to good civilian use. They hardly had a right to exclude anyone who had already met the test of the army in wartime, and now requested the recompense of uplift. The black soldiers who wrote to Colonel Reeves made their requests for entrance in these terms, hoping that this new American standard applied to them as well.

Higher education in the United States during the same academic year, 1918–19, moved in the opposite direction from the de-militarizing tendency of the AEF University. Back in the United States, universities and colleges were militarized by the Student Army Training Corps (SATC) in order to prepare young college men for the trials and sacrifices of war. Student soldiers at American universities in the United States wore uniforms and marched in groups to class. They stood guard over buildings and checked the identity papers of their professors. These military activities took precedence over more scholarly pursuits, and performance in the traditional sciences and humanities suffered as a result.

On opposite sides of the Atlantic, American education moved in opposite directions. Institutions in the United States imposed military standards of disciplined behavior on their students. Columbia University led the way when her president Nicholas Murry Butler offered what he called his "army" of students and faculty for service to the United States in the Fall of 1917. In France, the army de-militarized soldiers, reducing their army duties almost to nothing. The standards of discipline and Americanness had been met during the fighting. Now that sacrifice had to be turned to some civilian good.[10]

The course in Citizenship that every member of any AEF school was required to attend on Saturday mornings attempted to translate military sacrifice into civic virtue. The centralization of the army's school organization permitted complete uniformity in the course all over France. An address was prepared by a well-known speaker, for example Raymond B. Fosdick spoke on social customs one week and Herbert Hoover spoke, at another time, on the world's food supply. The army printed these hour-long talks in bulletins for every member of the schools. Surrogate speakers, often drawn from the ranks of "four minute men," volunteers of the Committee on Public Information who spoke before movies and shows, delivered the talks to groups of 200 men in the first hour of school Saturday morning. Discussion, movies, and lantern slides followed for two more hours. The army's efficiency allowed famous men to make a uniform presentation to the thousands concentrated at Beaune and to multitudes all over France in a single Saturday morning without those celebreties necessarily being present at any school.[11]

Of the talks delivered at these Saturday Morning classes, "The Principles of Democratic Government" by William J. Newlin, Professor of Philosophy at Amherst College, gives the flavor of what was meant by citizenship and how the army and World War I contributed to that understanding. First, Newlin made the distinction between personal interests and common interests.

> Personal interests, it is true, may cause men to unite for a time in a common cause. It is more likely to divide them and make them bitter rivals. A gang of thieves will stick together against the police; yet they will fight among themselves for their booty when the time comes to divide.
>
> You know this is not the spirit of Democracy. It was not this that welded our people into an army, and fused the nations of the world into a victorious alliance.

He told the men that they had been part of a great welded unit that had first transcended the barriers of individuality and then joined together the people of different nations for a great achievement. He went on to interpret that experience for Americans using the images of war propaganda with which these men were so familiar.

One of the posters advertising the fifth, the "Victory" loan, shows America pointing to a "Roll of Honor" on which are inscribed 17 names – names of 17 American soldiers who gave their lives in fighting for a common cause. Those names are the names of one of 17 different nationalities – from English to Greek, from French to Slav – Americans all. What force welded such widely diverse elements into unity? Something that makes them give up life itself if thereby they can help to win for their fellows that which they all value in common – freedom and liberty and justice for all men, everywhere, the right of self-determination; and the opportunity for unhindered self-development.[12]

That Americans had died in World War I, according to Newlin, required Americans to take away some important lessons which he was ready to supply. The lessons Americans should take from the war were that individuals from different nations, welded by a common cause, can achieve great things, and that World War I provided the big issues capable of this sort of metallurgy. These issues or forces, included "freedom and justice for all" from the new "Pledge of Allegiance," self-determination from Wilson's "fourteen points," and a phrase from the rhetoric of uplift: "unhindered self-development." In Newlin's message, Wilson's rhetoric about the rise of nations is inextricably linked to a notion of personal advancement, one of the progressive glues for a diverse society. Nations were to rise as a result of World War I, but just as surely, individual Americans were to experience advances too.

Death had played just as important a part in unifying the seventeen men of Newlin's example as the issues for which they died. Immigrant blood and flesh had mingled in common graves, and this had created a united American population. In the strictest sense, of course, only the dead had been fused into this Americanism. But, Newlin's audience, by their association with the dead in the same army characterized by standardized values and reactions, shared the Americanism of their dead comrades. They owed it to the dead to adhere to this American piety. The sacrifice would have meant little otherwise.

Army training and the kind of standard suggested by the movies of Frank Gilbreth became a model for good citizenship of the future as Newlin continued.

Even as drill practice, and training made you better soldiers, so thoughtful attention to some of the problems of citizenship may enable you to be better and more efficient citizens. What you have won by fighting must be held by voting. Marksmanship is as important when aiming the ballot as when aiming the bullet.[13]

He attached typical progressive rhetoric to the imagery of military training. These men should vote for cleaner cities, cleaner government, better schools, all to preserve the gains for the world won by the sacrifice that had unified them. The progressive goal of assimilation had already been achieved by the war. The course in citizenship served to underline those gains, and exhorted the men to preserve them through vigilance.

The uplift resulting from the war could also be expressed in art, and the AEF included art at the University at Beaune, and in its education schemes elsewhere too. A lecture in the importance of art was included in the Saturday morning course in citizenship attended by all the thousands of soldier students in the AEF. The lecture by George S. Hellman called "Applied Arts and Education" explained that the standard of danger, hardship and bravery established by the war had liberated American men to become artistic.

We are henceforth done with the old belief that art is a thing apart, a frill, a mere ornament of life – something almost effeminate. We can learn at this very University that hands which held firmly the bloody bayonet are now eager to grasp the architects's T-square, the painter's palette, the chisel of the sculptor.

Just as war had established a standard of citizenship that only needed to be pointed out, it had established a standard of American manliness that had made the arts respectable. No example of a veteran who wished to trade in his bloody bayonet for an artist's tools needed to exist. The possibility existed. "In the years to come," said George Hellman's surrogates to the thousands of American soldier-students in France, "it is our land that will wrest from Europe the leadership in the realm of art; for Europe is old and weary and we are fresh and young."[14]

The paintings and sculptures actually produced by those students showed little promise of a new, vigorous American style imbued with a fighting masculine spirit. An issue of the *Revue de Bourgogne* entirely devoted to the AEF University presented a selection of the student art. There were impressionistic pictures of the French countryside, drawings of medieval streets in Beaune, a Hercules, and, astonishingly for art produced by veterans of the war that ushered in modernity, a picture of putti harvesting wheat.[15] The more advanced students at the AEF Art Training center at Bellevue, near Paris, showed a strict adherence to the models of traditional French Beaux Arts training. Soldiers learned interior decoration in the styles of the various French kings. They created architectural drawings on the same subjects given for the French academic competitions of 1919: a riding school, and a restaurant by a lake.[16] To look for signs of a liberated American originality, some sort of vigor enhanced by the war, is to miss the point. The war provided a common experience after which unity, masculinity and loyalty to America could all be assumed.

Soldier-students of the AEF left few detectable traces of what they actually thought of the educational program they received. Few soldiers recorded any kind of formal education in their diaries and letters. Years later, when they filled out the survey of the United States Army Military History Institute, they remembered how badly their benefits compared with the GI bill of rights after World War II, but not the educational opportunities offered by the AEF. The lack of echoes of that AEF education may reflect how brief and insubstantial that education finally was. The AEF University, after all, lasted only a matter of months. However ambitious to return improved citizen soldiers to the United States, the program never had the resources of the GI Bill that held out the possibility of years of higher education to over ten million soldiers (but not female military personnel) in the 1940s.[17] Colonel Reeves and his collaborators improvised the program after World War I. It should hardly come as a surprise that the major trace of their work was their hopeful language.

That hopeful language of practical idealism did have its effect on some students. Student interest in business and practical training was noted in the Beaune Register. Business courses were especially in demand and copies of texts on business and salesmanship out-number by hundreds other books available at the university's library. Soldier-students connected cultural exchange

with making money. As one administrator noted, they saw France
as a business opportunity.

> French instruction seems to me of the utmost importance since
> many of the men who are asking for it have in mind future
> business relations with the French, and are extremely serious
> in wishing a practical grasp of the language.[18]

Eight hundred men had petitioned for further instruction in
French. The language of uplift and business opportunity was the
language they had chosen to use for their request. Whether or
not these soldiers were sincere, they had learned how to present
an argument that would appeal to their progressive superiors.

Soldier students often made the connection between business,
culture and uplift. The business courses that so many of them
took at the AEF University certainly aimed them in that direction. Popular publications available to soldiers also made this
point. And many returning soldiers found it to their advantage to
emphasize how the war had improved them for American life
and for business. Self-promotion, promotion of the AEF University, and promotion of the importance of the American contribution to the war were not particularly distinct ideas.

Finding a way to translate the victory in Europe into personal
victories of social advancement was an important part of how
veterans talked and wrote about the war. Popular magazines
made the future of the doughboy their special concern. Self-
help literature poured out a stream of optimism on the subject.
Some soldiers contributed to this torrent, others must have consumed it.

The process of this translation of war into peacetime progress
has come down to us in a negative form in the novels of the
expatriate American writers of the 1920s and 1930s. It could not
be done according to the literary. Ernest Hemingway's characters
resisted the translation of their wartime achievements and assured
sense of masculinity into success in commercial American terms
just as surely as they preferred not to return to America. John
Dos Passos's *The Big Money* examined this translation more
directly, complete with a post-1929 criticism about business
culture. Descending a ladder of degradation, Dos Passos's fiction-
al Charlie Anderson, a returning flying ace, contributed his
wartime experience first to the new aeronautics industry, but
eventually to financial manipulations on Wall Street. He ends up

a high-living drunk, crushed in an automobile accident shortly before the market crash of 1929. The romantic appertainances with which F. Scott Fitzgerald endowed Jay Gatsby included a military decoration from Montenegro, and a period at Oxford University provided by the AEF's education program along with the officer's uniform that first won him access to the house of his love, Daisy. These signs of respectability and substance proved hollow for Gatsby was a bootlegger redeemed by his strength as a dreamer.[19]

Just after the war, the language of ordinary Americans, how-ever, more closely resembled the boosterism of magazine articles than postwar literary disillusion. Some tried a direct approach, fitting their experience into the traditions of inspirational uplift and success literature. Lt. John Seerly, an ace from a flying squadron, let it be known in *The New Success*, a magazine promoting Horatio Alger-like notions of self-help, that the war had prepared him uniquely for business. It had taught him the value of training, it had taught him to "look at everything from its larger aspect." He seems to have thought of his relations with the army and with other members of the AEF as a business contract to beat the Kaiser. He had:

> shaken hands, figuratively, with every man in the American army, on the biggest bet any of us had ever made – namely, that together we could squelch the kaiser, we "got together" in a comradely fashion that would have stopped class struggles over here long ago if each of us had not been too stubborn in the past to give way an inch on account of misunderstanding. A better world and a better spirit of business is bound to come with the returning soldier.[20]

Seerly's position as a former ace perhaps gave him a certain advantage over many regular soldiers coming out of the war. His record of "nearly a score," of destroyed German planes in his five months of flying had made him a celebrity. In fact, he had never been without advantages. Before his flying career, he had at-tended the University of Chicago and had planned to enter law school. His successes during the war changed the course of his life from law to business. He gave his reason for this change of plan in *The New Success*. War had in some way removed prejudices from people's view of college men, "War showed that college men were all right. They responded to a man when the call came.

This fact has helped to remove a heap of prejudice against them."
In his view, before the war, college had been a disadvantage in
business, and had fit him only for the law or some other
profession. After the war, which he called the best preparation for
American business, he was ready to fit into the American world
of business, a seemingly higher, more American and more manly
calling than law. Education, once suspect in the American setting,
had become acceptable after the test of war.

The New Success made a cult of returning American war heroes.
Theodore Roosevelt Jr., who had attained the rank of Lt. Colonel
in the AEF, was hailed in an article called "Theodore Roosevelt
Jr., in His Father's Political Footsteps." The article recounted Lt.
Colonel Roosevelt's path to success. He had attended Groton and
played football for Harvard. After graduating early from Harvard, he had worked his way from the "bottom up" in a carpet
manufacturing firm. From there, he moved to the bond department of a Wall Street firm, and from there to the army. During
the war, he rose in rank, was wounded several times and
decorated. After the war, he devoted himself to the formation of
the American Legion. *The New Success* felt this would make the
basis for a political career. The narrative of his life presented in
its pages moved from success on the college football field to
business success, to military success and bravery, to the possibilities of political success, as if success in each of these realms
logically led to the next.[21] *The New Success* and its editor, the great
spokesman for American uplift, Orison Swett Marden, saw the
war as an agent that perfected Theodore Roosevelt, Jr. for the
highest level, politics, where a man would need the approbation
of the American people, not skills and privileges gained in elite
educational institutions. In war, the stigma of privilege had
rubbed off Roosevelt, as it had rubbed off the new businessman
Seerly. Roosevelt had learned to live and soldier, and his values
had become adjusted according to the same American standard
held by the Americans who whould be his constituents.

Marden and his magazine, so enthusiastic for advancement
brought on by the war, admitted few difficulties even for the
wounded and disabled. An article described the life of American
soldiers in a New York hospital as something of a miracle of
progress because of the size of the enterprise. The Army had
taken over one of the great abandoned department stores on
lower Fifth avenue and turned it into the "biggest hospital in the

world." It could hold 4,000 soldier patients in its 600,000 square feet of space. The biggest war ever required the biggest hospital ever, and that looked like progress. Any destructive and tragic aspect of the war receded. Wounded men became the neutral cause for all the useful activity and organization of American doctors and nurses. The wounded soldiers soon would share a picture of progress with the rest of the country.[22]

War at its most horrific, where it had torn limbs off men's bodies, could be transformed into a positive good. "It is a seeming paradox that a war-disabled man should find his disability the means of his real success, but it is absolutely true," proclaimed an article in *The New Success*.

> Take the instance of that bakery-wagon driver and clerk who received $11 a week before he volunteered: He came back with valvular heart-disease and neurasthenia, was re-educated in the commercial course, and is now a stenographer at $100 a month. Or one of the many farmer boys: This one lost his left foot. As a farm laborer, he was doing well to be paid $30 a month and board. He took the farm-tractor course, and is employed at $100 per month and board, operating the tractor which pulls a battery of gangplows, harrows, seeders. There are dozens of other farmer boys who have done as well . . . The disabled veteran of to-day doesn't want charity. All he wants is a chance! He wants a chance to slip back into a place in civil life where he can make his way on his merits, even as he made his way forward in France.[23]

The article described many examples of men who had suffered agonies in the trenches of France, in the same conditions that scarred a generation of Europeans, but who through re-education, made available to them by the army, had actually improved their station in life.

Richard M. Huber has described Orison Swett Marden as someone who "bobbed along atop the currents of fashion, carried first in one direction, then in another, drifting with the strong tides of the success idea." In the year following the Armistice, he found it easy to relate the success of American soldiers in France to all kinds of success in the United States in spite of evidence to the contrary. No strong tide of disillusion washed these shores yet.[24]

The optimistic language of men like Marden contrasted sharply with the record of reintegrating soldiers, especially the wounded, into American society. Investigators of the scandals of the Harding administration eventually revealed the dismal success rate of the federal efforts to rehabilitate soldiers in the early years after the war. Education, vocational training, rehabilitation and medical benefits for the estimated 200,000 disabled veterans became the province of the well-funded Veterans Bureau. *The New Success* reported conditions with astonishing optimism considering the corruption of the Veterans Bureau during the Harding administration under Charles R. Forbes, and of the Federal Bureau for Vocational Rehabilitation that preceded it. Hundreds of millions of dollars disappeared. Contracts for the construction of hospitals were signed but the buildings were not built. To receive benefits, former soldiers had to offer substantial proofs that they had indeed been injured in the war while letters supporting their claims were left unopened. At the beginning of the 1920s, though staffed with thousands of clerks, the Federal Bureau for Vocational Rehabilitation had accepted only 24,000 men of an estimated 110,000 eligible, and because of incompetence and delays, had a 30 per cent drop-out rate. By the early 1920s, the organization had only retrained 217 men.[25]

In 1919, two million former soldiers returning from Europe and two million released from training camps, all looking for work, strained a job market, already hurt by a post-war slow down in production. With these conditions coming after wartime inflation it is not surprising that 1919 saw thirty-six hundred strikes, the re-emergence of radical political parties on the left, and accompanying suppression from attorney general, A. Mitchell Palmer. Studies linked criminality with military experience in the 1920s. Former medical officers, who made a psychiatric study in Wisconsin where 20 per cent of prison inmates were veterans, concluded that "Nothing in war is uplifting, at least not for the humbler participants."[26]

The preparation of soldiers for their return to the United States and to civilian life had not been adequate and their integration took place under difficult circumstances to say the least. However, some men could speak of that time with superlative optimism: "I learned America was the best place to live on Earth."[27] Men with ambition used that training's enthusiastic language and attempted to rise in business while they still wore the uniform of the AEF. They felt that they lost time while away from business in the army. Soldiers could remain optimistic about their chances, however, and could hope that their experience would make them worth more to a business than they had been before. Clarence Akerley wrote to his step-father, who ran the family business,

> I am very anxious to step out and get down to business again, as two years is quite a length of time to lose especially when a person has to drop everything as I did, after doing so well. I am hoping that I will be able to step into broader steps for the future.[28]

This soldier admitted the time lost but had no doubts that it could be made up and saw himself as moving into a position of greater responsibility, perhaps as a result of his war experience.

The war could be so short for some Americans that it hardly interrupted their business lives. One man, whose first preserved letter to his wife from France bore the date November 3, 1918, only stopped thinking about his business in America long enough to condemn France and England. On November 10, 1918, he wrote,

> I dream and dream of those good times that we are planning ... I sometimes wonder just what the condition of business will be and just what I should do. I suppose I should go over to Chicago for a few weeks and get that special work ... I have seen some of England and part of this country and I will never have a desire to see these countries again. The US is so far ahead of England and France that I wonder at there being as many inhabitants in these countries as there are.[29]

His experience of war confirmed his belief in American business. His American dream had the strength to carry him "over to Chicago for a few weeks," even while he remained under military discipline half a continent and an ocean away.

When there was a story to tell, a veteran could assume a promotional tone. There is nothing of the reticent man who has seen too much pain to speak in the regimental history related by George Beekman.

> The story I am going to tell has not been dug out of musty manuscripts, nor is it concerned with the remote past. It comes

hot from the lips of men who know whereof they speak, and it deals with the terrific experiences and glorious achievement of a regiment which has played a vital part in the winning of this greatest and latest of wars.[30]

This man created an historical archive of his unit in order to write a regimental history. Promoting his unit and the "greatness" of the war appeared compatible.

Veterans made speeches and told the stories of their experiences to business men's luncheons, to Rotary Club meetings, and to hometown newspapers. Some encountered difficulty relating what they had learned in Europe at these boosterish functions. But the personal nature or harsh reality of the experience did not cause the problem. The problem arose from the increasingly negative interpretations of the results of the war as the 1920s progressed and America turned isolationist.

Personal experiences of war recounted before such an audience could only be positive, after all the speaker had survived something terrible, and here he was at home, in a better place, working towards a prosperous future. But the US Senate's rejection of the Versailles Treaty separated the American political consequences of war from its positive personal memory and any on going European reality. That separation of memory from political reality made the war tales difficult to tell if they included too much information about 1920s Germany. Mervyn Burke, a member of the returning Army of Occupation tried to explain the resentment felt by Germany to the Treaty of Versailles and what he called the "fifteen points" to a Rotary Club luncheon, as late as 1923.

> It was my first time at one of these "knife and fork" club affairs and I was given quite an introduction. Not one of these business leaders of Santa Rosa, [California] had a single question as to conditions in Germany. After that I kept off the subject.[31]

His status as veteran had earned him an introduction to and luncheon with the business leaders of his town. They wished to hear the uplifting story of his struggle in war that earned him his place. By 1923, the Rotary Club must have known that it could integrate veterans and their experiences into the business life of the community. If anything, the business community had learned to integrate a positive post-war feeling too well, and excluded any new information.

Burke embarked on a new stage of his life when he gave that Rotary Club talk. He had just left the army and these quotations from his memoir put a period to that piece of writing. Like so many other soldier-diarists, he kept his war experience in a separate volume from the rest of his life.

> Back to San Francisco and the final formalities, physical exams, etc., and I was out of the army. Thus ended seven years that had been rather eventful for what started as a pretty green country kid. It also marked the beginning of a new adult civilian life with new responsibilities and the foundation of a family life that has continued almost sixty years.[32]

Looking back at his life, this veteran found that his years in the army and the time he spent in France during World War I prepared the way for his adult life.

Living through a destructive war might have caused soldiers to reject ideas of taking up their domestic place in an industrial society. They might easily have rejected the positive interpretations that were thrown at them by various propaganda agencies. Having lived for several years in the embrace of positive slogans, soldiers seem to have accepted them, if not as literally true, at least as a necessary part of sustained military effort, like uniforms. Criticism of the war slogans and a relentlessly positive interpretation of the war, at least as it appeared in *The Stars and Stripes*, rather than presenting an opposing point of view only took the position that the war rhetoric could have been better, more original, and more varied. It did not criticize the idea that Americans should be provided with slogans, it only criticized the quality and quantity of those slogans.

> "Do our bit" and "do our darnedest," "slacker," "bomb-proof" and the rest,
> Of the hackneyed war-terms bore me like a bullet from the Boche;
> "Crown the Crown Prince!" Bean the Bertha" – oh, they're all a blooming pest,
> And if they don't stop saying 'em, I'll squeal to General Foch.
> "Ships will win the war, and aeros," – I have heard that line before;

"They shall not pass" – I weary of the finest of the bunch!
They all were grand the first time, but, repeated o'er and o'er,
The best of war-time slogans sure is bound to lose its punch.

Can't they issue us new sayings as they issue us new pants?
Can't they put originality in patriotic spiels?
Can't they think up something peppy, new, to get the boys
    in France,
Or are we to be handed out the same old verbal deals?
Our grub's the same from day to day, our clothes are all one cut,
Our drills, and our policing with monotony are rife;
Oh, I wish on those old war-cries that the trap-door firm
    would shut –
They were great once; but variety's the spice of Army life![33]

The author and the editors of *The Stars and Stripes* – and the
editors may sometimes have written anonymous poetry like this
– said here that they and their soldier readers understood and
could accept opinion formed by central slogan smiths, as long as
those slogans were made interesting, and made to suit, like a new
pair of pants, fit for consumption. The striking metaphors from
the consumer market suggest that soldiers neither resisted the
propaganda handed out to them consistently, nor accepted it
whole. Rather they made "verbal deals," picking and chosing
among opinions provided centrally for their consumption.

Perhaps *The Stars and Stripes* could not come much closer than
this to direct criticism of anything so central to the American war
effort as the creation and dissemination of positive war rhetoric
and propaganda. After all, *The Stars and Stripes* itself was an
important and privileged part of the army's opinion-making
system. In fact, *The Stars and Stripes* often struck this mild
humorous note on potentially troublesome shortcomings of army
life. But the feelings that the paper, written by and for soldiers,
chose to evoke must have already existed among the soldiers. If
they could not recognize themselves in the stories and poetry of
their newspaper, it would not have been effective.

Published soldier poetry could be critical, but always in a
humorous way. A signed poem offered a critique of the direction
American life seemed to be taking during the war. The regimentation of army life in "Line Up! Fall In!" has overtaken its
author's life until all he remembers of his tour of Paris is waiting
in line for tour literature and metro tickets. He wonders,

> . . . if, when I get home
> To wear a derby on my dome
> And strut around in civvy pants,
> I'll find things there as here in France!
> And it 'twill be, as it has been
> For everything, Line Up! Fall in!
>
> Line up to greet the folks and girl,
>   Fall in for civvy life,
> Line up to get your old job back,
>   Fall in to get a wife;
> And when you quit this vale of woe
>   To pass to realms on high,
> Line up to catch your death of cold,
>   Fall in, at last, to die![34]

So accustomed had this soldier become to army ways, to regimentation and standardization, that he could easily imagine these qualities dominating his homelife. He was certain he would not like such a change in his country nor in himself. In the last verse, satire only narrowly overcame his dispair of salvaging any individual life from the power of wartime organization.

Americans did not understand the war and its accompanying efficiencies and standardizations as unalloyed opportunity and progress. But if they had doubts about these effects of the war, they had still learned to look for them and respect them and connect progress with the United States. In this respect, the more soldiers learned about Europe, the better America looked. Even the American Army of Occupation's tasks looked more like a tour than an invasion of Germany. Ultimately, these tours taught Americans more about America than about Europe. One soldier explained how exposure to Europe had intensified his feelings for home in verse.

> Yes, Coblenz town's a fine town, as towns
>   in Europe go,
> But give me towns to westward, where
>   life moves not so slow,
> With fewer castles, maybe, – more future
>   and less past,
> And then I'll give up roaming, and settle
>   down at last.[35]

Unit newspapers that printed poems like this disseminated propaganda as much as they represented the thoughts of soldiers. Such newspapers existed as a meeting ground of opinion somewhere between a YMCA man's speeches and the letters of soldiers. Many American themes – and an Americanization that could only be accomplished by seeing the old world and thus learning about the new – were represented here: America became the land of progress; Europe of the past. Americans can visit that past, appreciate it; but Americans choose to settle down somewhere less slow than Europe. In fact, the contents of Europe, whatever they were, could only be a lesson in the appreciation of America.

Some Americans considered the dissemination of an American tourist's assurance of his home's superiority to have been among the greatest boons of the war. John Kendrick Bangs, through his connection with the "Comrades in Service," an "instrument of Morale Preservation which in the difficult days following the Armistice rendered invaluable service in upholding the 'Hold Together spirit of our lads not now fighting but marking time,' " wrote of this aspect of the war as if, for the men, reaffirmation of their loyalty to America had been the purpose of the war.

In his contact with American soldiers, he had found them uninterested in President Woodrow Wilson's Fourteen Points and the Wilsonian idea of Peace Without Victory. He had likewise found them irritated by the muddy degrading trenches, and the remoteness of their enemy in this modern war. American soldiers wished to beat Germany and individual Germans decisively. They desired, according to Bangs, a man-to-man confrontation. Like any organism in a Darwinist universe, they felt compelled to compete for the position of the best.

> They wanted to get out into the open and show Hans and Fritz that back in America a real fight was a face to face affair, in which the Party of the First Part was a Man and not a Mole, who wanted nothing so much as direct individual results that he could see with his own eyes, whether the Party of the Second Part was a bigger man than he or not.[36]

Bangs's words left the impression that Europeans were content being moles, not men, and were not so interested in comparing themselves with their adversaries. In his view, men's nationalism expressed itself in their preferences for certain types of battle.

How a soldier thought about his country, and how the war had stimulated those thoughts, interested Bangs even more than a soldier's preference for open battle. Through his liking for face-to-face confrontation, he might show his superiority to Europeans, but the ever-hopeful Bangs looked for evidence of war-improved Americans as well. He found this evidence in the new self-consciousness of their nationality that many soldiers gained from exposure to a foreign place. "Oh _ ll, yes _ Paris is all right; but, d _ n it ain't Fort Wayne!!" was the type of reply that most pleased Bangs when he spoke to American soldiers about the wonders of Europe. According to Bangs, such a reply showed,

> That while in all probability the bulk of our sons overseas had always in the past taken their own country for granted, and had thought little, if at all, on the values of American Citizenship, they were coming back not better Americans perhaps, but more devoted, and more appreciative sons of America than they had ever been before. Which is one of the benefits that, like a lovely flower having its roots in mire, have sprung up out of the chaos of muddy, bloody ruin into which the War has plunged the world.[37]

For Bangs, the war had improved American participants not by teaching them anything about the world or foreign culture, not by toughening them, or teaching them to act well under pressure, or teaching them any other martial virtue, but the war had improved them because it had made them into more loyal Americans. It had made them more loyal Americans simply by pitting their national identity against the national identities of others.

Just as the influential Orison Swett Marden's idea of success had changed during the war, so had John Kendrick Bangs's notion of an improved American changed because of the war. Marden's idea of success had started the war as character-building, self-discipline and active self-help that would improve and strengthen body and spirit and allow his disciples to win life's contest. After the war, he promoted the notion that positive thinking alone would attract success the way money in the bank attracted interest. For Bangs, the war provided a test of survival for Americans, but the most important change in them had not been any improvement, physical or mental. The war had not weeded out the bad Americans and strengthened the good. Rather Americans had learned to profess faith in their country. They had all learned a positive American rhetoric. That rhetoric, and the positive image of America it propagated, was "like a lovely flower" to these men who wished to publicize some gain from war.

Publicists of success and former progressives who had attached themselves to the reforming aspects of the war effort searched out this positive direction in the thought of the returning American soldiers. Many soldiers seem to have been ready to provide such evidence. Any number of soldier letters express the opinion that the writer would do anything to get home as quickly as possible, that France and the French were backward and strange, and that America was the best place on earth. "America was the burden of [soldiers'] thoughts," during that period after the Armistice and before soldiers could return home, according to John Kendrick Bangs, but "to concrete their ideas definitively was of course impossible, and it was here that Comrades in Service rendered a signal service not only to the men themselves, but to those of us at home as well who seek a leading insight into the innermost recesses of the soldier mind."

In May of 1919, prizes of 500, 250, and 100 francs were offered for the best essays written by a soldier still in Europe under the title, "Home – Then What?" The editors of the Paris editions of *The New York Herald, The Chicago Tribune,* and *The London Daily Mail* judged several hundred essays. The three prize winners, and excerpts from many others, were published under the title of the essay.[38] The contest motivated soldiers to write down positive ideas about America while they still held those ideas against the sharp relief of their European surroundings. Through publication, those American beliefs could be disseminated in the United States.

Private Marcelle H. Wallenstein of Atchison, Kansas, who won the first prize, believed American soldiers would return to the United States with a sense of American superiority enhanced. Europe had taught Americans something about the enjoyment of leisure and how to make a town square more picturesque, but Americans could easily reproduce these things at home now that they understood them through their education as tourists. Such things could be consumed and required no shift in cultural values, or any Europeanization. On the contrary, he believed soldiers had become isolationist and that America should cautiously stay clear of European and Asian affairs. American soldiers had newly confirmed their love for liberty and for the United States, which led them to believe in defense at home first.

Private Wallenstein felt soldiers had learned a combination of American "pep" and European enjoyment of life. The pep of army life had made soldiers ambitious. Each soldier would want his old job back and, "if that is not as good as he believes himself capable of holding, then he will have a better one, and to get it and keep it he is willing and eager to prove himself able. For some endeavours, he is better equipped mentally and even technically than when he put on the uniform." Thus, soldiers should improve their lot moving up the labor hierarchy as a result of the war experience.

According to Wallenstein, the farmer soldier had learned something more from Europe. "The superiority of his people in many accomplishments remains uppermost in his mind; he scorns certain antiquated methods of Europe, but things he has seen have left their mark." He had seen the intensive cultivation of the Rhine vineyards and the thrifty husbanding of resources in the French countryside. Typically, however, what the Frenchman or German practiced as thrift, the American saw as opportunity. An American returning to a farm had learned how to produce on what he had considered waste land. "If he has no farm to go to," he would lite out for the territory in the oldest tradition of American expansion and, "combine Yankee ingenuity and pep with European thoroughness and kick a perfectly good living out of the acres open to homesteaders."[39]

For men like Private Wallenstein, soldiering in Europe, which read much like touring Europe in his essay, had only reinforced love for America and would lead to isolationist politics:

> From the vantage point of soldiers we have had a bird's eye view of the nations of the earth. We have had a panoramic view of Europe from Russia to Italy and the more we see of the world the better we love America. Regardless of what our politics have been in the past our votes in the future will be controlled by one policy – America first.

Private Joshua B. Lee of Norman, Oklahoma, the second prize winner, reiterated much of what the first prize winner had said in an extended agricultural metaphor. Returning American sol-

diers would neither be stumps in the way of the plough of
progress, nor weeds sapping the strength of commerce, nor
Johnson Grass, an obnoxious plant he likened to the *Bolsheviki*.
But Private Lee went beyond Wallenstein, and Bangs too, and
found that not only had Americans become more loyal to
America through the experience of the war, but that they had
become better Americans, physically as well.

> While soldiering our blood has reddened, our muscles have
> hardened. The tooth-brush, the daily drill, the regular meals,
> the smooth shave, the clean shirt, the daily bath, the easy
> footwear, have all played their part. We are heavier, we are
> taller, we are stronger, and returning, we will infuse the iron
> of our blood into the nation and give her vigour.[40]

He made the point that those characteristics of Americans that
the French constantly remarked on as typical – glabrous appearance, size, insistence on cleanliness[41] – were characteristics
learned in the army: a set of American qualities standardized by
the army's great opportunity for socialization.

Upon the return of these paragons to the United States, the
general population would accept their standards of hygiene and
health. Standardization would cross old regional American barriers and take America to new heights.

> We learned that filth and disease are the greatest enemies to
> mortal men. We know the importance of ventilation and
> drainage. We prefer the "pup tent" to the stuffy tenement cell.
> We are returning to practice what we have learned. As U.S.
> troops entered hundreds of French villages and cleaned them
> up just so will discharged soldiers return to every corner of
> America and apply the laws of sanitation.
>
> Not only that but we have become acquainted with our-
> selves. The lad from the North was the pal of the lad from the
> South, the chap from San Francisco buddied with the boy
> from New York. Our world enlarged as we came to know each
> other. Acquaintance meant friendship, and what will this
> friendship mean to America when we return? New bonds will
> draw us together, new interstate commerce will arise and the
> fabrics of the nation will be strengthened.

It is difficult to say with certainty how a soldier from Norman,
Oklahoma, understood the preference he expressed for the "pup

tent" over the "stuffy tenement." His time in the AEF, however, had reinforced his understanding of a whole progressive reform platform. However sincere these men may or may not have been when writing for this contest, they had certainly mastered the rhetoric of American progress. This man received 250 francs or about 50 dollars for his efforts along with recognition and publicity. He predicted far greater gains in the future through increased business connections engendered by the war.

He ended his essay with an evocation of the American Dream, whose details he took from the illustrations of publications made available in the AEF.

> In the recreation rooms, the magazine pages that have pictures of cosy corners and neat little bungalows are thumbed and worn to tatters. Does that not hint as to the general trend of the A.E.F. mind? . . . Where is the soldier whose pulse does not quicken at the thought of a beautiful little cottage with morning-glories trellised over the window, and a swinging seat on the porch, a fresh green lawn with pansies along the walk and roses in the garden, a car in the garage and a girlish little somebody to help enjoy it all? Whether we admit it or not, we all alike have dreamed that same dream. It is the propeller of our lives.[42]

Ironically, the wartime army, with the help of magazines, the YMCA and other agencies, had taught this consumerist idea of American domesticity, a standardized, Levittown image a quarter of a century before Levittown existed. This dream of consumer culture had become identified with a propeller which, whether of an airplane or troop transport ship, not only had a connotation of war to a man from Oklahoma, but also was a manufactured part of a machine. The magazines that many soldiers must have seen regularly for the first time in those recreation rooms, the same magazines that spread an image of American life through advertising in American middle-class homes, mass-produced this compelling image of a life occupied with efficient commerce among people of different regions who finally recognized no differences between themselves.

Bangs and the newspaper editor judges of the contest probably chose the winning essays for their focused, positive, uplifting sentiments. His organization also published bits of more disjointed essays. Sometimes these demonstrated a willingness by soldiers to write in the manner of the four minute men. The inventive wildness of some of their language indicated that many soldiers could adopt a Wilsonian rhetoric even if they had not quite mastered President Wilson's sense of balance. "This world war has raised it [civilization] to a higher plane," wrote an anonymous entrant. "Morality has taken to aviation. The aims of this war are essentially moral and religious."[43] They wrote of the prospects of returning soldiers: "Undoubtedly you are better fitted for success than ever before; you are bringing home a keener mind than you took away."[44] And, very often, they compared American hygiene, public and private, with that of the French. Along with the American dream of cosy cottages and an automobile went frequent bathing and tooth-brushing. Certainly the advertising of those magazines that furnished the recreation rooms and the pages of *The Stars and Stripes* were full of the images, and carried the message, of regular shaving, mouthwash, tooth brushes and all the other products of standard American hygiene.

Again and again contributors to *Home then What?* help up the differences between France and the United States as the catalyst that should form "The greatest thing that America has gained in this combat . . . national consciousness."[45] This national consciousness started with personal and civic hygiene. The many manure piles that American soldiers had removed from French villages could become a metaphor for cleaning up politics in the United States. From that metaphor, the logic took off, thanks to the broadening experience of the war, to extend to the new position of the United States.

> Idle will be the citizen who does not measure up to the required standard and negligent will be the people who heed not the voice of those who successfully emerged from the period of trial with a greater knowledge and a broader experience. In no place more than our own America will this be more typically exemplified. Of all the nations, we to-day stand pre-eminent carrying with that position a host of new responsibilities which can not and must not be gainsaid.[46]

In his labored prose, this man expressed his belief that Americans, set to a standard by the war, would keep their country in the lead of progress. That European countries had destroyed their Empires and spent their capital in the United States played no part in her "pre-eminent" position. That position had been gained by Americans passing the test of war successfully and adhering to a standard.

An unfavorable comparison of France, and of Europe in general, with all locations in the United States, appeared often in soldier letters. American soldiers cleared the manure piles from the streets of French villages before they settled into billets. They wrote about this as though they had introduced the concept of cleanliness to the French. If the Comrades in Service presented a distorted view of soldiers' thoughts, it did so only by exaggerating the logical connections between these themes and the progressive politics of cleaning up corrupt government.

If soldiers had taken to this kind of uplifting rhetoric, they had done so partly for the same reasons that they took to frequent showers and brushing their teeth. It all seemed to be part of a materially better way of life. But the lessons some learned in the AEF and brought back to the United States with them included the desire for the continuation of their participation in life's improvements, along with a lesson about learning lessons and learning a language in which to repeat them. There was much to learn from the advertising in *The Stars and Stripes*, from uplifting articles about AEF bravery, and from lessons about hygiene from four-minute men. Taken together, the message seemed to be that spiritual enthusiasm and material prosperity could serve each other.

The questionnaire distributed among World War I veterans by the United States Army Military History Institute sheds some light on how soldiers came out of the war and how they thought of America at the moment of their return. Question 43, near the end of the questionnaire, asked "Since the World War I era was a great national experience, did you learn anything about America or Americans?" Veterans who did not always answer every question, answered this question often and most often in words that played on the theme that heads this chapter: that they had learned that America was the best place on earth.

If uniform response lends importance to any answer given to a question, this response should carry great weight. These men responded to those questionnaires in the 1970s, however. They must have made their responses in light of World War II, the

Korean War, the Vietnam War and the popular protests around it, to name only events that would come immediately to mind while thinking of American military experience. Thus, even their widely shared statements of loyalty to the United States have to be seen in the light of other questions: "Was your service during World War I of any specific benefit (or detriment) when you returned to civil life?" "What did you do after you were discharged?" What were your expectations of civilian life upon leaving service (postwar America, G-I benefits, educational and career opportunities)?" These questions came together at the end of the questionnaire. Not all veterans answered them all or answered all parts of them. Some patterns emerge from their responses nevertheless.

Most men in a sample of 102 gave neutral responses to the question about the possible specific benefits or detriments of their service. If these men are divided into more educated and less educated groups, the more educated men, who had been more likely to go into the war with high expectations for adventure and experience, tended to come out of the war disappointed: four out of five gave neutral responses, about one in eight gave negative responses. "Lost two years of college which was unable to make up," said one. "Still felt the effects of the war. 5 prep school classmates dead, one cousin dead, one wounded," said another who had waited for the draft and then joined enthusiastically with his friends. Only about one in twenty of this group found in the war the positive influence on their lives they had expected. On the other hand, one in five of the soldiers who had entered as laborers said they experienced some sort of social or career advantage because of the war while about one in ten answered negatively.[47]

The comments veterans made in the 1970s about their experiences of 1919 and the very early 1920s were often mixed messages. "Invalided home. Glad to be out of service – we are still tough," wrote a man from the Thirty-second Division. He had no regrets about leaving the service, though he connected his time in the army in some way with his toughness. Or he may have meant that his generation still had some fight left in them. Other veterans, perhaps in light of the controversy surrounding the Vietnam War, had re-evaluated the point of their having fought at all. "I wanted to become a civilian again. Perhaps it was a mistake, but I had entered service for a purpose and that purpose had been realized," wrote one, seemingly defending his actions. Such statements resisted categorization as positive or negative.[48]

When answering questions in the 1970s, many veterans of World War I thought of their postwar reactions in terms of the veteran bonus marches of the Great Depression and in comparison to the more generous benefits awarded to World War II veterans. The benefits for World War I soldiers had more uplifting puff than substance to them. They received $10,000 in life insurance if they continued to pay the premium, a suit of clothes, $60 as a bonus, and a train ticket home. Benefits like the education program ended for most soldiers with the discharge from the army in 1919. Women attached to the army as nurses and telephone operators found it almost impossible to receive even these benefits. The few women attached to the US Marines did receive their insurance and $60.[49]

The army presented education, and the life insurance, however, as a boon to a man's advancement. The AEF addressed the concept of life insurance at the AEF University at Beaune in courses on salesmanship and modern finance. No books appeared in greater numbers in the universities stock of texts than *Life Insurance Salesmanship* (1,050 copies on hand April 4, 1919) and *What Life Insurance Is and What it Does* (1,358 copies on the same date).[50] And in a demobilization pamphlet, the army presented life insurance as the sign of social advancement. "There is nothing which makes for self-respect so much as a consciousness that one is insured. There is no greater boon in our modern civilization than life insurance." The pamphlet ended on a threatening and cryptic note, "The man who can't afford to die can't afford to live."[51] Just how many soldiers can have appreciated this addition to their self-respect even from a pamphlet subtitled in their own slang, "The Real Dope"?

In the 1970s, many remembered with some bitterness the $60 and railway ticket home that they received with their discharge papers. "We still want a pension," said one. "Korean war vets get more. Why?" said another. And yet even while wondering about this neglect, this last veteran wrote that World War I was a most important war and that he did not regret having fought. A farmer who had seen combat regreted the lost opportunities of the wartime agricultural boom. "I learned a lot, but I wouldn't give a nikel to go through it all again," he added. Another farmer who had seen no combat insisted, "I learned to love my country." Others connected the experience with business success: "I have learned a great deal about America and Americans, since I was successful in my business, which later enabled me to go to college ... God Bless America."[52]

In some cases, they expressed themselves in the language of the AEF. "My opinion of America never changed – 'nation under God with liberty and justice for all,' " wrote Sergeant John K. Montgomery. The familiar words he used came from the "Pledge of Allegiance," an oath to the flag of the United States written for an 1892 edition of *Youth's Companion* when this soldier was a baby. The pledge became popular in the army during the war, and by the 1920s appeared in army training manuals.[53] He most likely learned the pledge in the army.

When they responded negatively, veterans wrote of adverse effects on their own lives. The better educated soldiers had had higher expectations and were more negative, but their criticisms were personal like that of the man who lost his school friends. Actual judgments against the war only took the ambivalent form of the question, "Perhaps it was a mistake?" And even counting personal loss, veterans were likely to reiterate their loyalty to America and insist that America was a better place than any other.

This lesson learned after the war solidified all their other perceptions from their time in France. A migration involving 2,000,000 young men and women from America had taken place. The experience of these young people was apparently not the shattering, oppressive four years in trenches that their European counterparts suffered. The Americans did not watch their civilization destroy itself. Unlike the Europeans, their nerves and sensibilities were not pounded into a jelly and allowed to reform in a desolate environment of mud and dead comrades. Accounts of the battle by American soldiers are bloody and full of the terror of surrounding death, but they are also breathless with the sheer effort of occupying trenches as fast as the Germans abandoned them. Subsequent battles were fought more bitterly, but the fact remains that most Americans did not encounter the frustrating, stagnating time in the trenches that characterized the war for the British, French and Germans. The war could not shake American optimism and in fact made the language of that optimism a universal among Americans.

The symbols that Americans formed around World War I could absorb war into the stream of American triumphal and commercial progress as well as memorializing sacrifice. The American military graveyards in France not only became a beachhead of American culture in the Old World, demonstrating not just American loss, but also American strength and grandeur. They became a touristic site, a destination that has allowed travelers to consume as tourism what might otherwise have been interpreted as a great waste of life and effort.

Battle experience itself, devastating as it must often have been, could become subsumed in all the other new experiences Americans acquired. After all, combat occupied an especially small proportion of the American Expeditionary Force's time. One soldier summed up his diverse experiences of battle and tourism in a couple of pages. Of battle, he wrote,

> Many of these events were very serious at the moment, but later when the emergency was over and I was alive and all in one piece, it was funny.

Of a visit to Paris, a few pages later, he reported,

> Many of us were from the country or small towns and had always heard of Paris as such an unusual city with museums, beautiful women, excellent wine, and the Eiffel Tower. We found Paris all we had heard about it and more so. The women were nice looking but no more so than the girls back home but those girls were there and the girls in Paris were here . . . The memories of our visit to Paris were things to hold on to!

Then the soldier's description of his trip to Paris melted into a description of a trip to Donremy, the birth place of Joan of Arc:

> Most of us had heard all about here [*sic*] when we were in school, but we never dreamed that we would ever be in her birth place. She crusaded for freedom, and we felt that we were doing the same.[54]

This soldier from Indiana who served in the Sixteenth Infantry of the First Division – a unit whose time and intensity of combat ranked near the top of the AEF – hardly privileged his battle experience at all. It had become an amusing anecdote no more important than the "hilarious" visit he made to Paris. He returned to his experience of battle, however obliquely, when he wrote of Joan of Arc. Like her, he and his comrades had fought for freedom. For Americans, the industrial nightmare of World War I could not shake this conviction in a good purpose. Americans could believe in this positive image of the war not only because their involvement in it covered so brief a period, but also because, behind the confusing official causes and purposes of the war, existed simple direct reasons for individual Americans "from the country or small towns" to take away a positive memory of the war. They learned that their women were as pretty as the Parisians of legend, and they learned that they shared the same historic purpose with Joan of Arc.

Conclusion

A cultural artifact, made in France and imported to the United States, demonstrated very well the power of American optimism to transform the war, and make it part of American progress. One of the souvenirs Americans brought back home from World War I was the brochure advertising and explaining a piece of memorial war art. As early as the end of 1914, a group of French artists started their great work commemorating World War I, *Le Panthéon de la Guerre*. They painted it on 5,400 square feet of canvas, 360 feet long and 45 feet high. In an effort recalling a story of Jorge Luis Borges where a map is contemplated, so detailed it will cover the area it represents, their intention was to immortalize all the allied heroes of the war. They included, "thousands of heroes, officers of all ranks and soldiers, footmen, gunners, horsemen, sailors, aviators, all very like and chosen among those mentioned in dispatches and having the war cross."

The artists had acted fast to capture accurately what they wished to preserve. "It would be too late to attempt this work of glorification after the war. Documents may get lost and, surely, the martial bearing of these men will disappear when peace sets in again. For the moment, they are nothing but soldiers, any other industrial stamp has faded away owing to the war, to their sacrifices, adventures and honour."

The two principal artists, Pierre Carrier-Belleuse and Auguste-François Gorguet, had had their pamphlet printed with commentary by René Bazin, a member of the Académie Française. By 1918, when many American soldiers visited their Paris studio to look at the painting, and take the brochure away with them as a souvenir, the brochure had been translated into English and the painting had undergone many expansions. The war had engulfed the world and the artists had added canvas. Starting with France, Britain and Belgium, they ended with those plus Italy, Portugal, China, several South American countries, The United States, – "what an exact comprehension of America in the double portrait of President Wilson and of General Pershing," they said – Greece, Montenegro, Serbia, Japan, Russia, Roumania . . .[1]

Looking upon this work, soldiers saw thousands of documented heroes accurately reproduced from photographs and enhanced by the artistic process that the pamphlet described: "True artists invent what is real. Those masters of endless travels through Fairyland, received a marvelous gift: they see and hear better the secret of this world." The painted heroes stood on memorial architecture, itself standing on the battlefields of France accurately reproduced from maps and aerial photographs. Testimonials from generals and flyers assured the viewer of the accuracy of this representation improved by art.

Though the landscape would only be familiar to those who had seen it from outside the trenches, the way the people looked in the painting was entirely familiar. Illustrated newspapers and magazines of the time frequently reproduced paintings that combined a photographic accuracy with an artist's use of heightened contrast and dramatization. Before photographs themselves dominated news magazines, paintings, often reproduced in tones of sepia or blue gray and white, appeared in their place depicting celebrated events and people. The portions of the painting reproduced in pamphlets and on postcards and kept by soldiers, when not in full color, have the same look as magazine illustrations of the time.

When they printed their pamphlet, the artists had not finished their representation of America: President Wilson could be identified, but not General Pershing. Some naval personnel were the merest ghosts sketched in, with the more substantial architectural features of the Panthéon showing through. But still, the pamphlet was an ideal souvenir for Americans. America, and Americans, had arrived in the Panthéon of European heroes and history, if only just in time. In the heart of Paris, they had been immortalized, becoming part of a new monument among all the other Paris monuments. Like the heroes of other countries, the artists had captured some American heroes in their moment of martial glory before peace set in again and reasserted its less glorious industrial stamp. The artists had gathered documentation and testimonials to set a standard of authenticity for these heroes.

Le Panthéon de la Guerre placed the whole United States, her war heroes, and by extension, every American, on a ladder of comparative patriotism and essential worth, with the other countries and peoples of the world, save Germany, her people and sympathizers. All Americans involved in the war were joined in a current feeding a larger and larger stream of ever greater and seemingly irresistible significance. *Le Panthéon de la Guerre* represented the whole triumphant swirl of allied humanity flowing about its painted cenotaphs.

The giant canvas enjoyed a notable success in Paris until 1927. Then it was shipped to the United States in a crate nine feet square at the ends and fifty-two feet long. Special trains transported it to a ship that carried it on deck heavily wrapped. In the United States, the private Panthéon Corporation exhibited the panorama in Madison Square Garden, in Washington and, finally, at the Chicago International Exposition of 1933. Later, a speculating bar owner from Baltimore bought it to decorate his drinking establishments. An exotic group of French African calvalry decorated the bar he built, but today, most of the painting resides at the Liberty Memorial Museum in Kansas City, Missouri. It has been cut up and rearranged. Now the figures representing the United States hold center stage. France, England, various Balkan states and colonies are grouped around the sides.[2] Once shipped to America, such a transformation was inevitable. The representatives of American heroism could not remain simple participants on the margin. They moved to the center where they set the tone at a touristic sight in the center of the United States.

Le Panthéon de la Guerre and its little known history has preserved, in the form of an image, a certain kind of American optimism from World War I. The *Panthéon*, with its idealized architecture placed fancifully in front of the landscape of the western front distorted history. And it, in turn, was distorted – cut up and rearranged – for its permanent display in America. Yet, it represented a part of themselves that its viewers recognized, either when they visited it in Paris or during its peregrinations around the United States. American heroes of the war could be seen not alone in their struggles with fear or doubt or physical hardship, but together with literally thousands of other heroes. The *Panthéon* made sense of the mass sacrifice of the war by showing documented heroic men and women with photographic precision, in large numbers. And the *Panthéon* included American heroes in this discourse of the place of individuals in a mass event.

This study started with the subject of motivation and combat, finding American World War I soldiers in transition from the soldiers of the American Civil War, who believed in battle as a test of individual courage in defense of a cause, to the Americans of World War II, that S. L. A. Marshall described as motivated by the small group of men around them, with little reference beyond that group. The American soldiers of World War I were somewhere between the men motivated by faith and abstraction in the one war, and the men whose field of vision has been so narrowed in the other. The technological and cultural changes that brought about this transformation had started to act in World War I. The combination of machine gun and trench had reduced the soldiers' vision considerably. The organization of supply and troop replacement that could sustain battles for weeks, months – and even years for European soldiers who started earlier – narrowed the soldier's time for reflection and for abstraction while near the battle. The Civil War soldiers whom Gerald Lindermann or James McPherson quoted could move to and from the battle quickly and could find themselves safe with paper and pencil and alone or with a few comrades, yet within sight of other regiments marching into the fight, of officers moving about on their urgent business. World War I soldiers seem to have been completely occupied with the task of surviving while at the front. The increased intensity of modern weapons had produced a mental void. The well organized and specialized services of propaganda stepped into this space supplying abstract and uplifting interpretations. The World War I soldier seems hardly to have been alone with his thought when away from combat.

Under these circumstances, references to courage continued to exist, but as a standard of courage in relation to that quality in others. The references to causes exist as well, but the causes and the words to express them, abstract in the extreme, were created far from the battle. In World War I, the relationship between the individual and the mass seems to have been at a turning point made manifest in official representations of the war, and in the way soldiers wrote and thought about it.

Soldiers and nurses had their own reactions, but those reactions were guided. They were alone with their emotions of fear or courage, but they said they felt just like everyone else. They traveled to a distant country with a different language and culture against which they could test their identity with their own culture, but they were guided in this as well. They became tourists, led to foreign sites in the company of other tourists. As such, they learned sensitivity to the foreign, the strange or beautiful. The tourist perceives the foreign site or the foreign

culture alone, but has been lead to react to it like his fellow
tourists. They can all be moved by the cathedral, statue,
landscape or folk dance, but they are instructed to feel the same
thing.

Even the symbols of loss and sacrifice from World War I
reproduce the tension between individual identity and the larger
society that could produce so massive a sacrifice. The individual
grave markers have to be seen against the myriad other grave
markers in a perfectly ordered cemetery, just as the individual
hero portraits in *Le Panthéon de la Guerre* must be seen with the
thousands of other portraits.

Some soldiers could still escape from the standard instructions
of mass society. Many could move back and forth across the
frontiers of mass national culture and the older culture where an
individual had been constrained only by more local influences.
The men who deserted leave trains, only to turn up again with
their unit later, crossed and recrossed such boundaries. So did the
letter or diary writers critical of army propaganda or authority on
one page and repeating some YMCA message on another. The
men who married French women had ignored the army's attempts to prevent any profound sentimental attachments in a
foreign place, and rejected the projection of American woman-
hood as an ideal to pursue, but when they carried their brides
back to the United States they may have returned across the
borders of mass culture as well. And those who reclaimed the
body of a loved one for burial in a family plot did so against the
background of that other national body returned to the United
States as well, the unknown soldier.

Some American participants in World War I were almost
excluded from the national standards of service, courage, sacrifice
and citizenship. African-Americans were mostly kept from battle,
were sent to different leave areas, were under-represented – if
present at all – at the AEF University and did not sing the same
songs learned from Broadway shows and gramophone records as
their white comrades. Some of them sang instead melancholy
songs of their own invention with a message critical of the AEF
and its enterprise. Upon their return to the United States, they
gained little on the strength of their war record. White resistance
to such a notion resulted in the rash of race riots and lynchings
across the country in 1919. The cemeteries of the AEF, however,
were integrated. The black labor battalions that buried the dead

assisted in the creation of a symbol of integration more complete than the United States has yet achieved. Amid the crosses and stars of David, no distinction between officers and men and no distinction between races is visible.

Americans could move back and forth across the boarder of new mass culture, but the war and the manner in which the United States pursued the war had provided compelling symbols and language to attach individuals to the mass culture at many levels. Whether appreciating cultural sites, personal character, a life's work or death, national standards and symbols now existed for the interpretation and comparison of personal achievements.

Notes

1 American Participants' Understanding of their Involvement in World War I

1. S. L. A. Marshall, *Men Against Fire: The Problem of Battle Command in Future War* (Washington, D.C.: The Infantry Journal, 1947); Samuel A. Stouffer et al., *The American Soldier* (Princeton, New Jersey: Princeton University Press, 1949).
2. James M. McPherson, *What They Fought For, 1861–1865* (New York: Anchor Books, Doubleday, 1994) 4; Bell Irvin Wiley, *The Life of Johnny Reb: The Common Soldier of the Confederacy* (New York: Bobbs-Merrill, 1943); Wiley, *The Life of Billy Yank: The Common Soldier of the Union* (New York: Bobbs-Merrill, 1952); Reid Mitchell, *Civil War Soldiers: Their Expectations and Experiences* (New York: Viking, 1988); Gerald Linderman, *Embattled Courage: The Experience of Combat in the American Civil War* (New York: The Free Press, 1994).
3. Samuel Eliot Morison, *Three Centuries of Harvard* (Cambridge: Harvard University Press, 1965) 450–1. Quoted in Phyllis Keller, *States of Belonging: German-American Intellectuals and the First World War* (Cambridge: Harvard University Press, 1979) 69.
4. Woodrow Wilson, Address delivered at Joint Session of the Two Houses of Congress, April 2, 1917 (US 65th Congress, 1st Session, Senate Doc. 5).
5. Responses of the Thirty-sixth Division, US Army Military History Institute World War I Survey, Carlisle Barracks.
6. The data in these paragraphs have been collected from the first section of the US Army Military History Institute Survey distributed to World War I veterans of the Thirty-second and Eighty-fifth Divisions, Carlisle Barracks. The Thirty-second Division was made up largely of volunteers from Michigan and Wisconsin. The Eighty-fifth Division was drafted from the same states. They were chosen for the frequency of German communities in those states.
7. Because of the difficulty in creating statistics from the responses to the US Army Military History Institute Survey, these percentages indicate tendencies.
8. See responses of the Ninety-second and Ninety-third Divisions, US Army Military History Institute World War I Survey, Carlisle Barracks. No fully reliable statistical analysis is possible as the number of respondents is too small.
9. George L. Bell, "Americanization as a Necessity to National Defense," Address at the State Convention of C. F. W. C., Pasadena, California. Pamphlet dated as a gift to the University of California, May 2, 1918. War Pamphlet Collection, Vol. 27, University of California at Berkeley.
10. *The American Red Cross Magazine*, XIV, 2, 40.
11. The quotes in the above paragraphs, including those from the *Indian Leader* of Lawrence, Kansas, were taken from "A Brief Sketch of the Record of

the American Negro and Indian in the Great War," Boston Hampton Committee, March, 1919, War Pamphlet Collection, Vol. 25, University of California at Berkeley. The pamphlet itself quoted Emmet J. Scott, secretary of the Tuskegee Institute who served as special assistant to the Secretary of War, in a speech to the Tuskegee Negro Conference in January 1919.

12. Editorial, *Crisis*, June 16, 1918, 60. Grace B. House, *Soldiers of Freedom*, (n.p., n.d.) 8. Quoted in Arthur E. Barbeau and Henri Florette, *The Unknown Soldiers* (Philadelphia: Temple University Press, 1974) 7.

13. Responses from the Ninety-second Division, US Army Military History Institute World War I Survey, Carlisle Barracks.

14. John Niles, *Singing Soldiers* (New York: Charles Scribner's Sons, 1927) 50 and 54. Niles had set out to record the songs of the war. Finding that white soldiers took their music from Tin Pan Alley, he concentrated on the songs of black soldiers. The first of these he heard while gangs of African- American soldiers loaded and unloaded trucks. Soldiers washing pots and pans in a canteen sang the second.

15. Michael Rogin, "The Sword Became a Flashing Vision": D. W. Griffith's "The Birth of a Nation," in *Representations* 9 (Winter, 1985).

16. Larry Wayne Ward, *The Motion Picture Goes to War, The US Government Film Effort During World War I* (Ann Arbor, Michigan: University of Michigan Press, 1981) 36.

17. Richard Hofstadter, *Social Darwinism in American Thought* (Boston: Beacon Press, 1992) Chapter 9, "Racism and Imperialism," 170–200.

18. Herman Hagedorn, *Leonard Wood, A Biography* (New York: Harper and brothers, 1931) vol. II, 173.

19. Richard Hofstadter, *Social Darwinism*, 203.

20. H. H. Houston Woodward to his parents, April 19, 1917, *A Year for France: War Letters of Houston Woodward* (New Haven: Yale Publishing Association, 1919) 59.

21. Alan Seeger, *The Letters and Diary of Alan Seeger* (New York: Charles Scribner's Sons, 1917) 186.

22. Alan Seeger, in an article for *The New Republic*, quoted in Irving Werstein, *Sound no Trumpet: The Life and Death of Alan Seeger* (New York: Crowell, 1967) 100.

23. See, McPherson, *What They Fought For*; Mitchell, *Civil War Soldiers*; Linderman, *Embattled Courage*. Linderman and Mitchell both refer to the importance of peer pressure.

24. "Alan Seeger, Poet Killed in France – The Poet of the Foreign Legion," *Scribner's Magazine*, LXI, 1 (January, 1917) 123–5.

25. Alan Seeger, "A Message to America," *The Poems of Alan Seeger* (New York: Charles Scribner's Sons, 1916) 162–5. The stirring poems were rushed into print shortly after Seeger's death during the Battle of the Somme, July, 1916.

26. Henry Howard Houston, II, to "Vava" (Susanna Valentine Mitchell) April 21, 1917. Houston was a volunteer in a French transport section. Private collection, Taconic, Connecticut.

27. Houston to Susanna Valentine Mitchell, May 13, 1917.

28. Houston to Susanna Valentine Mitchell, May 14, 1917.

29. Clifton Cates to his mother, February 4, 1918. Personal Papers Collection, Marine Corps Museum, Washington Navy Yard. Cates had a distinguished career, becoming eventually Marine Corps Commandant.
30. *The American Red Cross Magazine*, XII, 8, September, 1917.
31. *The Stars and Stripes*, Undated reproduction [most likely 1919], R. Norris Williams Collection, University of Pennsylvania.
32. Malcolm Aitken, Second Division, 5th Marines. Scrapbook, "Letters from a Marine to His Mother," US Army Military History Institute, Carlisle Barracks. Emphasis in original.
33. Cliffton Cates to his mother and sister, Summer, 1917, undated.
34. Ethel D. Warner, undated memoir, Ethel D. Warner Collection, Red Cross Museum, Washington, D.C.
35. Theodore Roosevelt, "The Great Adventure, Present-Day Studies in American Nationalism," included in *The Works of Theodore Roosevelt*, Memorial Edition (New York: Charles Scribner's sons, 1923–26), XXI, 263. "The Great Adventure" was written during World War I.
36. Paul Fussell, *The Great War and Modern Memory* (New York: Oxford University Press, 1975), see Chapter V, "Oh What a Literary War," and Chapter VI, "Theater of War," for his discussions of the strategies soldiers took to rectify the conflict between civilian reality and war reality through fiction or theater.
37. Klaus Theweleit, *Male Fantasies* (Minneapolis: University of Minnesota Press, 1987) vol. 1, Chapter 1, "Men and Women," 3–228.
38. See Lewis Erenberg, *Steppin' Out: New York Nightlife and the Transformation of American Culture, 1890–1930* (Westport, Connecticut: Greenwood Press, 1981); Kathy Peiss, *Cheap Amusements: Working Women and Leisure in New York City, 1880–1920* (Philadelphia: Temple University Press, 1986) as well as Theodore Dreiser, *Sister Carrie* (New York, 1932).
39. The speech of this unnamed war worker is quoted by Daniel Halévy, *Avec les boys américains* (Paris: Berger-Levrault, 1918) 17–19.
40. In English in *The Stars and Stripes*, Vol. I, no. 22, July 12, 1918, 1. In French, *Le Figaro*, 4 Juillet 1918, 2.
41. *The Stars and Stripes*, Vol. I, no. 22, July 5, 1918, 4.
42. *The Stars and Stripes*, Vol. 1, no. 23, July 12, 1918, 1.
43. "But that 4th in Paris," *The Stars and Stripes*, Vol 1, no. 23, July 12, 1918, 4.

2 The Meaning Americans Gave to Action at the Front in World War I

1. Joseph Shapiro, unpublished poem, 1919, rewritten 1976. Joseph Shapiro Papers, Fourth Division, US Army Military History Institute, Carlisle Barracks.
2. Gerald F. Linderman, *Embattled Courage: The Experience of Combat in the American Civil War* (New York: The Free Press, 1987) 61, 64–5.
3. Linderman, *Embattled Courage*, chapter 3, "Courage as the Cement of Armies," 34–60. Dwight D. Eisenhower quoted in Linderman, 18.

4. John Keegan, *The Face of Battle: A Study of Agincourt, Waterloo and the Somme* (New York: Penguin, 1978) 277.
5. Keegan, *The Face of Battle*, 276.
6. Edward M. Coffman, *The War to End All Wars: The American Military Experience in World War I* (Madison, Wisconsin: University of Wisconsin Press, 1986) 245.
7. General Erich von Ludendorff quoted in S. L. A. Marshall, *World War I* (Boston: Houghton Mifflin, 1987) 388.
8. Coffman, *The War to End All Wars*, 283.
9. Russell Weigley, *The American Way of War* (Bloomington, Indiana: Indiana University Press, 1977) 203.
10. Paul Fussell in *The Great War and Modern Memory* (New York: Oxford, 1975) located the origins of modern irony in the battle experience of the war. The divorce rate after the war as a possible result of the trauma of the war was a concern in the popular press of the 1920s; Stephen Kern, "The Cubist War," in *The Culture of Time and Space* (Cambridge, Mass: Harvard University Press, 1983). · Kern related the spreading understanding of the modernist innovations and perceptions of the early 20th century to the " 'composition' of the fighting itself."
11. *Over There! A Journal of the First World War*, Vol. 1, No. 4 (Winter, 1988): 1. Marine Corps Museum, Washington Navy Yard.
12. Captain R. R. Meigs to his wife, Summer, 1918, and an unidentified newspaper clipping enclosed in a letter from Mrs. R. R. Meigs to Captain R. R. Meigs, September 12, 1918. Private collection, Philadelphia.
13. For example, John Dollard and Donald Horton, *Fear in Battle* (Washington: The Infantry Journal, 1944). The authors concern themselves with motivating soldiers to choose courage; Charles McMoran (Baron Moran), *Anatomy of Courage* (London: Constable, 1966) takes this matter of choice as its starting point.
14. See, for example, Anthony Kellett, "Beliefs, Values, and Commitment," in *Combat Motivation: The Behavior of Soldiers in Battle* (Boston: Kluwer-Nijhoff Publishers, 1982) 165–97, who traced the diminution of the importance of individual beliefs and values and the increasing importance of the military unit to soldier motivation through this century; William Darryl Henderson, *Cohesion, The Human Element in Combat* (Washington: National Defense University Press, 1985), located American military weakness in the independence of soldiers to make their own choices due to high pay and too great contact with surrounding society, emphasized loyalty to the small group around an individual soldier and the authority of noncommissioned officers; Morris Janowitz and Roger Little, *Sociology and the Military Establishment* (New York: Russell Sage Foundation, 1965), also emphasizes loyalty to a small group and is much cited by others presenting this argument; Elmar Dinter, *Hero or Coward* (London: F. Cass, 1985), emphasizes unit cohesion and relies heavily on the work of Samuel Lyman Atwood Marshall during and after World War II and the Korean War; see Marshall's *Men Against Fire: The Problem of Battle Command in Future Wars* (Washington: Infantry Journal, 1947).
15. McMoran, *Anatomy of Courage*, 3.
16. McMoran, *Anatomy of Courage*, 61.

17. Because of the extensive portrait photography of Matthew Brady and others, the US Army Military History Institute at Carlisle Barracks, Pennsylvania, is attempting to create a photographic record of every single member of the Civil War armies.

18. Edward Bellamy, *Looking Backward* (New York: New American Library, 1960).

19. Reports from the Présidence du Conseil, Commissariat Général Des Affaires de Guerre Franco-Américaines, 15 N 59, French military archives, Vincennes.

20. Walter Benn Michaels, "An American Tragedy or the Promise of American Life," in *Representations* 25 (Winter, 1989): 71–98. Michaels wrote that the concept of individuality destabilized as a result of mass production after the Civil War. He found that progressives redefined the individual as only existing against a standard, or machine background and "systematic management." Michaels used the example of Civil War uniforms found in Egal Feldman, *Fit for Men: A Study of New York's Clothing Trade* (Washington, D.C., 1960) 97; the United States Army in World War I made an excellent testing ground for "systematic management," see Michael O'Malley, *Keeping Watch* (New York: Viking, 1990) 250–3; Fred Davis Baldwin, "The American Enlisted Man in World War I," doctoral dissertation, Princeton, 1964, especially, "Results of the Army's Testing program," 70, and "The Army's Education Program," 116.

21. Henry H. Houston, II, to Susanna Valentine Mitchell, March 12, 1917. Private collection, Taconic, Connecticut.

22. Henry H. Houston to Suzanna Valentine Mitchell, March 12, and April 21, 1917.

23. Joseph Brown, to his wife, June 23, 1918.

24. Joseph Brown, to his wife, June 23, June 28, and July 31, 1918.

25. Joseph Brown, to his wife, July 31, 1918.

26. Joseph Brown, to his wife, June 23, 1918. Letter #20. Joseph Brown destroyed the diary he kept in Belleau Wood and that he sent to his wife. In letter #22, June 28, 1918, he writes of the diary, "I shouldn't have sent thee any French diary but I mean all I said even now when I'm no longer nutty."

27. Clyde A. Hunsucker, letter to his mother, December 11, 1918. Thirty-sixth Division, US Army Military History Institute, Carlisle Barracks.

28. Robert Sawyer, memoir entry for approximately October 10, 1918. Thirty-sixth Division, US Army Military History Institute, Carlisle Barracks.

29. Robert Sawyer, August 31, 1918.

30. Robert Sawyer, October 9, 1918.

31. Earl R. Poorbough, undated journal entry, First Division, US Army Military History Institute, Carlisle Barracks.

32. John F. Dixon to his sister, received August 8, 1918. Anna Russell Collection, Hoover Institute Archives, Stanford University.

33. Henry I. Craven, Ninety-second Division, US Army Military History Institute World War I Survey, Carlisle Barracks.

34. Austin Roberts, Ninety-second Division, US Army Military History Institute World War I Survey, Carlisle Barracks.

35. Leonard Bogart, Thirty-sixth Division, US Army Military History Institute World War I Survey, Carlisle Barracks.

36. Quotes taken from responses of the Ninety-second and Ninety-third Divisions to the US Army Military History Institute World War I Survey, Carlisle Barracks.

37. Bertram Lawrence, Ninety-second Division, US Army Military History Institute World War I Survey, Carlisle Barracks.

38. This paragraph and the following quotes, including those from the *Indian Leader* of Lawrence, Kansas, were taken from "A Brief Sketch of the Record of the American Negro and Indian in the Great War," Boston Hampton Committee, March, 1919. War Pamphlet Collection, Vol. 25, University of California at Berkeley.

39. Samuel Kent, unpublished journal, July 29, 1918. Samuel Kent Papers, Thirty-second Division, US Army Military History Institute, Carlisle Barracks.

40. Raymond Austin to his mother July 31, 1918. Raymond Austin Papers, Sixth Artillery, First Division, US Army Military History Institute, Carlisle Barracks.

41. Austin, July 31, 1918.

42. William Mitchell, *Memoires of World War I: "From Start to Finish of our Greatest War"* (New York: Random House, 1960) 10, quoted in Weigley, *The American Way of War*, 203.

43. Raymond Stenbeck in *The Way it Was*, Vol. II, Humbolt State University, Retired Senior Volunteer Program, 1980. Raymond Stenbeck Papers, Sixth Marine Rgt. 73rd Co. Second Division, US Army Military History Institute, Carlisle Barracks.

44. Stenbeck, letter, November 16, 1918.

45. Samuel Kent, September 2, 1918.

46. *The History of the Provost Marshall*, National Archives, Record Group 120, #57, gives no figure for such executions, nor does the report on stragglers and desertions prepared by the Army War College for World War II, Carlisle Barracks; John J. Pershing, *My Experiences of the World War* (New York: Frederick A. Stokes Company, 1931) vol. II, 98. Pershing mentions forty-four death sentences in all, and thirty-three executions, all for murder or rape. Many soldiers, however, wrote that they believed desertion to be punishable by summary execution.

47. Unsigned letter to Blanche C. Matthias, November 29, 1918. Blanche C. Matthias Collection, Hoover Institute Archives, Stanford University.

48. Provost Marshall, *History of the Provost Marshall*, Vol. 1, 11, Record Group 120, #57, National Archives, Washington, D.C.

49. Provost Marshall, *History of the Provost Marshall*, Vol. 1, Record Group 120, #57, National Archives, Washington, D.C.

50. "Trials of an MP," *The Stars and Stripes*, May 2, 1919, anonymous poem reprinted in Alfred E. Cornebuise, ed., *Doughboy Doggerel* (Athens, Ohio: University of Ohio Press, 1985) 19. This question and answer remained a joke in the army through World War II.

51. Unsigned letter to Blanche C. Matthias, November 29, 1918. Blanche C. Matthias Collection, Hoover Institute Archives, Stanford University. Spelling and Grammatical mistakes in the original.

52. Eric Leed, *No Man's Land: Combat and Identity in World War I* (New York: Cambridge University Press, 1979), see chapter 4 "Myth and Modern War," 115–62.

53. "Private Burningham's Story," in *Defenders of Democracy* (New York, 1919) 112. The anonymous editors of this book collected the testimony of hospital patients in the New York area, just after the war.

54. "Private Bolin's Story," *Defenders of Democracy*, 60–71.

55. "Private Walter Stanley's Story," *Defenders of Democracy*, 228.

56. "Corporal Berney Tovin's Story," *Defenders of Democracy*.

57. Bertram Lawrence, Ninety-second Division, US Army Military History Institute World War I Survey, Carlisle Barracks.

58. Harry Croft, quoted in Stanley Weintraub, *A Stillness Heard Round the World* (New York: Dutton, 1985) 170.

59. Frank Sibley, *With the Yankee Division in France* (Boston, 1919) quoted by Weintraub, *A Stillness Heard Round the World*, 170.

60. Kent, unpublished diary, November 12, 1918.

61. Kent, November 11, 1918.

62. Weintraub, *A Stillness Heard Round the World*, "Final Shots," and "The Stillness," 169–225.

63. Tony Ashworth, *Trench Warfare, 1914–1918: The Live and Let Live System* (New York: Macmillan, 1980).

3 Americans' Encounter with French Culture

1. Alden Brooks, *As I Saw It: Battle in 1918, Seen by an American in the French Army* (New York: Alfred A. Knopf, 1930) 108.

2. Samuel Kent, unpublished diary, August 24, 1918, 43. Samuel Kent Papers, Thirty-second Division, 128th Infantry, US Army Military History Institute, Carlisle Barracks.

3. Jonathan Culler, "The Semiotics of Tourism," *Framing the Sign: Criticism and its Institutions* (Norman, Oklahoma: University of Oklahoma Press, 1988) 153–67.

4. Dean MacCannell, *The Tourist: A New Theory of the Leisure Class* (New York: Schocken Books, 1989) chapter 1, "Modernity and the Production of Touristic Experiences," 37.

5. For the history of the CTCA, see Nancy Bristow, *Making Men Moral: Social Engineering in the Great War* (New York: New York University Press, 1995), especially chapter 3, "Reformers Between Two Worlds: The Battle Against Tradition and Working-Class Modernism."

6. Newton D. Baker to Woodrow Wilson, April 2, 1917, Arthur Link ed., *The Papers of Woodrow Wilson* (Princeton, New Jersey: Princeton University Press, 1966–1980) vol. 41, 527.

7. For the progressive development of a new society in the war see Bristow, *Making Men Moral*, Chapter Two, " 'Full-Orbed Moral Manhood': Cultural Nationalism and the Creation of New Men and Women."

8. Newton D. Baker to Woodrow Wilson, April 2, 1917 in Link, *Papers of Woodrow Wilson*, vol. 41, 527.

9. Among the lessons the army took away from World War I was the necessity of leave and leave areas in overseas theatres of war. A course on recreation was eventually taught to army officers. It emphasized practical military concerns like reducing desertion and raising morale rather than following the more progressive ambitions of men like Baker. W.P. #25, G.1. Theatre of Operations Lecture delivered at the Army War College, Fort Humphreys, D.C., March 28, 1935. Army War College Historical Section, Carlisle Barracks.

10. John J. Pershing, *My Experiences in the Great War* (New York: Frederick A. Stokes, 1931) Vol. I, 214.

11. Report of the Commander of the Leave Area Bureau quoted in Col. C. F. Martin, "Military Leaves and the Leave Area System," 1943, Army War College, Historical Section, Carlisle Barracks. This is one of a series of studies of World War I executed during American involvement in World War II, designed to use the lessons of the previous war.

12. Col. C. F. Martin, "Military Leaves and the Leave Area System," 1943, Army War College, Historical Section, Carlisle Barracks.

13. The records of all district liaison officers contain complaints from the French. See Record group 120 #51, Box 3485–3487, US National Archives. Also see Provost Marshal's Reports for crimes requiring investigation or disciplinary action by the army, Record group 120 #61, Box 1, National Archives.

14. For the assumption that American drinking habits differed from those of the French, see for example, Theodore Roosevelt, Jr., *Average Americans* (New York, 1919) 51.

15. With great frequency and not a little anxiety, the spread of the martini cocktail or dry martini is chronicled in the *Physionomie de Paris*, from late 1917 to the Summer of 1919, Musée de la Gendarmerie.

16. If an American soldier received all his pay, he received far more than the men of other armies. But with various allotments, for bonds, family support and insurance, his pay could be greatly reduced. Purchasing bonds and life insurance was made obligatory in some units in order to reduce the purchasing power of the men.

17. *Physionomie de Paris*, 16 Décembre 1917, Musée de la Gendarmerie [Author's translation].

18. Prefectorial Reports found at the *Archives Nationales* on economic conditions throughout France from June 1917 to June 1919 backed up with statistical and anecdotal evidence, point to the very real problem of inflation brought about by American soldiers allowed to feed themselves. Throughout American involvement in the war, a series of economic measures were taken to prevent this inflation. See also reports of the *Contrôle Postal*, Archives Militaires, Vincennes.

19. *Physionomie de Paris*, 19 Janvier 1918, Musée de la Gendarmerie.

20. The pattern of rising prices after Americans arrived can be seen all over France, and was a constant subject in the reports of the *Contrôle Postal*, and in the reports of various administrators. Measures were taken to control this: Americans were only permitted to purchase at certain times and in certain places, for example. See Yves Henri Nouaillat, *Les Américains à Nantes et St. Nazaire* (Paris: Les Belles Lettres, 1972), chapter 3 and

Conclusion, see also André Kaspi, *Le Temps des Américains: Le concours américain à la France en 1917–1918* (Paris: Université de Paris I, 1976).

21. Lt. John W. Kress, PFC, 314th Infantry, Seventy-ninth Division, US Army Military History Institute War I Survey, Carlisle Barracks.

22. Andrew J. Kuchich, PFC, 314th Infantry, Seventy-ninth Division, US Army Military History Institute, World War I Survey, Carlisle Barracks.

23. Provost Marshal's reports contain records of the investigation into this activity. A pattern also formed in which American service men supplied goods to French girlfriends. Record Group 120, Entry 61, Box 1, National Archives.

24. Col. Robert C. Humber, "Absences and Desertions During the First World War," November 1942, US Army War College Historical Section, Carlisle Barracks; Col. William H. Dodds, Jr., G-1 Theatre of Operations Lecture delivered at the Army War College, Fort Humphreys, D. C. March 28, 1935, Army War College Historical Section, Carlisle Barracks.

25. Franklin S. Edmonds, Divisional Secretary, Savoie, *The Leave Areas of the AEF* (Philadelphia: The John C. Winston Co., 1928) 6.

26. Andrew J. Kuchick, PFC, Seventy-ninth Division, US Army Military History Institute, World War I Survey.

27. *L'Avenir*, Aix-les-Bains, 23 Février, 1918.

28. Colonel C. F. Martin, "Military Leaves and the Leave Area System, AEF," Historical Study no. 41, prepared January, 1943, Historical Section Studies, US Army War College Curricular Archives, US Army Military History Institute, Carlisle Barracks.

29. Col. Martin, "Military Leaves."

30. Col. Humber, "Absences and Desertions."

31. Col. Martin, "Military Leaves."

32. *The Stars and Stripes*, vol. 1, no 1, 1.

33. Edmonds, *The Leave Areas of the A.E.F.*, 4.

34. Edmonds, *The Leave Areas of the A.E.F.*, 5.

35. *L'Avenir*, January 19, 1918. Quoted in Geneviève Frieh and Pierre Rault, *Le Grand Cercle d'Aix-les-Bains* (Paris, 1978) 244.

36. *L'Avenir*, January 26, 1918, 1.

37. *L'Avenir*, January 26, 1918.

38. *L'Avenir*, January 26, 1918.

39. *L'Avenir* doubled in size for its February 9 issue, in time to greet the American soldiers. On February 23, it printed an article, cited above, describing the arrival of the first American soldiers. Thereafter this newspaper, that concerned itself mostly with promoting the town and its hotel business, hardly mentioned the presence of the Americans. The soldiers on leave were no longer controversial. They had become tourists, and they didn't read French newspapers.

40. "Paris for Englishmen and for Americans," from James Weirich Papers, Third Division, US Army Military History Institute, Carlisle Barracks. Other examples from miscellaneous pamphlets, Mumford Collection, University of Pennsylvania.

41. Baudry de Saunier, *The American's Guide Book in France*, published by *Office National Du Tourisme*, Bibliothèque internationale de documentation contemporaine, Nanterre.

42. Estimates vary between these two figures. YMCA figures tend towards the higher number.

43. Robert Edward Allen, Sr., Duty Sgt. US Military History Institute, Carlisle Barracks.

44. Anonymous diary, Seventy-ninth Division, US Military History Institute, Carlisle Barracks.

45. Winston Churchill, "A Traveler in War-time," *Scribner's Magazine*, LXIII (February, 1918): 129–37.

46. Herbert Adams-Gibbons, "The A.E.F. at Play," in *The Century* (1918): 441–53.

47. Bob Howe, Jr., "Sammy 'Mangers,' " in *The Gas Attack*, Christmas, 1918, 6–7, newspaper of the 27th Division, the New York Division, R. Norris Williams Collection, University of Pennsylvania.

48. Sgt. Seth T. Williams, "Henry's Pal to Henry," 26. Undated reprint from *The Stars and Stripes*, R. Norris Williams Collection, University of Pennsylvania.

49. Eugene Kennedy, "Observations of a Local Boy in France," in *The Enterprise Times* (Lancaster, New York), May 22, 1919. Clipping, Eugene Kennedy Collection, Hoover Institute Archives, Stanford University.

50. Cpl. Duncan D. Hutchinson, printed in an unidentified newspaper, Clarence Hackett Collection, US Army Military History Institute, Carlisle Barracks.

51. Responses to World War I Research Project question #10, by Cpl. John Cornett, Cpl. Francis Buhler, Howard David Hanks, Pvt. Arthur J. Nelson, Cpl. A.C. Hatch, all of the Ninety-first Division, and Virgil B. Ragsdale of the Ninety-second Division. US Army Military History Institute World War I Survey, Carlisle Barracks.

52. YMCA Handbook, R. Norris Williams Collection, University of Pennsylvania. For statistics of YMCA activities, see Dwight F. Davis to Franklin S. Edmonds, March 14, 1928, published in Edmonds, *The Leave Areas of the A.E.F.*, 1.

53. Letter writing was taught with model sentences expressing respect and gratitude to the army and patriotism. Army Education Pamphlet, World War I Pamphlet Collection, Berkeley University, California.

54. This figure was derived from a count of the sample used for leisure activities who stated their former occupation as farmer.

55. In my search of French marriage registers, discussed more fully in Chapter 4, I found no marriages of American officers to French women. In newspaper reports, I found two.

56. Austin Raymond to his mother, May, 1918. US Army Military History Institute, Carlisle Barracks.

57. Austin Raymond, to his wife, June 1, 1918.

58. Alan Seeger, *The Letters and Diary of Alan Seeger* (New York: C. Scribner's Sons, 1917) 61.

59. Col. A. B. Miller, Diary entry, Sunday December 16, 1917. (During the war he held lower ranks). Personal Papers Collection, Marine Corps Museum, Washington Navy Yard.

60. An indication of American familiarity with this song is that it is the only French song included in the compendium of AEF songs compiled by John

Niles, *Songs My Mother Never Taught Me* (New York: The Macaulay Company, 1929).

61. Col. A. B. Miller, Diary entry, November 23, 1917.
62. Major Samuel W. Flemming, "World War One Service," unpublished memoir, 1928, 87. US Army Military History Institute, Carlisle Barracks.
63. Col. A. B. Miller, Diary entry, December 25, 1917.
64. *The Martian*, Christmas issue, January 5, 1919. *The Martian* was the newspaper for the Red Cross Hospital near St. Pierre Le Moutier. Red Cross History Collection, Red Cross Museum, Washington, D.C.
65. Lt. John W. Kress, 314th Infantry, Seventy-ninth Division, unpublished memoir, 1924, US Army Military History Institute, Carlisle Barracks.
66. Lieutenant Joseph Brown, letters to his wife, Summer 1918, Third Division, US Army Military History Institute, Carlisle Barracks.
67. Captain Robert R. Meigs to his wife, May, 18, 1918. Private Collection, Philadelphia.
68. Franklin S. Edmonds to E. D. Carter, Chief Secretary, YMCA, AEF, February 16, 1919. Quoted in Edmonds, *The Leave Areas of the A.E.F.*, 10.
69. Herbert Adams-Gibbons, "The A.E.F. at Play."
70. Sergeant Alexander Woollcott, "A Friendly Guide" (Paris, 1919). R. Norris Williams Collection, University of Pennsylvania.
71. Nurse Nellie Delisle Collection, Red Cross History Collections, World War I, Box #1, Red Cross Headquarters, Washington, D.C.
72. Casper Schwartz, Diary, February 3, 1919, US Army Military History Institute, Carlisle Barracks.

4 Sexual Attitudes of Americans in World War I

1. Edward M. Coffman, *The War To End All Wars: The American Military Experience in World War I* (Madison, Wisconsin: University of Wisconsin Press, 1986) 133.
2. Richard Holmes, *Acts of War: The Behavior of Men in Battle* (New York: The Free Press, 1985) 95.
3. This point was made by David M. Kennedy in *Over Here: The First World War and American Society* (New York: Oxford University Press, 1980) 187.
4. Quoted in Coffman, *The War to End All Wars*, 133.
5. See for example the postcards in the collection of Captain Robert Grier St. James, Seventh Infantry, Third Division, US Army Military History Institute, Carlisle Barracks.
6. *The American Red Cross Magazine*, Vol. 13, no. 1 (August 1918): 7.
7. The emasculating quality of defensive trench warfare has long been connected with World War One. See Eric Leed, *No Man's Land* (New York: Cambridge University Press, 1979), chapter 3, "War in the Labyrinth: the Realities of War," and Paul Fussell, *The Great War and Modern Memory* (New York: Oxford University Press, 1975), chapter 2, "The Troglodyte World." Both talk about the shock of modern mechanized war on standards of masculine behavior. More recently, Susan Gubar and Sandra Gilbert have argued that women took over so much of English and

American civilian life during World War One that men were doubly emasculated, once at the front where they passively endured bombardment in the significantly named "No Man's land," and once when they returned to a home that had become "Her Land." Sandra Gilbert and Susan Gubar, *No Man's Land: The place of the Woman Writer in the Twentieth Century, Vol. 2, Sex Changes* (New Haven: Yale University Press 1988), chapter 7, "Soldier's Heart: Literary Men, Literary Women, and the Great War." Ernest Hemingway's war novels, *The Sun Also Rises* (New York: Scribner's, 1926), and *A Farewell to Arms* (New York: Scribner's, 1929) contain the best known American instances of this phenomenon.

8. Richard Holmes, *Acts of War* (New York: The Free Press, 1985) 56 and section, "Venus and Mars," 93–108.

9. Alan Hanbury-Sparrow, *The Land-Locked Lake* (London, 1932). Quoted in Holmes, *Acts of War*, 93.

10. Captain R. R. Meigs to his wife, April 24, 1918. Private collection, Philadelphia.

11. Otis Emmons Briggs, unpublished letters, collected 1920, 72. Otis Emmons Briggs Collection, Hoover Institute Archives, Stanford University.

12. Briggs, letters, 95.

13. Briggs, letters, 71.

14. Briggs, letters, 107.

15. Briggs, letters, 71.

16. Both the *Physionomie de Paris*, BA/1587–1588, and the collection of songs submitted for censorship, BA/697–698, are at the Archives de la Gendarmerie, Paris. This subject is ubiquitous in these sources.

17. Memorandum circulated to all the American Expeditionary Forces, R. Norris Williams Collection, University of Pennsylvania.

18. Earl R. Poorbaugh, Thirty-first Infantry, First Division, US Army Military History Institute, Carlisle Barracks. Text reproduced without corrections.

19. Translation by Captain Fithian, the American Liaison Officer XIème Région, of a letter by Général Coutanceau, commanding XI Région to Colonel Chief of the Base No. 1, St. Nazaire, January 30, 1919, Record Group 120 #51, Box 3485, National Archives.

20. Alain Corbin, *Les filles de noces: Misère sexuelle et prostitution aux 19e et 20e siècles* (Paris: Aubier, 1978) section, "Les belles heures de la guerre," 486–9.

21. All verses of "Mademoiselle from Armentières" are taken from John J. Niles and Douglas S. Moore, *Songs My Mother Never Taught Me* (New York: Macaulay, 1929).

22. Colonel E. G. Johnston, unpublished memoir, 20, First Division, US Army Military History Institute, Carlisle Barracks.

23. Niles and Moore, *Songs My Mother Never Taught Me*, 15.

24. Niles and Moore, *Songs My Mother Never Taught Me*, 55. Niles had collaborators on this book, their names were listed as John J. "Jack" Niles, Douglas S. "Doug" Moore, and A. A. "Wally" Wallgren. [Author's Translation]

25. John J. Niles, *Singing Soldiers* (New York: C. Scribner's Sons, 1927), vii.

26. Niles and Moore, *Songs My Mother Never Taught Me*. [Author's translation]

27. Clifton Cates, to his mother, July 13, 1918. Personal Papers Collection, Marine Corps History Museum, Washington Navy Yard.

28. Françoise Thébaud, *La femme au temps de la guerre de 14* (Paris: Stock, 1986) 300.

29. Kathy Peiss, "Charity Girls and City Pleasures: Historical Notes on Working-Class Sexuality, 1880–1920," in Kathy Peiss and Christina Simmons with Robert A. Padgug, eds, *Passion and Power, Sexuality in History* (Philadelphia: Temple University Press, 1989) 57–69. Kathy Peiss has found that limits on intimacy and standards of respectability were negotiated between working-class men and women, but that men, who "treated," had the upper hand. Accounts of Red Cross nurses dancing and dating enlisted men as a special favor can be found throughout nurses' diaries. See, for example, Ethel D. Warner, unpublished journal, Red Cross Museum, Washington, D.C.

30. "My Angel of the Flaming Cross," song by Byron Gay. Sheet music artist Alice R. Gordon, (New York, no date). "The Girl with the Little Red Cross (on her sleeve)," song by Buck Rodgers and John Itell (New York, no date). "My Red Cross Girlie the Wound is Somewhere in My Heart," song by Leo Feist, (New York, no date). World War One Collection, Red Cross Museum, Washington, D.C.

31. Samuel Kent, unpublished diary, September 4, 1918, 49. 128th Infantry, Thirty-second Division, US Army Military History Institute, Carlisle Barracks.

32. *The Stars and Stripes*, Friday, May 10, 1918, 1.

33. *The Stars and Stripes*, Friday, May 3, 1918, 1.

34. Bulletin R. 46, General Headquarters, Chaumont, May 10, 1918. Quoted in John J. Pershing, *My Experiences in the War*, Vol. 2 (New York: Frederick A. Stokes, 1931) 38.

35. "Mother's Day on the Rhine," War Pamphlets Collection, University of California at Berkeley.

36. Howard W. Munder, Bugler, to his mother and father, September 30, 1917. Twenty-eighth Division, US Army Military History Institute, Carlisle Barracks.

37. Harold Lee, Ninth Infantry, booklet of undated war poems published posthumously by the Women's Christian Temperance Union, 1918. Several concern the love of mother. Second Division, US Army Military History Institute, Carlisle Barracks.

38. Quoted in Thébaud, *La femme au temps de la guerre de 14*, 137.

39. Fred Davis Baldwin, "The American Enlisted Man in World War I," dissertation, Princeton, 1964. Baldwin's extensive search turned up no articles on the subject of Franco-American unions save two articles presenting the formalities regulating these marriages and estimates of the number of those marriages. See "Cupid Has Had to Print a Set of Rules for the Doughboys in France," in *Literary Digest*, July 12, 1919, quoted in Baldwin, 215–16.

40. For information on the US Army's policy on marriages in following paragraphs, I am indebted to Lt. Col. Albert B. Kellogg, "Marriages of Soldiers," Army War College Historical Section Report, July, 1942, 2. US Army Military History Institute, Carlisle Barracks. Col. Kellogg pieced

together his report from the correspondence of General Headquarters on the subject.

41. Kellogg, "Marriages," 4.
42. Kellogg, "Marriages," 4.
43. Kellogg, "Marriages," 5.
44. Kellogg, "Marriages," 8.
45. Kellogg, "Marriages," 9.
46. Kellogg, "Marriages," 9.
47. Kellogg, "Marriages," 4.
48. *Oo La La Times*, St. Nazaire, Vol. I, no. 1, October 30, 1917, 3. Bibliothèque Nationale.
49. *Oo La La Times*, St. Nazaire, Vol. 1, no. 1, October 30, 1917. British soldiers used the expression "French letter," to refer to condoms, which meaning would make this quotation improbably crude, but quite in keeping with the newspaper's subsequent attacks against the reputations of soldiers' French girlfriends.
50. *Oo La La Times*, St. Nazaire, Vol. 1, no. 2, Christmas, 1917.
51. *Oo La La Times*, St. Nazaire, Vol. 1, no. 3, January, 1918.
52. *Oo La La Times*, St. Nazaire, Vol. 1, no. 3, January, 1918.
53. *Oo La La Times*, St. Nazaire, Vol. 1, no. 5, February 22, 1918.
54. *Oo La La Times*, St. Nazaire, Vol. 1, no. 8, June 16, 1918.
55. *Oo La La Times*, St. Nazaire, Vol. 1, no. 5, February 22, 1918.
56. *Oo La La Times*, St. Nazaire, Vol. 1, no. 7, May 12, 1918.
57. For this study, I have examined fully the Marriage Registers for 1917–19 at the État Civil of Brest (a port of embarkation), Dijon (a town with an American hospital nearby), Beaune (the site of the American Expeditionary Forces University), Aix-les-Bains (the largest of the leave areas), and Chambéry (a leave area reserved for black soldiers).
58. Orders of Colonel Reeves, March 2, 19, 1919, Record Group 120, #414, Box 1944, National Archives.
59. Lieutenant W. D. Haselton, unpublished diary, First Division, January 3–5, 1919. US Army Military History Institute, Carlisle Barracks.
60. These statistics, and those in subsequent paragraphs, are derived from my examination of the Marriage Registers of the État Civil of representative French communes chosen for their proximity to American camps, hospitals or leave areas.
61. Nouaillat, *Les Américains à Nantes et St. Nazaire 1917–1919*, chapter 3.
62. Ethel D. Warner, unpublished memoir, World War I History Collection, Box 3, Red Cross Museum.
63. Warner, memoir, 7.
64. Niles, *Singing Soldiers*, 13.
65. Niles, *Singing Soldiers*, 138.
66. Niles, *Singing Soldiers*, 49. Niles called this song the Blacks' equivalent of "Mademoiselle from Armentières."
67. Addie W. Hunton and Kathryn M. Johnson, *Two Colored Women with the A.E.F.* (Brooklyn, New York: The Eagle Press, 1971, reprint of 1921 edition) 182–4.

68. Quoted in Bernard C. Nalty and Morris MacGregor, eds, *Blacks in the Military* (Wilmington: Scholarly Resources, 1982) 88. Also a copy found in the French Military Archives, Vincennes.

69. I have compiled this information on marriages from an extensive examination of the marriage registers of the *État Civil* of Chambéry, Aix-les-Bains, Brest and Beaune. A comparative study appears in Nouaillat, *Les Américains à Nantes et St. Nazaire 1917–1919*, chapter 3.

70. Hunton and Johnson, *Two Colored Women*, 137–8.

71. *Yank Talk* (Paris, 1918). R. Norris Williams Collection, University of Pennsylvania.

72. *Le Réveil Artistique*, 28 décembre 1918. Quoted in Nouaillat, *Les Américains à Nantes et St. Nazaire*, 188–9. Nouaillat used this quote to indicate the possibility of deceptive American soldiers, but the article came early enough to serve as a warning. Also it seems mostly to express a certain amount of jealousy on the part of the French.

73. Captain R. R. Meigs to his wife, April 23, 1918. Private collection, Philadelphia.

74. I have tried to demonstrate this system at work in soldiers' experience of organized leave and in combat in the previous chapters. Nancy Bristow has demonstrated this purpose at the training camps of World War I in America in *Making Men Moral: Social Engineering in the Great War* (New York: New York University Press, 1995), especially Chapter Two, "Full-Orbed Moral Manhood": Cultural Nationalism and the Creation of New Men and Women."

75. John D. Clark, Fifteenth Field Artillery, Second Division, Letter to Dr Richard Sommers, March 30, 1975, US Army Military History Institute, Carlisle Barracks.

76. Emma Marie Zangler, unpublished diary, with John D. Clark Collection, Fifteenth Field Artillery, Second Division. US Army Military History Institute, Carlisle Barracks.

5 American War Dead of World War I

1. "I've Got a Grave-diggin' Feeling in my Heart," in John Niles, *Singing Soldiers* (New York: C. Scribner's Sons, 1927) 131–2. Niles recorded the song as sung by African-American labor units working for the Graves Registration Service.

2. See Thomas W. Lacqueur, "Memory and Naming in the Great War," in John R. Gillis, ed., *Commemorations: The Politics of National Identity* (Princeton, New Jersey: Princeton University Press, 1994) 157.

3. Lacqueur, "Memory and Naming," 160–1 and 165.

4. Mark Meigs, "La mort et ses enjeux: l'utilisation des corps des soldats américains lors de la première guerre mondiale," *Guerres Mondiales et Conflits Contemporains* 175 (Juillet 1994): 135–46.

5. Elaine Scarry, *The Body in Pain: The Making and Unmaking of the World* (New York: Oxford University Press, 1985) 63, and chapter 2, "The

Structure of War: The Juxtaposition of Injured Bodies and Unanchored Issues," 60–157.

6. John Dos Passos, *Nineteen Nineteen* in *USA* (London: Penguin, 1966) 722. First published in the US, 1932.

7. US Army Quartermaster Corps, *History of the American Graves Registration Service, Q.M.C. in Europe* (undated, 1922?) 22. Other versions of this ceremony exist, perhaps because it has so much significance in the symbology of the country. David Kennedy described a blindfolded sergeant dropping a white carnation on the coffin of the unknown soldier, in *Over Here: The First World War and American Society* (New York: Oxford University Press, 1980) 368. John Dos Passos finished the *Nineteen Nineteen* section of *U.S.A.* casting sardonic aspersions on the choosing and meaning of this soldier, Dos Passos, "The Body of an American," *Nineteen Nineteen*, 722–7.

8. G. Kurt Piehler, "The War Dead and the Gold Star: American Commemoration of the First World War," in John R. Gilles, ed, *Commemorations: The Politics of National Identity*, 175.

9. For the choosing of the "Unknown Soldier" for Vietnam and the medical advances made in this century for identifying even incomplete bodies, see Susan Sheehan, "A Missing Plane, Identification," in *The New Yorker*, May 19 (1986): 78. For information about Arlington National Cemetery, I am indebted to Thomas Sherlock, the Historian of the Arlington National Cemetery.

10. Walter Benn Michaels, "The Souls of White Folks," in Elaine Scarry, ed., *Literature and the Body: Essays on Populations and Persons* (Baltimore: Johns Hopkins University Press, 1988) 205. Michaels found in Ernest Hemingway and F. Scott Fitzgerald the invention of a racism that protected itself by disguise as an American aesthetic. Jake in *The Sun Also Rises* establishes racial criteria to distinguish people and finds the Jewish character Cohn lacking. Nick in *The Great Gatsby*, seems at first to condemn the racist brutality of Tom Buchanan, but by the end escapes back to Minnesota to contemplate his version of American History that does not require Buchanan's brutal attempts at its preservation, but neither does it include Gatsby and his boundless optimism.

11. Dos Passos, *Nineteen Nineteen*, 724.

12. Alice Fahs, "Writing the Civil War", dissertation research, New York University, 1990.

13. Eugène Dédé, "American Ballade," BA/698, Archives de la Gendarmerie.

14. Field Marshal Paul von Hindenburg, *Out of My Life*, quoted by John J. Pershing, *My Experiences in the World War* (New York: Frederick A. Stokes, 1931) vol. II, 162.

15. Pershing, *My Experiences in the World War*, vol. II, 211.

16. Pershing, *My Experiences of the World War*, vol. II, 389.

17. Pershing, *My Experiences of the World War*, vol. II, 389.

18. Theodore Ropp, *War in the Modern World* (Durham, North Carolina: Duke University Press, 1959) 201.

19. John Keegan, *The Face of Battle* (New York: Penguin, 1984) 216.

20. Ivan S. Bloch, *The Future of War* (Boston, 1903), Vol. 6, xxxi. Quoted in Ropp, *War in the Modern World*, 201.

21. Ropp, *War in the Modern World*, 200–4; Jack Snyder, *The Ideology of the Offensive: Military Decision Making and the Disasters of 1914* (Ithaca, New York: Cornell University Press, 1984) 104–5.
22. Snyder, *The Ideology of the Offensive*, 199.
23. Tony Ashworth, *Trench Warfare 1914–1918: The Live and Let Live System* (New York: Macmillan, 1980).
24. Snyder, *The Ideology of the Offensive*, 125.
25. Alfred von Schlieffen, *The War of the Future* (Berlin, 1913), quoted in Ropp, *War in the Modern World*, 204.
26. For ideas on the strategy of attrition, see Gil Elliot, *Twentieth Century Book of the Dead* (New York: C. Scribner, 1972), chapter 2, "The European Soldier in the First World War."
27. "They Have not Died in Vain," program to the First Annual Belleau Wood Day Memorial Service, US Marine Corps club of St. Louis, June 11, 1922, World War One Miscellaneous, Marine Corps Museum, Washington Navy Yard.
28. Captain Charles C. Gardner of the Second Division made a collection of this kind of material: Edwin L. James' article, *The New York Times*, undated; Special Information Bulletin, Second Division, December 17, 1918; reprints of the Bulletin in *The New York Times* and *The Baltimore Sun*, November 17, 1918. Charles C. Gardner Papers, Second Division, US Army Military History Institute, Carlisle Barracks. See also "Marines in Combat: The Gallant Breed," a PBS program aired January 10, 1990, in which casualty rates of as much as forty per cent are cited with unalloyed pride.
29. Loren Duren, unpublished memoir, 3. Fourth Division, US Army Military History Institute, Carlisle Barracks.
30. Ralph Williams, *The Luck of a Buck* (Madison, Wisconsin, 1985), US Army Military History Institute, Carlisle Barracks.
31. Murvyn Burke, "Summary of the Battle of Cantigny," read to the members of the East Bay Retired Officers Association, May 28, 1981, First Division, US Army Military History Institute, Carlisle Barracks.
32. Arnold Toynbee, "Death in War," in Robert Fulton, ed., *Death and Dying Challenge and Change* (Reading, Massachussets: Addison-Wesley Publishing Co., 1978) 368.
33. Liddell Hart, *A History of the World War* (Boston: Little, Brown, 1935) 585.
34. Hart, *History of the World War*, 9–10.
35. Scarry, *The Body in Pain*, 73–81.
36. Scarry, *The Body in Pain*, 75.
37. Scarry, *The Body in Pain*, 65.
38. Clarence L. Mahan, "Hoosier Doughboy with the First Division WWI, 1917–1919," unpublished memoir, 33. US Army Military History Institute, Carlisle Barracks.
39. Mahan, "Hoosier Doughboy," 41.
40. John Blaser Papers, Fourth Division, US Army Military History Institute, Carlisle Barracks.
41. Howard Munder Papers, Twenty-eighth Division, US Army Military History Institute, Carlisle Barracks. The papers and diary were transcribed by William Bell Clark.

42. Howard Munder to his parents, Summer 1917. Howard Munder Papers, US Army Military History Institute, Carlisle Barracks.
43. Samuel Kent, unpublished diary, April 5, 1919, Thirty-second Division, US Army Military History Institute, Carlisle Barracks.
44. Charles Robinson Papers, Eightieth Division, US Military History Institute, Carlisle Barracks. Captain Bersky's letter is undated. Lieutenant Kleinstuber's letter is dated March 5, 1919.
45. Colin V. Dyment, "Casualty Reports of the Ninety-first Division", Ninety-first Division Papers, Hoover Institute Archives, Stanford University.
46. Loren Duren, unpublished memoir, 20. Fourth Division, US Army Military History Institute, Carlisle Barracks.
47. Loren Duren, unpublished memoir, 23.
48. *The Absolute Truth*, photographs taken by the US Signal Corps and reproduced by the American Field Service, Neal Betoth Papers, Second Division, US Military History Institute, Carlisle Barracks.
49. Ethel D. Warner, unpublished memoir, 1919?, Box #3, World War I Collection, Red Cross Museum, Washington, D.C.
50. Charlotte Gailor to the parents of Clarence Hackett, Aug 12, 1918. Clarence Hackett Papers, Second Division, US Army Military History Institute, Carlisle Barracks.
51. Ernest W. Wood to the parents of Lieutenant Quentin Robertson Logie, undated, Quentin Logie Papers, Second Division, US Army Military History Institute, Carlisle Barracks.
52. *The Martian* (Hospital Newspaper of Mars, Savoie), April 27, 1919, Box #3, World War I Collection, Red Cross Museum, Washington, D.C.
53. Daniel Halévy, *Avec Les Boys Américains* (Paris: Berger-Levrault, mai 1918) 55–6. Halévy took his text from General Bordeaux's speech given at the burial service. The speech was printed in English and widely distributed. Copies are especially prevalent among the papers of First Division Veterans.
54. Pershing, *My Experiences of the World War*, vol. I, 217.
55. *The New York Times*, November 10, 1917, 9.
56. *The New York Times*, November 7, 1917, 8.
57. *The New York Times*, November 28, 1917, 1.
58. "Transportation of the Graves Registration Service," Lecture, delivered in 1922, at the Quartermaster Corps Motor Transport School, Camp Holabird, Baltimore, Maryland. Army War Callege Historical Section, Carlisle Barracks.
59. "Transportation of the Graves Registration Service," Quartermaster Corps Motor Transport School.
60. Hunton and Johnson, *Two Colored Women with the A.E.F.*, 234.
61. Ralph Haze, "The Care of the Fallen: A Report to the Secretary of War on American Military Dead Overseas" (Washington, D.C., 1920), US Military History Institute, Carlisle Barracks.
62. Haze, "The Care of the Fallen," 4–6.
63. Haze, "The Care of the Fallen," 12–24. Organizations of the American funeral industry made important contributions to the movement to repatriate the dead and did publish optimistic speculation about the money to be made by repatriation, Piehler, "The War Dead," 171–2.
64. "Transportation of the Graves Registration Service", 22.

65. Lt. Col. James A. O'Brien, "Loss of Effects of Deceased Officers and Soldiers, WWI," August 1942, Army War College Historical Section, Carlisle Barracks.
66. US Army Quartermaster Corps American Graves Registration Service, *History of the American Graves Registration Service*, Vol. II, 151–65.
67. Henry Bartol, Liaison Officer XIV Region, Lyon, to Graves Registration, Tours. Record Group 120, box 3485 #51, National Archives. The correspondence of Bartol and Forbes, who were both liaison officers, gives a very good record of the bureaucratic difficulties encountered during the war by energetic officers with the best possible will.
68. Mervyn Burke Papers, US Military History Institute, Carlisle Barracks.
69. Piehler, "The War Dead," 173.
70. Hunton and Johnson, *Two Colored Women*, 238.
71. Philippe Ariès, *Western Attitudes Toward Death from the Middle Ages to the Present* (Baltimore: Johns Hopkins University Press, 1974) 73–4.
72. Stanley French, "The Cemetery as Cultural Institution: The Establishment of Mount Auburn and the 'Rural Cemetery Movement,'" with Philippe Ariès et al. in David E. Stannard, ed., *Death in America* (Philadelphia: University of Pennsylvania Press, 1975) 69.
73. Annette Becker, "Les deux rives de l'Atlantique. Mémoire américaine de la Grande Guerre," *Annales de l'Université de Savoie*, 18 (janvier 1995): 29.
74. David Kennedy gives the figure 30,000 and called it "more than half," *Over Here*, 367. G. Kurt Piehler wrote that 70 per cent of American bodies were repatriated; using the GRS figure of 45,588 repatriated and 764 sent out of France, that places the number of dead buried in France at a low 19,538, "The War Dead and the Gold Star: American Commemoration of the First World War," in John R. Gillis, ed., *Commemorations: The Politics of National Identity*, 173.
75. Becker, "Les deux rives de l'Atlantique," 27.

6 Lessons for the Doughboys' Return

1. Alexander Woollcott, quoted by Howard Teichmann, *Smart Aleck: The Wit World and Life of Alexander Woollcott* (New York: William Morrow, 1976) 80.
2. Mark Meigs, "Crash-Course Americanism: The AEF University, 1919," *History Today* 44, 8 (August 1994): 36–43.
3. General Order No. 30, "Educational Work in the A.E.F." James W. McAndrew, Chief of Staff, General Headquarters, A.E.F., France, February 13, 1919. US Army History Institute, Washington, D.C.
4. General Order No. 30, February 13, 1919.
5. Colonel Ira L. Reeves to Dr John Erskine, February 27, 1919. Record Group 120, #E409, Box 1956, National Archives, Washington, D.C.
6. Minute of the University Council, March 2, 1919, American E. F. University Bulletin #91, *The Register* (Beaune, 1919) 14. Archives Municipales, Beaune, Côte d'Or.
7. American E. F. University Bulletin #91, Part II, *The Register*, xi. Archives Municipales, Beaune, Côte d'Or.

8. *The Register*, xi.
9. Correspondence of Colonel Ira L. Reeves, 1919. Record Group 120, #E409, Box 1956, National Archives, Washington, D.C.
10. For a good account of the state of higher education in the United States during World War I, see Carol S. Gruber, *Mars and Minerva* (Baton Rouge: Louisiana State University Press, 1975).
11. *The Register*, 33–4.
12. William J. Newlin, "The Principles of Democratic Government," Headquarters American E. F. University Bulletin No. 92, 1. Bibliothèque internationale de documentation contemporaine, Nanterre.
13. Newlin, "Principles of Democratic Government," 4.
14. George S. Hellman, "Applied Arts and Education," Headquarters American E. F. University Bulletin No. 93, 1. Bibliothèque internationale de documentation contemporaine, Nanterre.
15. *Revue de Bourgogne*, Septième Volume, Numéro 4, Juin 1919.
16. Report of the American E. F. Art Training Center Bellevue, Seine et Oise, March-June 1919. Bibliothèque du musée de la ville de Paris.
17. For comparisons of benefits to military personnel after World War I and World War II, see Richard Severo and Lewis Milford, *The Wages of War When American Soldiers Came Home, from Valley Forge to Vietnam* (New York: Simon and Schuster, 1989).
18. Memorandum, Dr John Erskine to Colonel Ira L. Reeves, March 14, 1919. Record Group 120, #408, Box 1809, National Archives, Washington, D.C.
19. See for example, Ernest Hemingway, "Soldier's Home," *In Our Times* (New York: Charles Scribner's Sons, 1924); John Dos Passos, *The Big Money* (New York: Penguin, 1966, first published 1936); F. Scott Fitzgerald, *The Great Gatsby* (New York: Charles Scribner's Sons, 1925).
20. Harriet Nixon Pettibone, "The Uniform Behind the Office Desk, Lieutenant John Seerley Tells Why Returning Soldiers Have Learned Many Things That Will Make Them Better Business Men," *The New Success*, Vol. III, No. 4 (April, 1919).
21. "Theodore Roosevelt Jr., in His Father's Political Footsteps," in *The New Success*, Vol. III, No. 6 (June, 1919): 7–9. Roosevelt died in France in 1944 with the rank of Brigadier General.
22. John H. Perry, "How Your Wounded Boy Is Cared For in New York," *The New Success*, Vol. III, No. 2 (February, 1919): 28–9.
23. Garrard Harris, "Uncle Sam as a Gloom Chaser, How He Helps Soldiers to Find their Way Thru Disabilities," in *The New Success*, Vol. III, No. 4, April, 1919, 25–6.
24. Richard M. Huber, *The American Idea of Success* (New York, McGraw-Hill, 1971) 163.
25. Severo and Milford, *The Wages of War*, 248–9.
26. Severo and Milford, *The Wages of War*, 240.
27. Alfred G. Beekman, Question #43, US Army Military History Institute World War I Survey, US Army Military History Institute, Carlisle Barracks.
28. Clarence Akerley to Murray Laidlaw, March 27, 1919. Laidlaw Papers, Bancroft Library, University of California at Berkeley.

29. Bernard R. Gay to his wife, November 10, 1918. First Division, US Army Military History Institute, Carlisle Barracks.

30. George Beekman, undated typescript history of the 16th Infantry. From an archive of the 16th Infantry created by George Beekman, US Army Military History Institute, Carlisle Barracks.

31. Mervyn Burke, unpublished memoir, 105. Mervyn Burke Papers, US Army Military History Institute, Carlisle Barracks.

32. Burke, memoir, 113.

33. Anonymous, "Canned War Cries," *The Stars and Stripes*, June 28, 1918, in Alfred Cornebise ed., *Doughboy Doggerel: Verse of the American Expeditionary Force, 1918–1919* (Athens, Ohio: University of Ohio Press, 1985) 113.

34. Sgt. A. W. Bowen, "Line Up! Fall In!," *The Stars and Stripes*, May 9, 1919, in Cornebise, *Doughboy Doggerel*, 60.

35. "Deauboie," "Farewell to Coblenz," *The Amaroc News*, August 31, 1919, in Cornebise, *Doughboy Doggerel*, 76.

36. John Kendrick Bangs, ed., *Home then What?* (Paris: Comrades in Service, 1920) x.

37. Bangs, *Home then What?* vii.

38. Bangs, *Home then What?* xviii–xix.

39. Marcelle H. Wallenstein, PFC, 104th Aerial Photo Section, "Home then What? First Prize," in Bangs, *Home then What?* 25–31.

40. Joshua B. Lee, Pvt. Base Hospital 43, "Home then What? Second Prize," in Bangs, *Home then What?* 32–8.

41. See, for example, Daniel Halévy, *Avec les boys américains* (Paris: Berger-Levrault, 1918) and André Chevrillon, *Les américains à Brest* (Paris: Chapelot, 1920). French authors created a stereotyped American, vigorous, clean shaven, naïve, and easily adaptable to Taylorite methods of mass production.

42. Joshua B. Lee, in Bangs, *Home then What?* 32–8. It is interesting to note that James Jones' protagonist in *From Here to Eternity* (New York: Scribners, 1951) receives an education in middle-class images from magazine advertisements in a barracks recreation room, twenty-five years later.

43. An anonymous contribution in Bangs, *Home then What?* 51.

44. Newton S. Bement of Ann Arbor, Michigan in Bangs, *Home then What?* 58.

45. Roy E. B. Bower, Pvt. Med. Dept. in Bangs, *Home then What?* 61.

46. Lawrence L. Cassidy, Ordnance Sergeant in Bangs, *Home then What?* 77–8.

47. These proportions were generated by an examination of the United States Military Institute World War I Survey returned by former members of the Thirty-second, Seventy-ninth, Eightieth and Eighty-fifth Divisions, Carlisle Barracks.

48. Quotations from a random sampling of the United States Military Institute World War I Survey returned by former members of the Thirty-second, Seventy-ninth, Eightieth and Eighty-fifth Divisions, Carlisle Barracks.

49. Severo and Milford, *Wages of War*, 300–1.

50. Text Book Report No. 8, April 8, 1919, R.G. 120 #E 409, National Archives, Washington, D.C.

51. "Where do we go from here: This is the Real Dope," AEF demobilization pamphlet. James Weirich papers, Third Division, US Army Military History Institute, Carlisle Barracks.

52. Rizieri D'Ariano, Eightieth Division, US Military Institute World War I Survey, Carlisle Barracks.
53. John K. Montgomery, Thirty-sixth Division, US Army Military History Institute, Carlisle Barracks. For the "Pledge of Allegiance," see US Army Military History Institute Reference File on the flag prepared by John Slonaker, Chief Reference Librarian.
54. Clarence L. Mahan, "Hoosier Doughboy," unpublished memoir. First Division, US Military History Institute, Carlisle Barracks.

Conclusion

1. "Panthéon de la Guerre, par Pierre Carrier-Belleuse et Auguste-François Gorguct," Pamphlet, (Paris, no date, probably 1918). Frank Franek papers, Second Division, Third Infantry Brigade, US Army Military History Institute, Carlisle Barracks. The length of the canvas multiplied by the height gives the figure 16,200 square feet far greater than that given in the pamphlet. Either the canvas was not rectangular, or some error was made translating from meters into feet. In any case, the work was immense. Several examples of this pamphlet, and of a smaller version, were found among the personal papers of World War I soldiers at Carlisle Barracks.
2. François Robichon and Edith Herment, "Le 'Panthéon de la guerre,' une victoire démesurée," *Hommes de Guerre*, 13 (Novembre 1988): 32–4.

Bibliography

UNPUBLISHED, OFFICIAL DOCUMENTS

France

Archives Militaires, Vincennes
Contrôle Postal, 1917–1919.
Reports from the Présidence du Conseil, Commissariat Général Des Affaires de Guerre Franco Américaines, 15 N 59.

Archives Nationales, Paris
Prefectorial Reports on economic conditions throughout France, June 1917 to June 1919.

Bibliothèque Internationale de Documentation Contemporaine, Nanterre
Hellman, George S. "Applied Arts and Education." Headquarters American E. F. University Bulletin No. 93.
Newlin, William J. "The Principles of Democratic Government," Headquarters American E. F. University Bulletin No. 92, 1.

Bibliothèque du Musée de la Ville de Paris
Report of the American E. F. Art Training Center Bellevue, Seine et Oise, March-June 1919.

État Civil et Archives Municipales
American E. F. University Bulletin #91, *The Register* (Beaune, 1919), 14.
Archives Municipales, Beaune, Côte d'Or.
Archives Municipales for 1917–1919 at Aix-les-Bains, Beaune, Brest, Chambéry, Dijon.
Marriage Registers for 1917–1919 at the État Civil of Aix-les-Bains, Beaune, Brest, Chambéry, Dijon.

Musée de la Gendarmerie, Paris
Physionomie de Paris, B A/1587–1588, April, 1917 to August, 1919.
Songs submitted for censorship, B A/697–698, 1917–1919.

USA

National Archives, Washington, D.C.
Erskine, Dr. John, Academic Director of the AEF University at Beaune, Correspondence, Record Group 120, #408, Box 1809.

Provost Marshal. *History of the Provost Marshall.* National Archives, Record Group 120, #57.

Provost Marshal's Reports for crimes requiring investigation or disciplinary action by the army, Record group 120 #61, Box 1.

Quartermaster Corps Motor Transport School. "Transportation of the Graves Registration Service," Lecture, 1922, Camp Holabird, Baltimore, Maryland.

Records of district liaison officers in France, Record group 120 #51, Box 3485–3487.

Reeves, Colonel Ira L. Orders. Record Group 120, #414, Box 1944. – Correspondence. Record Group 120, #E409, Box 1956.

Stanford University, California. Hoover Institute Archives
Ninety-first Division Papers.

University of California at Berkeley Doe Library
World War I Pamphlets Collection.

US Army History Institute, Washington, D.C.
General Orders, General Headquarters, AEF, France, 1917–1919.

US Army War College Historical Section, and US Army Military History Institute, Carlisle Barracks, Pennsylvania
Dodds, Col. William H. Jr. G-1 Theatre of Operations Lecture delivered at the Army War College, Fort Humphreys, D. C. March 28, 1935.

Haze, Ralph. "The Care of the Fallen: A Report to the Secretary of War on American Military Dead Overseas." Washington, D. C., 1920.

Humber, Col. Robert C. "Absences and Desertions During the First World War," November 1942.

Kellogg, Lt. Col. Albert B. "Marriages of Soldiers," Report, July, 1942.

Martin, Colonel C. F. "Military Leaves and the Leave Area System, AEF," Historical Study no. 41, prepared January, 1943.

O'Brien, Lt. Col. James A. "Loss of Effects of Deceased Officers and Soldiers, WWI." Army War College, August 1942.

Slonaker, John Chief Reference Librarian, US Army Military History Institute, Reference Files.

CONTEMPORARY WORKS, WORKS BY PARTICIPANTS, FICTION, POETRY

Adams-Gibbons, Herbert. "The A.E.F. at Play," *The Century*, 1918.

Bangs, John Kendrick, ed. *Home then What?* Paris: Comrades in Service, 1920.

Bourne, Randolph S. *War and the Intellectuals, Collected Essays, 1915–1919.* New York: Harper and Row, 1964.

Brooks, Alden. *As I Saw It: Battle in 1918, Seen by an American in the French Army.* New York: Alfred A. Knopf, 1930.

Chevrillon, André. *Les américains à Brest*. Paris: Chapelot, 1920.

Churchill, Winston. "A Traveler in War-time." *Scribner's Magazine*, Vol. LXIII, February, 1918.

Defending Democracy. New York, 1919. Interviews with wounded soldiers.

Dos Passos, John. *USA*. London: Penguin, 1966. (first published, New York, 1936).

Edmonds, Franklin S. Divisional Secretary, Savoie, *The Leave Areas of the AEF*. Philadelphia: The John C. Winston Co., 1928.

Fitzgerald, F. Scott. *The Great Gatsby*. New York: Charles Scribner's Sons, 1925.

Halévy, Daniel. *Avec les boys américains*. Paris: Berger-Levrault, 1918.

Hemingway, Ernest. "Soldier's Home," *In Our Times*. New York: Charles Scribner's Sons, 1924.

– *The Sun Also Rises*. New York: Charles Scribner's Sons, 1926.

– *A Farewell to Arms*. New York: Charles Scribner's Sons, 1929.

Hunton, Addie W. and Kathryn M. Johnson. *Two Colored Women with the A.E.F.* Brooklyn, New York: The Eagle Press, 1971. (reproduction of 1921 edition).

Mitchell, William. *Memoires of World War I: "From Start to Finish of our Greatest War."* New York: Random House, 1960.

Niles, John J. *Singing Soldiers*. New York: Charles Scribner's Sons, 1927.

Niles, John J. and Douglas S. Moore, *Songs My Mother Never Taught Me*. New York: Macaulay, 1929.

Pershing, John J. *My Experiences in the Great War*. 2 vols. New York: Frederick A. Stokes, 1931.

Roosevelt, Theodore Jr. *Average Americans*. New York: 1919.

– *Rank and File; True Stories of the Great War*. New London, Connecticut: C. Scribner's sons, 1928.

Saunier, Baudry de. *The American's Guide Book in France*. Paris: *Office National Du Tourisme*. 1918[?].

Seeger, Alan. *The Poems of Alan Seeger*. New York: Charles Scribner's Sons, 1916.

– *The Letters and Diary of Alan Seeger*. New York: C. Scribner's Sons, 1917.

Stenback, Raymond. *The Way it Was*, 2 vols. Humbolt, Washington: State University Retired Senior Volunteer Program, 1980.

Woodward, H. H. Houston, *A Year for France, War Letters of Houston Woodward*. New Haven: Yale Publishing Association, 1919.

PERSONAL PAPERS

Private Collections

Henry Howard Houston Collection, Taconic, Connecticut.

Robert Rodgers Meigs Collection, Philadelphia.

Public Collections

Bancroft Library, University of California at Berkeley
Laidlaw Papers.

Marine Corps History Museum, Washington Navy Yard
A. B. Miller Collection.
Clifton Cates Collection.
"They Have not Died in Vain," program to the First Annual Belleau Wood Day Memorial Service, US Marine Corps club of St. Louis, June 11, 1922.

Red Cross Museum, World War One Collection, Washington, D.C.
Delisle, Nurse Nellie. Collection
Warner, Nurse Ethel D. Journal and memoire.

Stanford University, California Hoover Institute Archives
Agnes Wright Spring Collection
Anna Russell Collection
Blanche C. Matthias Collection
Eugene Kennedy Collection
Otis Emmons Briggs Collection

US Military History Institute World War I Survey, Carlisle Barracks, Pennsylvania

Collections
Aitken, Malcolm, 5th Marines, Second Division. Scrapbook.
Austin, Raymond, Sixth Artillery, First Division.
Beekman, Alfred G. Undated typescript history of the Sixteenth Infantry.
Betoth, Neal, Second Division.
Blaser, John, Fourth Division.
Brown, Lt. Joseph, Third Division.
Burke, Murvyn, First Division. Memoir.
Clark, John D. Fifteenth Field Artillery, Second Division.
D'Ariano, Rizieri, Eightieth Division.
Duren, Loren Fourth Division. Memoir.
Flemming, Major Samuel W. "World War One Service." Memoir, 1928.
Franek, Frank, Third Infantry Brigade, Second Division.
Gardner, Captain Charles C., Second Division.
Gay Bernard R., First Division.
Hackett, Clarence, Second Division.
Haselton, Lt. W. D., First Division. Diary.
Hunsucker, Clyde A., Thirty-sixth Division.
Johnston, Col. E. G., First Division. Memoir.
Kent, Samuel, Thirty-second Division, 128th Infantry. Diary.
Kress, Lt. John W. 314th Infantry, Seventy-ninth Division. Memoir, 1924.
Lee, Harold, Ninth Infantry, Second Division. War poems published posthumously by the W.C.T.U., 1918.
Logie, Lt. Quentin Robertson, Second Division.
Mahan, Clarence L., First Division. "Hoosier Doughboy with the First Division WWI 1917–1919." Memoir.

Montgomery, John K. Thirty-sixth Division.
Munder, Howard W., Bugler, Twenty-eighth Division.
Poorbaugh, Earl R. First Division. Journal.
Robinson, Charles.
St. James, Capt. Robert Grier, Seventh Infantry, Third Division.
Sawyer, Robert Thirty-sixth Division. Diary.
Schwartz, Casper. Diary.
Shapiro, Joseph. Fourth Division.
Stenback, Raymond, Sixth Marine Rgt. 73rd Co. Second Division.
Weirich, James, Third Division.
Williams, Ralph. *The Luck of a Buck.* Madison, Wisconsin, 1985.
Zangler, Emma Marie. Diary, with John D. Clark Collection.

Responses to the US Military History Institute World War I Research Project Questionnaire
Allen, Robert Edward Sr., Duty Sergeant.
Bogart, Leonard, Thirty-sixth Division.
Buhler, Cpl. Francis, Ninety-first Division.
Cornett, Cpl. John, Ninety-first Division.
Craven, Henry I., Ninety-second Division.
Hanks, Pvt. Howard David, Ninety-first Division.
Hatch, Cpl. A. C., Ninety-first Division.
Kress, Lt. John W., 314th Infantry, Seventy-ninth Division.
Kuchich, Andrew J., 314th Infantry, Seventy-ninth Division.
Lawrence, Bertram, Ninety-second Division.
Nelson, Arthur J., Ninety-first Division.
Ragsdale, Virgil B., Ninety-second Division.
Raymond, Austin.
Roberts, Austin, Ninety-second Division.

University of Pennsylvania, Philadelphia
Mumford Collection
R. Norris Williams Collection

PERIODICALS

American Red Cross Magazine, Vols. 12, 13, 14, 1917–1919.
L'Avenir (Aix-Les-Bains), 1918–1919.
Le Figaro, 1917–1919.
Martian (Hospital Newspaper of Mars, Savoie), 1918.
New Success, 1919.
New York Times, 1917–1919.
Oo La La Times (St. Nazaire, France), 1917–1919. (In the Bibliothèque Nationale, Paris.)
Over There! A Journal of the First World War, 1984–1988.
Revue de Bourgogne, 1918–1919.

Stars and Stripes, 1918–1919.

PUBLISHED DOCUMENTS AND PAPERS, COLLECTED POEMS

Cornebise, Alfred, ed. *Doughboy Doggerel: Verse of the American Expeditionary Force, 1918–1919*. Athens, Ohio: University of Ohio Press, 1985.

Link, Arthur S., ed. *The Papers of Woodrow Wilson*. Vols 38 to 41. Princeton, New Jersey: Princeton University Press, 1966–1980.

Roosevelt, Theodore. *The Works of Theodore Roosevelt*. 24 vols. Memorial Edition. New York: Charles Scribner's sons, 1923–26.

US Army Quartermaster Corps American Graves Registration Service. *History of the American Graves Registration Service Q.M.C. in Europe*. 2 vols. 1922[?]

SECONDARY WORKS

Adams, Michael C. C. *The Great Adventure: Male Desire and the Coming of World War I*. Bloomington, Indiana: Indiana University Press, 1990.

Ariès, Philippe. *Western Attitudes Toward Death from the Middle Ages to the Present*. Baltimore: Johns Hopkins University Press, 1974.

Ashworth, Tony. *Trench Warfare 1914–1918: The Live and Let Live System*. New York: Macmillan, 1980.

Baldwin, Fred Davis. "The American Enlisted Man in World War I." dissertation, Princeton, 1964.

Barbeau, Arthur E. and Henri Florette. *The Unknown Soldiers: Black American Troops in World War I*. Philadelphia: Temple University Press, 1974.

Becker, Annette "Les deux rives de l'Atlantique. Mémoire américaine de la Grande Guerre," in *Annales de l'Université de Savoie*, 18 (janvier 1995).

Bond, Brian. *War and Society in Europe, 1870–1970*. New York: Oxford University Press, 1986.

Bristow, Nancy. *Making Men Moral: Social Engineering in the Great War*. New York: New York University Press, 1995.

Carnes, Mark C. and Clyde Griffen, eds. *Meanings for Manhood: Constructions of Masculinity in Victorian America*. Chicago: University of Chicago Press, 1990.

Coffman, Edward M. *The War To End All Wars: The American Military Experience in World War I*. Madison, Wisconsin: University of Wisconsin Press, 1986.

Cooper, John Milton, Jr. *The Warrior and the Priest: Woodrow Wilson and Theodore Roosevelt*. Cambridge, Massachusetts: The Belknap Press of the Harvard University Press, 1983.

Corbin, Alain. *Les filles de noces: Misère sexuelle et prostitution aux 19e et 20e siècles*. Paris: Aubier, 1978.

Culler, Jonathan. "The Semiotics of Tourism," in *Framing the Sign: Criticism and its Institutions*. Norman, Oklahoma: University of Oklahoma Press, 1988.

Dinter, Elmar. *Hero or Coward*. London: F. Cass, 1985.

Dollard, John and Donald Horton. *Fear in Battle*. Washington: The Infantry Journal, 1944.

Elliot, Gil. *Twentieth Century Book of the Dead*. New York: C. Scribner, 1972.

Erenberg, Lewis. *Steppin' Out: New York Nightlife and the Transformation of American Culture, 1890–1930*. Westport, Connecticut: Greenwood Press, 1981.

Fahs, Alice. "Writing the Civil War." Dissertation research, New York University, 1990.

Ferrell, Robert H. *Woodrow Wilson and World War I, 1917–1921*. New York: Harper and Row, 1985.

Fox, Richard Wightman and T. J. Jackson Lears, eds. *The Culture of Consumption: Critical Essays in American History*, 1880–1980. New York: Pantheon, 1983.

French, Stanley. "The Cemetery as Cultural Institution: The Establishment of Mount Auburn and the 'Rural Cemetery Movement,' " with Philippe Ariès et al. in David E. Stannard, ed., *Death in America*. Philadelphia: University of Pennsylvania Press, 1975.

Frieh, Geneviève and Rault, Pierre. *Le Grand Cercle d'Aix-Les-Bains*. Paris: 1978.

Fussell, Paul. *The Great War and Modern Memory*. New York: Oxford University Press, 1975.

George, Alexander and Juliette George. *Woodrow Wilson and Colonel House, A Personality Study*. New York: Dover Publications, Inc., 1956.

Gilbert, Sandra and Susan Gubar. *No Man's Land: The Place of the Woman Writer in the Twentieth Century, Vol. 2, Sex Changes*. New Haven: Yale University Press 1988.

Gruber, Carol S. *Mars and Minerva*. Baton Rouge: Louisiana State University Press, 1975.

Hagedorn, Herman. *Leonard Wood, A Biography*. 2 vols. New York: Harper and brothers, 1931.

Henderson, William Darryl. *Cohesion, The Human Element in Combat*. Washington: National Defense University Press, 1985.

Herment, Edith and François Robichon. "Le 'Panthéon de la guerre,' une victoire démesurée," in *Hommes de Guerre*, 13 (Novembre 1988).

Hofstadter, Richard. *The Age of Reform; From Bryan to F.D.R*. New York: Knopf, 1955.

– *Social Darwinism in American Thought*. Boston: Beacon Press, 1992.

Holmes, Richard. *Acts of War: The Behavior of Men in Battle*. New York: The Free Press, 1985.

Huber, Richard M. *The American Idea of Success*. New York, McGraw-Hill, 1971.

Janowitz, Morris and Roger Little. *Sociology and the Military Establishment*. New York: Russell Sage Foundation, 1965.

Kaspi, André. *Le Temps des Américains: Le concours américain à la France en 1917–1918*. Paris: Université de Paris I, 1976.

Keegan, John. *The Face of Battle: A study of Agincourt, Waterloo and the Somme*. New York: Penguin, 1984.

Keller, Phyllis. *States of Belonging: German–American Intellectuals and the First World War*. Cambridge: Harvard University Press, 1979.

Kellett, Anthony. "Beliefs, Values, and Commitment," in *Combat Motivation: The Behavior of Soldiers in Battle*. Boston: Kluwer-Nijhoff Publishers, 1982.

Kennedy, David M. *Over Here: The First World War and American Society*. New York: Oxford University Press, 1980.

Kern, Stephen. *The Culture of Time and Space.* Cambridge, Mass: Harvard University Press, 1983.

Knock, Thomas J. *To End All Wars: Woodrow Wilson and the Quest for a New World Order.* Princeton, New Jersey: Princeton University Press, 1992.

Lacqueur, Thomas W. "Memory and Naming in the Great War," in John R. Gillis ed., *Commemorations: The Politics of National Identity.* Princeton, New Jersey: Princeton University Press, 1994.

Leed, Eric. *No Man's Land: Combat and Identity in World War I.* New York: Cambridge University Press, 1979.

Levine, Lawrence W. *Highbrow Lowbrow: The Emergence of Cultural Hierarchy in America.* Cambridge, Massachusetts: Harvard University Press, 1988.

– *The Unpredictable Past: Explorations in American Cultural History.* New York: Oxford University Press, 1993.

Liddell Hart, Basil Henry. *A History of the World War.* Boston: Little, Brown, 1935.

Limon, John. *Writing After War: American War Fiction from Realism to Postmodernism.* New York: Oxford University Press, 1994.

Linderman, Gerald F. *Embattled Courage: The Experience of Combat in the American Civil War.* New York: The Free Press, 1987.

MacCannell, Dean. *The Tourist: A New Theory of the Leisure Class.* New York: Schocken Books, 1989.

MacGregor, Morris and Bernard C. Nalty, eds. *Blacks in the Military.* Wilmington: Scholarly Resources, 1982.

Marshall, Samuel Lyman Atwood. *Men Against Fire: The Problem of Battle Command in Future Wars.* Washington: Infantry Journal, 1947.

– *World War I.* Boston: Houghton Mifflin, 1987.

May, Henry F. *The End of American Innocence: A Study of the First Years of Our Own Time, 1912–1917.* New York: Alfred A. Knopf, 1959.

McMoran, Charles, Baron Moran. *Anatomy of Courage.* London: Constable, 1966.

McPherson, James M. *What They Fought For, 1861–1865.* New York: Anchor Books, Doubleday, 1994.

Meigs, Mark. "La mort et ses enjeux: l'utilisation des corps des soldats américains lors de la première guerre mondiale," *Guerres Mondiales et Conflits Contemporains* 175 (juillet, 1994) 135–46.

– "Crash-Course Americanism: The AEF University, 1919," *History Today* 44, 8 (August 1994): 36–43.

Michaels, Walter Benn. "The Souls of White Folks," in Elaine Scarry, ed. *Literature and the Body: Essays on Populations and Persons.* Baltimore: Johns Hopkins University Press, 1988.

– "An American Tragedy or the Promise of American Life," in *Representations* 25 (Winter, 1989).

Milford, Lewis and Richard Severo. *The Wages of War: When American Soldiers Came Home, from Valley Forge to Vietnam.* New York: Simon and Schuster, 1989.

Mitchell, Reid. *Civil War Soldiers: Their Expectations and Experiences.* New York: Viking, 1988.

Morison, Samuel Eliot. *Three Centuries of Harvard.* Cambridge, Mass: Harvard University Press, 1965.

Mosse, George L. *Fallen Soldiers: Reshaping the Memory of the World Wars*. New York: Oxford University Press, 1990.

Nouaillat, Yves Henri. *Les Américains à Nantes et St. Nazaire*. Paris: Les Belles Lettres, 1972.

O'Malley, Michael. *Keeping Watch*. New York: Viking, 1990.

Peiss, Kathy. *Cheap Amusements: Working Women and Leisure in New York City, 1880–1920*. Philadelphia: Temple University Press, 1986.

– "Charity Girls and City Pleasures: Historical Notes on Working-Class Sexuality, 1880–1920," in Kathy Peiss and Christina Simmons with Robert A. Padgug, eds. *Passion and Power, Sexuality in History*. Philadelphia: Temple University Press, 1989.

Piehler, G. Kurt "The War Dead and the Gold Star: American Commemoration of the First World War," in John R. Gillis, ed, *Commemorations: The Politics of National Identity*. Princeton, New Jersey: Princeton University Press, 1994.

Rogin, Michael. " 'The Sword Became a Flashing Vision': D. W. Griffith's The Birth of a Nation," in *Representations* 9 (Winter, 1985).

Ropp, Theodore. *War in the Modern World*. Durham, North Carolina: Duke University Press, 1959.

Scarry, Elaine. *The Body in Pain: The Making and Unmaking of the World*. New York: Oxford University Press, 1985.

Sheehan, Susan "A Missing Plane, Identification," in *The New Yorker*, May 19 (1986).

Snyder, Jack. *The Ideology of the Offensive: Military Decision Making and the Disasters of 1914*. Ithaca, New York: Cornell University Press, 1984.

Stouffer, Samuel A. et al. *The American Soldier*. 4 vols. Princeton, New Jersey: Princeton University Press, 1949.

Susman, Warren I. *Culture as History: The Transformation of American Society in the Twentieth Century*. New York: Pantheon, 1984.

Teichmann, Howard. *Smart Aleck: The Wit, World and Life of Alexander Woollcott*. New York: William Morrow, 1976.

Thébaud, Françoise. *Le femme au temps de la guerre de 14*. Paris: Stock, 1986.

Theweleit, Klaus. *Male Fantasies: Women, floods, Bodies, History*, vol. 1. Minneapolis: University of Minnesota Press, 1987.

Toynbee, Arnold. "Death in War," in Fulton, Robert, ed. *Death and Dying, Challenge and Change*. Reading, Massachussets: Addison-Wesley Publishing Co., 1978.

Trachtenberg, Alan. *The Incorporation of America: Culture and Society in the Gilded Age*. New York: Hill and Wang, 1982.

Vaughn, Stephen L. *Holding Fast the Inner Lines: Democracy, Nationalism, and the Committee on Public Information*. Chapel Hill, North Carolina: University of North Carolina Press, 1980.

Ward, Larry Wayne. *The Motion Picture Goes to War, The US Government Film Effort during World War I*. Ann Arbor, Michigan: University of Michigan Press, 1981.

Weibe, Robert H. *The Search for Order, 1877–1920*. New York: Hill and Wang, 1967.

Weigley, Russell. *The American Way of War*. Bloomington, Indiana: Indiana University Press, 1977.

Weintraub, Stanley. *A Stillness Heard Round the World*. New York: Dutton, 1985.

Werstein, Irving. *Sound no Trumpet: The Life and Times of Alan Seeger*. New York: Crowell, 1967.

Wiley, Bell Irvin. *The Life of Johnny Reb: The Common Soldier of the Confederacy*. New York: Bobbs-Merrill, 1943.

– *The Life of Billy Yank: The Common Soldier of the Union*. New York: Bobbs-Merrill, 1952.

Index

AEF (American Expeditionary
  Forces), 5, 39–41, 212
  and casualties, 158
  and desertion, 60–1
  and disruption of French life, 79
  and intelligence testing, 46–7
  and occupation, 69–70
  and presence in cemeteries, 184
  and strategy of attrition, 148
  and tourism, 83
AEF University at Beaune, 188–90,
  191–2, 224
  and African–Americans, 191
  art course, 195–6
  business courses, 196–7
  course in citizenship, 193–5
  as remembered by soldiers, 196
  see also education; progressive ethos
Absolute Truth (The), 171–2; see also
  photographs
Adams–Gibbons, Herbert, 92–3
African–Americans, 15
  and AEF University, 191
  assimilation through participation,
    17–20
  and battle experience, 54–5, 224
  and bravery, 54–5
  and burial of soldiers, 177–8,
    183–4
  in cemeteries, 224–5
  and marriage in France, 137
  opinions about enlistment, 15, 20
  songs of, 135–6, 224
  see also assimilation
Aisne-Marne campaign, 40
Aix-les-Bains, 81, 84–5, 92–3
  economic benefits from AEF, 85–6
  see also Leave Area System
alcohol, 74, 77, 78
American Soldier (The), see Marshall,
  S.L.A.
amputees, 64–5
  rejection of optimism, 55
  see also casualties; injury

Arlington National Cemetery, 142
  civil war dead at, 147
  see also cemeteries; memorials;
    Unknown Soldier
Armistice, 41, 66–8, 200
  and after, 69–70, 83, 188
  see also last shot
army of occupation, 69
  and Mother's Day, 124
  and tourism, 206–7
art and the AEF, 195–6
Ashworth, Tony, 155
assimilation, 16–19, 57
  in AEF education program,
    193–4
  for African–Americans, 17–20
  and death, 143–6, 147–8
  for Native Americans, 17–18
attrition, 42, 149–52, 154–6
  and belief in military expertise,
    149–52, 171
  and bodies, 144–5
  and German strategy, 155–6
  and memorialization, 144–5,
    148
  and soldier perception of
    casualties, 158
  see also strategy of attrition
Avenir (L'), Aix-les-Bains, 84, 85–6,
  234 n

Baker, Newton Diehl, 74–5, 108; see
  also progressive ethos
Baldridge, C. Le Roy, 187–8
Bangs, John Kendrick, purposes of
  the war, 207
  and renewed loyalty to the US,
    208–9
'Battle Cry of Peace (The)', 21
Beaune, Côte d'Or, 188; see also
  AEF University
Beekman, George, and history of
  the 16th Infantry, 202–3
Bell, George L., 16

259

Bellamy, Edward, 46
Belleau Wood, 39–40, 48–50, 119, 149–50
Benn Michaels, Walter, 45, 147, 230 n, 241 n
'Birth of a Nation (The)', 20–1, 74
Blackton, J. Stuart, 21
Bloch, Ivan S., 153
blockade of Germany, 11
bodies, 147, 161
    and burial, 177
    home reception of, 183
    and identification, 143, 181–3
    and memorialization, 143
    as seen by nurses, 173
    shipping of, 180
    and soldier perception, 169
    see also death; injury;
        memorialization; pain;
        Unknown Soldier
bravery, tests and standards of, 26, 36–8, 44–5, 47–52, 54, 59, 61, 157, 223
    for African–Americans, 54–5
    described by McMoran (Baron Moran), 44–5
    for MPs (Military Police), 62–3
    for Native Americans, 57
    and strategy of attrition, 154
Bring Home the Soldier Dead League, 179
burial of Americans, 145–6, 176–80, 185
    and African–Americans, 177, 183–4
    and chaplains, 173–4
    in Civil War, 148–9
    controversy over location, 179
    described by a nurse, 172
    described by soldiers, 169–70, 177, 181–2
    and French propaganda, 175
    repatriation of American bodies, 180–1
    see also cemeteries; death; Graves
        Registration Service;
        Unknown Soldier
business ethos, and WWI, 191, 196–7, 198, 201–3

and literary rejection of, 196–7, 217
    in magazines, 198–201
    and postwar salesmanship, 65–6
    and regimental history, 203
    and suppression of negative
        interpretation of war, 203–4
    see also progressive ethos; rhetoric
Butler, Nicholas Murry, 192

CPI (Committee on Public Information), 8, 9
CTCA (Commission on Training Camp Activities), 73–4; *see also* progressive ethos
Cantigny, 39, 158
Carrier-Belleuse, and *Le Panthéon de la Guerre*, 220
casualties, 39, 158, 162–9
    and amputees, 64–5
    at Cantigny, 158
    compared to Civil War dead, 144
    in Meuse-Argonne offensive, 151, 159
    and moral breakdown, 39–40, 51–3, 58
    theories on, 159–62
    and unit reputation, 157, 159
    see also attrition; bodies; injury
cemeteries, 184, 185, 224–5
    for American soldiers in France, 172, 180, 184–5, 218
    for British soldiers, 143–4
    and chaplains, 173–4
    of Civil War, 144, 148–9
    and integration, 224–5
    as tour sites, 185, 218
    and US democratic spirit, 184
    see also burial of Americans
chaplains
    and cemeteries, 173–4
    and French culture, 128, 130
    and French women, 128–32
    and marriages, 127–8
Château-Thierry, 39, 149–50,
    as touristic site, 104
Churchill, Winston (American novelist), 91–2

Civil War comparisons, 2, 5, 9, 21
    with WWI cemeteries, 144, 148,
        174
    with WWI soldiers, 17, 20, 24,
        37–8, 45–6, 222–3
Clausewitz, Karl von, 152
Clémenceau, Georges, 90, 108
'Comrades in Service,' 207
consumerism, of American soldiers,
        86–7, 223 n
    and magazine articles, 91–2, 212
    model of consumer rhetoric in
        The Stars and Stripes, 205–6
    among officers, 99–102
    see also tourism
continence, 107, 112
    and recreation, 107
Corbin, Alain, 115
courage, described by McMoran
        (Baron Moran), 44–5; *see also*
        bravery
Culler, Jonathan, 71–2, 91

Darwinism, in the American
        military context, 21–2, 207–8
    as explanation of wartime
        sexuality, 112–13
    in soldier opinion, 22, 207
    and strategy of attrition, 154–5
death, of American soldiers, 169–70
    and chaplains, 173–4
    as described by a nurse, 173
    division record of, 168–9
    and education in the AEF, 194
    in photographs, 171–2
    in *The Stars and Stripes*, 187–8
    see also casualties; injury;
        Unknown Soldier
desertion, from battle, 60–3, 231 n
    near AEF camps, 79
    and morale, 79
    see also MPs (Military Police)
destruction, of cultural sites, 71,
        105
    by American soldiers, 73, 77
diaries, *see* memoirs; narratives
domesticity, and soldiers, 110–11,
        135, 139
    in magazines, 212

mother as symbol of, 122
    in postcards, 109–10, 135
    and postwar France, 121
    and sexuality, 111–12
    in songs, 116
    see also marriages; women
Donremy (birthplace of Joan of
        Arc), 218
Dos Passos, John, 145, 147–8,
    rejection of business ethos,
        197–8
doughboys, 183
    future, 197
    and letters home, 26
    and participation in war, 34–5
    and tourism, 94–5
    and women, 107–9, 111–13,
        119–20
    see also interpretation of American
        involvement; voices of
        participants

education, 73, 75, 81–2, 143, 188,
        190–5, 211
    and AEF, 188
    and African–Americans, 191
    and art, 195–6
    and business, 196–7
    course in citizenship, 193–5
    and European universities, 189
    farm-school, 191–2
    high-schools, 189
    and letter-writing, 235 n
    and literature, 197–8
    as remembered by soldiers, 196
    technical schools, 189
    of wounded men, 201
    see also AEF University;
        progressive ethos; tourism
élan, 41; *see also* morale
expatriate writers, 23, 147, 197–8
    and rejection of business ethos,
        197–8

fear, in battle, 44, 54–5
    as motive, 38–9
Federal Bureau for Vocational
        Rehabilitation, 201
Field of Honor Association, 179

films, 20–1
    and time-motion studies, 46
    see also movies
'First to Go Home (The)', 187–8
Fitzgerald, F. Scott, and literary
    rejection of business ethos, 198
Foch, Ferdinand, 41
    and offensive strategy, 154
Forbes, Charles R., 207
Fosdick, Raymond, 108
France in the opinion of returning
    Americans, 217–19
French women, and American
    soldiers, 107–9, 111–13,
    119–20, 124–6, 128–31, 141,
    234 n
    in the AEF press, 128–32
    accosted by American soldiers,
        114–15
    accused of venality, 126–7
    and African–Americans, 135,
        137–8
    as factory workers, 119–20
    and marriage to American
        soldiers, 99, 124, 132–3,
        138–9
    and prostitution, 108–9, 114, 120
    in songs, 107, 115–17
    see also marriages; masculinity;
        sexuality; songs
Fussell, Paul, 30, 229 n, 236 n

gender roles, 120–1, 135–6; *see also*
    French women; masculinity;
    sexuality; women
Gilbreth, Frank B., 46, 194
Gorguet, François, and *Le Panthéon
    de la Guerre*, 220
Graves Registration Service (GRS),
    145–6, 176–7, 178–80, 185
    and accusations of negligence,
        180–1
    and creation of cemeteries in
        France, 180
    and problems of body
        identification, 181–2, 183
    and public opinion, 179, 180
    and recuperation of dead bodies,
        177–8

    see also burial of Americans;
        cemeteries; Unknown Soldier
Griffith, D.W., 20–1
group cohesion, 43; *see also* primary
    group cohesion

Hellman, George S., 195
Hemingway, Ernest, and literary
    rejection of business ethos, 197
Hindenburg, Paul von, and strategy
    of attrition, 150
Hofstadter, Richard, 21–2
Holmes, Richard, 110
Home then What?
    and American superiority, 209
    and domesticity, 212
    and progressive rhetoric, 211–14
    and traditional American values,
        210
    see also narratives; progressive ethos
Huber, Richard M., 200
hypernominalism, 145

identification of dead bodies, 181–2,
    183; *see also* Unknown Soldier
ideology, 9
    and the Civil War, 9
immigrants, involvement in war,
    14–15
individualism, 22, 25, 29
    and attrition, 154
    and death, 142
    and identity, 42, 44, 48
    and progressive ethos, 45–6
    in relation to a mass event, 4, 22,
        37, 47–52, 56, 63, 66–7
    and training, 43–6
    see interpretation of American
        involvement; voices of
        participants
injury, 162–9
    described to families, 163–8
    described by a nurse, 172–3
    in photographs, 171
    and rehabilitation, 201
    see also amputees; casualties
innocence, 4
intelligence testing in the AEF,
    46–7

interpretation
  of American involvement, 1,
    205–7, 208
  of combat, 42
  official and individual, 5
  of tourism and battle, 72, 87, 104
  see also individualism; voices of
    participants
isolationism, and soldiers, 209–10
  upon return, 203

Jewish Welfare Board, 73
Joan of Arc, 218, 219
Junger, Ernst, 63–4

Keegan, John, 38–9
Kennedy, David, 5–6
Knights of Columbus, 73

Lacqueur, Thomas, 143–4
last shot, 66–7; *see also* Armistice
Leave Area Bureau, 76, 81–2; *see
  also* Leave Area System
Leave Area System, 79–84, 103–4
  in US Army Military History
    Survey, 89–91
  see also tourism; YMCA
Leed, Eric, 63–4, 236 n
letters home, 26, 98, 224
  preservation of, 26–7
  printed in home town
    newspapers, 94–6, 164
  and progressive ethos, 98
  reporting death or injury, 163–8
  teaching soldiers letter writing,
    95, 235 n
  see also narratives; voices of
    participants
Liddell Hart, Basil Henry, 159–61
Lincoln, Abraham, 148–9; *see also*
  Civil War
Linderman, Gerald, 5–6, 9, 37, 223
'live and let live' systems, 155; *see
  also* attrition
Looking Backward, 46
Ludendorff, Erich von, 40
Lusitania, 11

MPs (Military Police), 61–2, 231 n

role in battle, 44, 60–3,
  see also desertion
MacCannell, Dean, 72–3, 75, 92, 99
'Mad'moiselle from Armentières,'
  115–17
manhood, *see* masculinity
Marden, Orison Swett, and *The New
  Success*, 199
  wartime shift from
    character-building to positive
    thinking, 208
marriages, of American soldiers,
    109, 239 n
  and African–Americans, 135,
    137–8
  and American officers, 131–2,
    134
  to American women, 134, 140–1
  army obstruction of, 126–7
  army rules regarding, 125–6,
    134
  in French marriage registers, 133,
    137–8
  to French women, 99, 124, 138–9
  and married couples prohibited
    from service, 125
  and socio-economic status of
    French brides, 133–4, 139
  in US Army Military Institute
    Survey, 135
  see also domesticity; French
    women; sexuality
Marshall, Samuel Lyman Atwood,
  8–9, 223
masculinity, 9
  and art, 195–6
  and battle, 110–11, 119–20
  and literature, 197–8, 236–7 n
  and military service, 9, 28–9, 30,
    139–40
  and self-control, 111–12, 113,
    139–40
  threat to, 25
  war as foundation for adult
    masculine role, 204
  see also bravery
May, Henry, 4
McMoran, Charles (Lord Moran), 44
McPherson, James, 9, 223

memoirs
  of doughboys, 5, 6, 10
  of Pershing, 75–6, 82, 186
  of veterans, 90
  see also narratives
memorialization, 143–4
  of battle experience, 51–8
  and cemeteries, 185–6
  and *Panthéon de la Guerre* (*Le*), 222
  and propaganda, 172, 176
  see also cemeteries; memorials;
    Unknown Soldier
memorials, and monuments, 144
  and African–Americans, 142,
    145–6
  in American towns, 157–8, 176
  in France, 180, 186, 218
  Panthéon de la Guerre (*Le*), 220–2
  Tomb of the Unknowns, 146
  see also cemeteries; Unknown
    Soldier
Men Against Fire, 8–9, 223
Meuse-Argonne offensive, 41, 59,
  154, 159; *see also* casualties
Michelin guides, 86
Mitchell, Reid, 9
Moltke, Helmuth von (the younger),
  155–6
morale, 41, 79
  and 'Comrades in Service,' 207
  and desertion, 79
  and tourism, 74–5, 79
mother, 122, 125, 134, 141
  and African–Americans, 136
  French women as threat to, 127
  Mother's Day soldier letters,
    123–4
movies, 20–1, 74
  comparisons to battle, 49
  and training, 46
  see also films

narratives
  of death, 168–9
  of domesticity, 135
  of last shot, 66–7
  of masculinity, 25–6
  of return, 202–4, 209–13
  of romance, 140–1

of tourism, 71, 92–3, 95–6,
  101–3
of under-fire bravery, 47–50, 51,
  52, 58, 59–60, 62–3
of women's work, 31–2
see also letters home; memoirs
nationalism, 159, 174, 207–8
  and identity, 145
Native Americans, 17–18
  in battle, 56–7
  and bravery, 57
  see also assimilation
New Success (*The*), 198–200
new woman, and war work, 30–2,
  141; *see also* nurses
New Yorker (*The*), in relation to *The
  Stars and Stripes*, 33–4; *see also*
  Woollcott, Alexander
Newlin, William J., 193–5
Niles, John J., 117–19, 135–6, 227 n
No Man's Land, 63–4, 236 n
Nouaillat, Yves Henri, 133
nurses, 29
  description of burial, 172
  description of wounds, 172–3
  and marriage, 134–5
  and relations with enlisted men,
    134
  and relations with officers, 132
  as sexual symbols, 121–2, 140–1
  see also marriages; new woman;
    women

offensives
  belief in, 154–5
  failure of, 153
  and German strategy, 155–6
  Meuse-Argonne offensive, 41,
    154, 159
  offensive à outrance, 154–5
  Somme offensive, 153
Office National du Tourisme, 87–8
Oo La La Times
  and French culture, 130
  and French women, 128–31
  and marriages to American
    officers, 131–2
optimism, and WWI, 4, 6, 64,
  200–2, 220

optimism (*contd*)
  and African–Americans, 54–5,
    183–4
  and American patriotism, 201,
    207, 210–11, 219
  in magazines, 198–9
  and *Panthéon de la Guerre (Le)*, 222
  and postwar expression by
    soldiers, 201–4
  rejected by amputees, 65
  as taught by AEF, 188–9, 196
  and trench warfare, 217
  and the wounded, 199–201
  see also progressive ethos; rhetoric;
    uplift

pain, 146, 160
  and death, 163–6
  and rhetoric of injury, 161, 174
  soldier interpretation of, 162
  see also structure of war
Palmer, A. Mitchell, 201
Panthéon de la Guerre (Le), 220–2,
  247 n
Paris, as leave destination, 69, 83,
  100–1, 218
patriotism, 9, 15–20, 146, 172
  of African–Americans, 19
  in battle, 57, 64
  and love of country, 168
  of Native-Americans, 18
  in Seeger, 23–4
  survey question on, 13
pay, of American soldiers, 77
  and effects on local economy, 78
  on leave, 80–1
  and marriage with French
    women, 126–7
peer pressure, 24
Pershing, John J., 3, 32–3, 41, 221
  and death of American soldiers,
    175–6, 179, 186
  and independent command, 40–1
  memoirs of, 75–6, 82, 186
  and morale, 79
  and Mother's Day, 124
  and progressive ethos, 75–6, 83
  and strategy of attrition, 150–1
  and tourism, 82–3, 186

and venereal disease, 107–8
  see also progressive ethos
photographs, 17, 171–2
  of Civil War compared to WWI,
    45–6
Physionomie de Paris, 77
  and sexuality of American
    soldiers, 113
postcard collections, 105, 109–10,
  135
preparedness, 8, 21
primary group cohesion, 9, 38,
  43–4, 229 n; *see also* bravery
progressive ethos, and WWI, 6,
  45–6, 74
  and art, 195
  and death, 143, 186
  and French society, 108–9
  and Pershing, John J., 75–6
  and prostitution, 108–9
  and sexuality of soldiers, 107–8
  and soldier education, 73–5,
    81–2, 108, 143, 188, 190,
    191–5, 211
  and soldier marriages, 109
  and Woodrow Wilson, 12, 22,
    207
  see also optimism; rhetoric; uplift
propaganda, 3–4, 7, 46, 172, 174,
  207, 224
  against Germans, 21–2
  and assimilation, 16
  and first US war dead, 175–6
  and persuasion, 33–4
  and slogans, 204–5
  see also optimism; progressive
    ethos
prophylaxis, 107, 109
prostitution, 30, 74, 77–8, 108–9,
  114–15
  in songs, 119
  see also sexuality
Provost Marshal
  and prostitution, 114
  reports on assaults, 77
  reports on desertion, 61–2
  see also MPs

quiet sectors, 155

recreation of American soldiers,
75–6, 80–3, 212; *see also* Leave
Area System; YMCA
Red Cross nurses, 29 *see also* nurses
Reeves, Ira L., 189–90, 196
repatriation of American bodies,
180–1; *see also* Graves
Registration Service
returning soldiers
and ideas about the US, 209–14
life in US, 215–16
in US Army Military History
Institute Survey, 214–17
see also narratives
Revue de Bourgogne, 196
rhetoric
of bravery, 53
of death, 171, 175
of optimism, 52–4
of personal improvement, 74
progressive, 46
slogans discussed, 204–5
of success, 4, 6, 57
of uplift, 82, 203–5, 208–9, 212
see also optimism; progressive
ethos; uplift
Roosevelt, Theodore, 21, 28, 183
Roosevelt, Theodore, Jr., 179, 199
Rotary Club, 203–4

SATC (Student Army Training
Corps), 192
Saint-Mihiel, 41
Salvation Army, 30
Scarry, Elaine, 144, 160–2
Schlieffen, Alfred von, 156
Seeger, Alan, 227 n
'Message to America,' 24–6
reasons for engagement, 23–5, 28
Seicheprey, 39
sexuality
of American women in France,
121, 122
and battle, 110, 119–22, 238 n
and continence, 107–8, 110–12
expressed in songs, 113, 115–19,
122
and French women in WWI,
112–13

in postcards, 109–10
reported by French civil
authorities, 114–15
reported in *Physionomie de Paris*,
113–14
and sex education, 108
threats to, 21–2, 25
and venereal disease, 107–8
and wartime polarization of
gender roles, 120–1, 135–6
see also domesticity; marriage;
masculinity; prostitution
shell shock, 63
and experience of American
soldiers, 50
Singing Soldiers, 135–6, 224; *see also*
Niles, John J.; songs
slogans, 204–5; *see also* propaganda
Snyder, Jack, 155
Soissons, 39–40
Somme, battle of, 153
songs
of African–Americans, 135–6, 224
and domesticity, 116
'Mad'moiselle from Armentières,'
115–17
and prostitutes, 119
and sexuality expressed in, 113,
115–19, 122
and sheet music, 122
see also Niles, John J.
Songs My Mother Never Taught Me,
115–17, 122
Stars and Stripes (The), 27–8
and formation of soldier opinion,
32–5, 187, 204–6
and image of Liberty, 122–3
and image of Mother, 122–3
and letters to mother, 123–4
poetry in, 205–6
see also propaganda
stragglers, *see* desertion
strategy of attrition, 42, 149–52,
154–6
and failure of offensives, 153,
and German strategy, 155–6
and memorialization, 144–5, 148
Meuse-Argonne offensive, 41,
154, 159

strategy of attrition (*contd*)
  and soldier perception of
    casualties, 158
  Somme offensive, 153
  see also attrition; casualties;
    offensives
structure of war, 144–5, 167–8; *see
  also* pain; Scarry, Elaine
submarine warfare, 11
survey of World War I veterans by
    the US Army Military History
    Institute, 3, 226 n
  on enlistment, 13–16, 22
  on learning about America, 214
  on leisure activities, 96–8
  on lessons of war and combat, 55
  on looting, 99
  on recreation, 89–90
  on return to civil life, 215–17
  see also US Army Military History
    Institute

technology
  effects on American soldier
    experience, 37–8, 41, 43, 46,
    47–8, 52, 64, 68, 103–4, 223
  effects on German soldier
    experience, 64
  effects on memorialization, 144
  and strategy of attrition, 152, 156
Thébaud, Françoise, 120; *see also*
    sexuality; women
theft, 100
  and Graves Registration Service,
    180
  and looting, 99–100
time-motion studies, 46; *see also* films
Tomb of the Unknowns, 146; *see
    also* memorialization
tourism
  and American patriotism, 207,
    210, 218
  and American soldiers, 70–3,
    85–90, 140, 188, 218, 223
  and battlefields, 70, 72, 104
  and the classless society, 92–4
  and experience of officers and
    men compared, 101–3
  in home town newspapers, 94–6

and Leave Area System, 79–84,
    103–4
  in magazine articles, 91–3
  and *Panthéon de la Guerre* (*Le*), 222
  and prostitution, 108–9
  in *The Stars and Stripes*, 94, 205–7
  and uplift, 73
  and Woodrow Wilson, 90
  see also Leave Area System; YMCA
Toynbee, Arnold, 158
trench warfare
  and American experience, 40, 41,
    217
  compared with war of movement,
    58, 207
  effect on German strategy, 156
  and European experience, 63–4
  and memorialization, 144
  see also attrition; strategy of
    attrition

US Army Military History Institute,
    WWI Survey, 3, 226 n
  and education in AEF, 196
  and lack of veteran benefits, 196
  and leisure activities of soldiers,
    96–9
  and lessons of WWI, 214–16
  and soldiers' reasons for
    enlistment, 13–15
  see also survey of World War I
    veterans
Unknown Soldier (the)
  and African–Americans, 146
  at Arc de Triomphe, 143
  at Arlington, 142
  choosing the body of, 145–6
  comparison with Civil War
    unknowns, 146–7, 148
  comparison with Vietnam
    unknowns, 147
  in literature, 147–8
  and meaning to soldiers and
    family, 166, 183
  at Westminster Abbey, 143
  see also attrition; burial; casualties;
    cemeteries; injury
uplift
  and Bangs, John Kendrick, 212

criticized by doctors, 201
criticized in postwar literature,
    197–8, 201
as morale boost after Armistice,
    188, 207
and postwar business ethos,
    196–7, 201
in postwar magazines, 198
and soldier opinion, 211
and tourism, 73–5, 83
see also optimism; progressive ethos

venereal disease, 107–8, 115
and venereal rate compared to
    other armies, 107
see also prophylaxis
veteran benefits, 216
in US Army Military History
    Survey, 196
for wounded, 201
Veterans Bureau, 201
victory
and American morale, 39–40,
    57
and German morale, 39
and positive interpretation of
    casualties, 54
voices of participants, 1, 5, 7,
    13–16, 18–20
of African–Americans, 15
of immigrants, 14–15
and motivation to combat, 38
of Native Americans, 17–18
and peer pressure, 24–5
in *The Stars and Stripes*, 32–3
and tourism, 70–2, 87, 104
of volunteers, 24, 26, 28
of women, 27
see also interpretation, of
    American involvement

War Risk Insurance, 80, 127, 216
What They Fought For, 9, 223
Wiley, Bell Irvin, 9
Wilson, Woodrow
and American entry into war, 8,
    11–13, 16, 221
and American involvement in
    war, 34

and progressive rhetoric, 13, 22,
    207, 213
and tourism, 69, 90
see also progressive ethos;
    rhetoric
women, 107, 109, 132, 135
African–American, 136, 138
and description of men after
    battle, 110
and domesticity, 110–16
and marriage, 109, 124
as mothers, 122–4, 127, 136–7
as nurses, 135–6, 140–1
as prostitutes, 107–8
as war workers, 30–1
see also French women; gender
    roles; new woman; sexuality
Woollcott, Alexander
and C. Le Roy Baldridge, 187
guide to battlefields, 104
see also New Yorker (The)
World War I
causes of, 10, 223
and entrance of the United States
    in, 8, 10–13
and the popular press, 16–17
and soldier opinion about
    entrance, 13–15
World War I, interpretations of
    soldiers, 218–19
and art, 220
and future opportunities for
    participants, 198, 202,
    203–4, 211, 217
and models for the study of other
    American wars, 6–7
see also interpretation, of
    American involvement;
    narratives; voices of
    participants
World War II, soldier experience of,
    2, 8, 9
comparison of veterans' benefits,
    196
comparison with WWI
    experience, 2, 37, 38, 223

YMCA (Young Men's Christian
    Association), 6, 212, 224

YMCA *(contd)*
  and African–Americans, 136–7,
    138, 176–7
  and education, 84, 86–7
  and guide books, 86–7
  hostesses, 30, 141
  and Leave Area System, 79–80,
    84, 98–9, 103–4
  and leisure activities of soldiers,
    73, 101
  and letters home, 224
  and mother, 124
  and propaganda, 4, 6
  and soldier sexuality, 111–12
  and tourism, 71–2, 103–5
  see also progressive ethos;
    propaganda; tourism